R-3903-USDP

Soviet Foreign Policy and the Revolutions of 1989 in Eastern Europe

Ronald D. Asmus, J. F. Brown, Keith Crane

Prepared for the
Under Secretary of Defense for Policy

WITHDRAWN

RAND

PREFACE

This report describes the revolutions of 1989 in Eastern Europe and the evolution of Soviet foreign policy toward the region in the 1980s. It was prepared for the Under Secretary of Defense for Policy under RAND's National Defense Research Institute, a federally funded research and development center supported by the Office of the Secretary of Defense and the Joint Chiefs of Staff. It is part of RAND's International Security and Defense Policy Program and should be of interest to policymakers, intelligence officers, and scholars concerned with Soviet policy toward Eastern Europe.

SUMMARY

The failure of communism in East-Central Europe can be traced back to its introduction after World War II. It was imposed rather than accepted, often brutally and always undemocratically, by the Red Army in the name of a nation most East-Central Europeans had traditionally hated or despised.

The subsequent inability of the local East-Central European communist regimes to acquire popular legitimacy and a relationship with their populations based on national identity ensured their eventual failure. (In the case of the German Democratic Republic the regime's task was made all the more difficult by the pressure of a democratic, prosperous West Germany and by its own total artificiality. It was a state always searching unsuccessfully for a nation.)

The communist system in Eastern Europe might have attained, if not legitimacy, then some degree of popular acceptance, had it been able to establish a rational and satisfactory economic basis that would ensure higher standards of living and at least approach popular expectations. This might also have softened nationalist resentment against Soviet-imposed communist rule, thereby narrowing the gulf between rulers and ruled. Poland, very briefly after 1956, seemed to have begun moving toward this relatively stable state of affairs. Hungary, between the early 1960s and the late 1970s, showed some signs of having achieved it. Czechoslovakia, had the Prague Spring in 1968 been allowed to continue, would almost certainly have gotten there. All these possibilities originated or were associated with the rule of Nikita Khrushchev in the Soviet Union.

But the Prague Spring, with its spirit of spontaneity and its combination of political and economic pluralism, prompted the new Soviet leadership under Brezhnev to deliver a hammer blow. Through its invasion of Czechoslovakia in 1968, the Soviet Union signaled to the whole of Eastern Europe that it would not allow any regime to regenerate itself in terms of its own national requirements. In doing so it sealed the fate of communism in Eastern Europe. Initiative would in future only come from *outside* the system, not inside, as had been the case with the Prague Spring. It would also eventually be aimed at destroying the system rather than reforming it.

The "Brezhnev system" in Eastern Europe, put in place between 1969 and 1975, was a conservative construction designed to restore cohesion and orthodoxy. A program of comprehensive integration unfolded—economic, political, military, ideological, and cultural—

designed to knit the alliance more closely and secure Soviet hegemony. The Soviet and East European leaderships, under pressure after the Prague Spring and the Polish riots in 1970, devised (or stumbled into) the economic policy of "consumerism." Viability and, hopefully, legitimacy were to be achieved through higher living standards, more plentiful food and consumer goods, and steadily rising real incomes. At the beginning of the 1970s global economic conditions were conducive to economic expansion and consumer boom. But the OPEC oil price explosion dramatically reversed this upward trend and put the East European economies on the road to ruin. Their course was only accelerated by the availability of Western credits. These had originally been intended to facilitate export-led growth, but they were now increasingly diverted to feed the consumer boom. By the middle of the 1980s all the East European economies were in crisis. Only systemic reform could possibly have saved them, but Moscow would not have permitted this, even if the East European leaderships had themselves been so inclined.

In these conditions of depression and failure, political opposition in the East-Central European states grew and solidified. This opposition brought together—although the strength and unity varied according to country—intellectuals, young people, and workers; sometimes, especially in the case of Hungary, these movements allied themselves with reformist members of the communist establishment. Just as important as this growing opposition was the fact that those sections of society that before had supported the regimes now began to withhold their support. The communist ruling elites then began to lose confidence in themselves. A prerevolutionary situation was in the making.

Two external factors played a role in this process of disintegration— one subsidiary, the other vital. The improvement of East-West relations that began in earnest in the late 1960s not only made most East European states economically dependent on the West but also brought their societies increasingly under Western influence. The process served both to soften communism and restrain it.

But the Western influence was slight compared with the Soviet impact under Gorbachev after 1985. Gorbachev (1) galvanized the reform elements that had already formed in Eastern Europe, making reform, if not mandatory, then at least *de rigueur*; (2) decisively demoralized conservative elements, which now realized they could no longer look to Moscow for support, even to ensure the survival of the system itself. The Brezhnev Doctrine, though not officially pronounced dead, expired as soon as Gorbachev assumed the Soviet leadership.

But Gorbachev, despite subsequent claims to the contrary, did not anticipate, still less connive at, the collapse of communism in Eastern Europe. He evidently believed the socialist basis there was sound enough to withstand the rigors of systemic change and that socialism would eventually emerge the stronger for it. Nor was his policy ever predicated on the eventual reunification of Germany. He may sincerely have worked for the overcoming of the division of Europe, but his vision of a united Europe involved two Germanies. Even when it was obvious that the rest of Eastern Europe was rejecting the system, Gorbachev still apparently believed that the GDR and East German socialism could survive.

In terms of its previous domination, any future Soviet role in Eastern Europe is likely to be minimal. In fact, some Soviet leaders and many decisionmakers fear a total exclusion from Eastern Europe and, by extension, from the new Europe itself. The only interaction with Eastern Europe, they feel, will entail the latter exporting eastward its destabilizing mix of nationalism, market capitalism, and liberal democracy. At present the main characteristic of the Soviet–East European relationship involves the East Europeans seeking to extricate themselves as smoothly as possible from the multilateral organizations like SMEA and the Warsaw Pact that were the expressions of Soviet domination. Eventually, however, the mutual advantages to be derived from economic relations and even cooperation should be enough to ensure the Soviets a continuing role in Eastern Europe. And the uncertainties and possible changes of the new European order might ensure a political and diplomatic role also. But it will be different, and it will be diminished.

CONTENTS

TABLES

I. GORBACHEV'S DILEMMAS IN EASTERN EUROPE

The impetus for change in Soviet policy toward Eastern Europe must be sought in the same factors that promoted radical changes in Soviet domestic and foreign policy—the growing recognition of the profound domestic and foreign policy crisis that confronted Soviet policymakers since the early 1980s.[1] At the same time, Mikhail Gorbachev's attempts to deal with Eastern Europe were plagued from the outset by the same contradictions and inconsistencies that characterized the first five years of his rule. Although Gorbachev has shown himself to be a masterful politician and tactician in consolidating his personal power, those qualities have not necessarily produced any lasting solutions in his attempts to deal with multiple and mounting crises. As Harry Gelman has written in an overview of the Soviet leader's first five years in power:

> Gorbachev's fundamental problem was thus not that he has tried to do too much on too many fronts, but rather that he lagged behind on some fronts while advancing rapidly on others. It is the resulting inconsistencies and "disconnects" that have been most destabilizing. . . . Over his first five years, Gorbachev did not have a consistent strategy or a single blueprint for reform because he lacked an integrating vision of how to coordinate advance in different spheres simultaneously. In addition, his notion of what he wanted in each arena has been continuously evolving—partly in reaction to the . . . failure of previous efforts, and partly in response to his sense of changing political pressures.[2]

Perhaps nowhere does Gelman's description hold more true than in the case of Soviet policy toward Eastern Europe. Gorbachev's approach to what Jim Brown, former research director of Radio Free Europe, termed the USSR's classic dilemma between "cohesion and viability" in Eastern Europe was radically different from that of his predecessors, but the changes in Soviet policy would unfold in a halting and inconsistent fashion. While Gorbachev would effectively dismantle the key pillars upon which previous Soviet policy was built, he failed to

---

[1]On the genesis of *perestroika* see Seweryn Bialer, "Domestic and International Factors in the Formation of Gorbachev's Reforms," *Journal of International Affairs*, Spring 1989, pp. 283–297.

[2]See Harry Gelman, *Gorbachev's First Five Years in the Soviet Leadership: The Clash of Personalities and the Remaking of Institutions*, The RAND Corporation, R-3951-A, May 1990, pp. 109–110.

replace them with a viable alternative; and even if the fate of Gorbachev's domestic policies is still uncertain, the results are surely in on his erratic efforts to reform Soviet–East European relations. Some Soviet academics have tried to paint a positive picture of the dramatic events of fall 1989, but it is difficult to escape the conclusion that the precipitous crumbling of East European communism was undesired and largely unforeseen, and that it means a major shift in the East-West balance and a decline in Soviet influence in Europe.[3] Nowhere does this hold more true than in the case of the GDR, where the collapse of communism confronted an unsuspecting Moscow with what in a matter of weeks became the seeming inevitability of German unification.

This report will examine in detail the complex web of factors that fostered the democratic revolutions of 1989. Eastern Europe was and is no monolith: each country had its own unique part to play in the fall of communism. But before telling those individual stories, it is helpful to set the stage by considering three questions: What was the link between the rise of *perestroika* in the USSR and the shifts in Soviet attitudes toward Eastern Europe? How did official Soviet policy toward Eastern Europe evolve under the aegis of Gorbachev? What forces did those policy changes set in motion?

Such questions are by no mens solely academic or historical. The issue of "who lost Eastern Europe" and, above all, "who lost Germany" is a real factor in the ongoing competition and power struggle that characterizes Soviet politics, as reflected in statements by Gorbachev and Foreign Minister Eduard Shevardnadze denying that they are to blame for the events of fall 1989. Moreover, one must first understand why Moscow was so unprepared for the political earthquake that shook Eastern Europe before attempting to assess its efforts to come to grips with the aftermath, especially its reaction to the question of a reunified Germany. Finally, as one Soviet academic wrote in the spring of 1990, although the fall of communism in Eastern Europe may have been inevitable, it is important to understand the details of the collapse, for that and the variances among different countries may also tell us something about the future influence of communism and Moscow in the region.[4]

---

[3]In the words of Sergei Karaganov: "The events which took place in Eastern Europe in the last months of 1989 were in many respects the crowning success of the recent Soviet European policy and they confirmed several very positive tendencies." See his article "The Year of Europe: A Soviet View," *Survival*, March/April 1990, pp. 121–128.

[4]In the words of Anatolii Butenko: "A system rotting to the core is doomed in all cases to its inevitable demise. However, the way in which it falls—in the form of a bloody fight, an uncontrolled mutiny, or a 'mild revolution'—and, above all, whether it crushes its creators under the ruins all depends on many circumstances and chiefly on the actions of communists, their efficiency and decisiveness." See his article "Time to

THE ORIGINS OF SOVIET REFORM AND THE IMPLICATIONS FOR EASTERN EUROPE

When Gorbachev came to power in 1985, he inherited a country and a system in a state of political, economic, and spiritual crisis. By the end of the Brezhnev era, Soviet society was chronically ill by almost any standard. In political terms, the country was suffering from growing apathy not only among the population but in important segments of the party itself, individuals and groups who found themselves estranged from their rulers. Economically, it was becoming clear that the extensive growth model had reached its limits and that its effectiveness was diminishing rapidly. Cheap sources of raw materials were exhausted. The input of ever-expanding capital expenditures was becoming increasingly difficult. The neglect of the economic infrastructure had created tremendous bottlenecks and widespread waste of materials and labor. In a speech at a party plenum in February 1988, Gorbachev admitted that in the 20 years before his accession to power the Soviet national income, with the exception of the production of alcohol, had not increased in real terms.[5]

The mounting internal imperatives for Soviet reform were augmented by international economic trends. By the early 1980s, for the first time in postwar history the USSR was falling further behind the major capitalist nations in key economic indicators. The technological gap between the Soviet Union and the advanced capitalist countries was widening sharply and ever faster. A growing sector of the Soviet elite realized that Soviet economic and technological stagnation, coupled with the explosive growth sparked in the capitalist world by the Third Industrial Revolution (microelectronics and telecommunications), threatened to have calamitous results for the USSR.

Moscow was also confronted with a deterioration in its international political position. In the late 1960s and early 1970s, the achievement of strategic parity and the onset of détente was seen in the USSR as signaling a basic shift in the correlation of forces between the capitalist and socialist systems. A central premise of Brezhnev's foreign policy was that the correlation of forces in the world, a concept that encompasses the ideological, political, economic, and military power of a state or alliance, was moving in favor of the socialist countries. By the early 1980s, however, the undeniable growth in Soviet military power had

---

Learn Some Lessons: What Events in Eastern European Countries Tell Us," *Nedelya*, No. 11, March 1990.

[5]See *Pravda*, February 19, 1988; see also Elizabeth Teague, "Gorbachev Tells Plenum Soviet Economy Has Stopped Growing," *Radio Liberty Research*, RL 74/88, February 22, 1988.

only provoked efforts to counterbalance that power. Even before the invasion of Afghanistan, Soviet policy had precipitated a backlash in American policy toward Moscow. The USSR's Afghan venture not only signaled the end of Soviet-American détente, but led to a new round in the arms race that increased the economic costs of geopolitical competition and fueled Soviet fears of an American technological breakout. The deployment of SS-20s in Europe and the subsequent anti-INF deployment campaign backfired; it would go down in Soviet diplomacy as a textbook example of a major military miscalculation followed by diplomatic clumsiness.

By the mid-1980s, the USSR was in a state of internal distress and external overextension. The domestic crisis, combined with the decline on the international scene, required an urgent reassessment of Soviet internal and external policy. The internal policy was and is Gorbachev's first priority. He and other leading officials have repeatedly stressed that the primary item on the Soviet Union's agenda is *perestroika* and internal reform, not foreign policy, and that the chief objective of foreign policy is the creation of an international environment that will permit the USSR to turn inward safely.[6] But at first there were few signs that Gorbachev would initiate the type of reforms that would unleash multiple pressures and processes for change in the USSR.[7] On the contrary, his earliest policies seemed to a large degree

---

[6]In Gorbachev's words: "I state with full responsibility that our international policy is more than ever determined by domestic policy, by our interest in concentrating on domestic endeavors to improve our country. This is why we need lasting peace, predictability, and constructiveness in international relations." "For a Nuclear-Free World, for the Survival of Mankind," *FBIS-SOV-87-031*, February 17, 1987, p. AA 17. According to Foreign Minister Shevardnadze, the key task of Soviet foreign policy is to ensure that "our country should not bear additional expenditures in connection with the necessity of supporting our defense capability and the defense of our legitimate foreign policy interests. That means that we must seek paths to the limitation and reduction in military rivalry, to the removal of confrontational moments in relations with other states, to the dampening down of conflicts and crisis." See his speech to a meeting of the Diplomatic Academy on June 27, 1987, published in *Vestnik Ministerstva Inostrannykh Del SSSR*, August 26, 1987.

[7]There is little evidence that Gorbachev harbored radical reformist views at the time of his elevation to the top echelon of the Soviet leadership, and some reason to assume he would not have been elected had this been the case. The initial biographies of Gorbachev that appeared in the West generally concluded that he was at best a proponent of limited reform and modernization. Yegor Yakovlev, chief editor of *Moscow News*, would describe the evolution of *perestroika* in the following terms: "I could perhaps name three stages in the development of the social consciousness of our country. At the very beginning of *perestroika* it seemed merely enough to change one's posture in one's armchair for everything to start smooth sailing. When it became clear that it would not be possible to overcome the past at once, we clamped down on the bureaucrat, whom we saw as the main adversary of the new, and suspected of all mortal sins. At the time we rather looked like those people who raised a pack of wolves, let them loose, and were now trying to catch them. Lastly, the third stage in the development of social thinking coincided

to be a continuation of the limited reforms initiated by Andropov—calls for greater discipline and efficiency, albeit in a younger and more dynamic guise. The emphasis was on economic restructuring and modernization, concepts that would only later be flanked by *glasnost* and democratization. Initially, Gorbachev maintained that the Soviet Union was facing what he termed a "precrisis," justifying his push for more reforms by maintaining that they were needed to ward off a more general crisis, to the brink of which the society and the economy had been brought by the Brezhnev leadership.

In any case, Gorbachev's attempts to cope with seemingly intractable problems would lead to a gradual transformation of his own agenda and policies. It was perhaps inevitable that initial reform attempts were partial, marked by compromise, and thus often inconsistent. As minor tinkering with the system failed to elicit the desired improvements, and as the depth of the problems facing the Soviet Union became more apparent, Gorbachev was forced to expand the scope of the reform debate via *glasnost* in an attempt to address the deeper root causes of existing problems and to find meaningful answers.

The evolution of Soviet "new thinking" in foreign and security policy must be seen in large part against this background. The core concepts of "new thinking"—mutual security, common human values over class values, global interdependence, and reasonable sufficiency in defense policy—did not of course spring full-blown from the pen of a Gorbachev speechwriter, but had a much longer intellectual gestation period and can be traced to the writings of a number of Soviet academics as far back as the late Brezhnev period.[8] But it was in the midst of the growing domestic crisis and the failures of Brezhnev's foreign policy that they now took hold. While this debate has been, first and foremost, a Soviet debate, it has had enormous ramifications for Eastern Europe. In the case of domestic reform in the USSR, the link is clear. Although the days when Eastern Europe emulated the Soviet domestic model in each and every detail have long been gone, Soviet ideologies and theories on a "developed socialist society" still established the broad parameters within which those allies pursued their national policies.

---

with the 19th party conference. It became self-evident that our existing political structures were reproducing anti-*perestroika*. For instance, how could the old Supreme Soviet be equal to the new tasks if it was of the same composition as before? The old structures, which provided a dependable foundation for stagnation, have become a Procrustean bed. At the time of renewal, a reform of the political system alone can ensure *perestroika*'s irreversibility." See his interview in *Moscow News*, No. 8, February 19, 1989.

[8]For a useful survey on the origins of this debate, see Stephen Shenfield, *The Nuclear Predicament: Explorations in Soviet Ideology*, Royal Institute of International Affairs, London, 1987.

Growing Soviet criticism of the Brezhnev period not only undercut the policies pursued in Eastern Europe in the 1970s and early 1980s; as scholars increasingly traced the origins of the USSR's crisis back to earlier phases of its history, above all the Stalinist experience, communist leaders in Eastern Europe began to be confronted by some touchy questions. While Gorbachev could openly claim that Soviet theory had stagnated since the 1940s and hark back to an earlier phase of ostensibly healthy pre-Stalinist socialism under Lenin, such an option simply did not exist for East European communist regimes that came into power in the late 1940s specifically as a byproduct of Stalin's foreign policy. The rise of such questions raised the issue of the legitimacy of regimes established in the late 1940s whose very existence was intertwined with the mantle of Stalin.[9]

Gorbachev's initial stance that the USSR's troubles were the result of mistaken policies of the past and the Brezhnevian period of stagnation must have discomfited those leaderships in Eastern Europe whose legacy seemed closely intertwined with Brezhnev's. Above all, it suggested that the diagnosis of the ills of the socialist system applied to Eastern Europe as well. While Gorbachev was careful not to destabilize regimes in Eastern Europe by pressuring them to adopt reform programs, the fact was that leading Soviet reformers increasingly argued that the problem was systemic in nature. The Institute for the Economics of the World Socialist System, headed by Academician Oleg T. Bogomolov, has been foremost among proponents of the view that the crisis facing the USSR is a crisis of socialism as a system, and that all socialist countries will sooner or later have to implement both political and economic reforms.[10] Bogomolov repeatedly went on record to

---

[9]One of the interesting and as-yet unanswered questions is what impact, if any, crises in Eastern Europe, especially in Poland, had on the genesis of *perestroika* in the USSR. See Elizabeth Teague, "Perestroika: The Polish Influence," *Survey*, October 1988, pp. 39–59.

[10]Bogomolov was a member of the special "Interdepartment Council" set up in 1983 to advise the Politburo, then headed by Yurii Andropov, on the relevance of economic reforms in Eastern Europe for the USSR, and as such had an opportunity to influence Gorbachev after his elevation to the CPSU Politburo. Bogomolov was also the first Soviet official to speak of the need for "reform," in an article in *Pravda* on March 14, 1983—long before Gorbachev or other party leaders felt able to do so. In the spring of 1988, Bogomolov revealed that he had sent a memorandum to the Politburo in January 1980 criticizing the Soviet invasion of Afghanistan and warning of the consequences for East-West relations in Europe. See his letter to the editor in *Literaturnaya Gazeta*, February 17, 1988. According to Bogomolov: "At the current stage [in the development of socialism] a certain commonality is manifesting itself in the problems that have cropped up even in the development of countries that are extremely different from one another. Almost all—without exception—countries of socialism are encountering quite complex economic problems and are at the peculiar stage of switching from an extensive-type economy to an intensive economy, and from the former command-edict model of economic management to a different mode. It is not only our country that is

emphasize that the problems in Eastern Europe came about because those countries were compelled to copy a model of socialism that was itself Stalinist and flawed.[11]

In addition to the delegitimizing criticism of past aspects of socialist rule, the fact that Soviet scholars looking for solutions also turned to Western models of political and economic management—ranging from the role of market mechanisms to the importance of constitutional reform and the separation of party and state—has inevitably legitimized an array of alternative concepts once rejected as unacceptable bourgeois thinking. This, coupled with Soviet statements that each socialist country has the right to seek its own national solutions to the problems it faces, has stoked a wide-ranging debate over political and economic reform. The fact that Moscow has not been able to produce a successfully functioning reform model has simply meant that an ideological Pandora's box was opened and never shut.[12]

The debate over "new thinking" in foreign and security policy also had profound ramifications for Eastern Europe. It was there that Soviet definitions of security and ideology merged in the early postwar period. Moscow's desire to have a security glacis on its Western

---

effecting this transition. It is of an international character and has become objectively necessary. So that even in those countries where there has been insufficiently broad discussion of questions of economic reform and new models of organizing the socialist economy, even in these countries such processes have become imminent and must, sooner or later, become the subject of conscious policy. This problem—the renewal of the economic system—is a common one. . . . But I think that politics also contains many problems that are common to many countries. The need, for instance, to democratize public life and to give new substance to the very concept of socialist democracy. . . . All the socialist countries face these problems." See his interview in *Komsomolskaya Pravda*, July 23, 1988, *FBIS-SOV-88-146*, July 29, 1988, pp. 4–6.

[11]According to Bogomolov, "I believe the point is that many socialist countries began to build a new society while strongly influenced by the model of socialism prevailing in the Soviet Union, which today is in need of restructuring. This model is of the lowest type, based on command-edict principles which preclude the development of real commodity-money relations and a genuine market. If we are talking about the political system, then it is the kind of model in which command-edict methods once again supplanted the development of democracy and the broad participation of the masses in decision making. *There is no doubt that this model was not only an example, but that to a certain extent it was foisted upon them, because the same principle of democratic centralism was in force in relations between socialist countries as was proclaimed in domestic policy development—subordination to the center imposition of* [Soviet] *experience, and the desire to unify the socialist world* [emphasis added]." See Bogomolov's interview in *Sovetskaya Kultura*, July 12, 1988, *JPRS-UIA-88-015*.

[12]In early October 1988, Politburo member and ideology chief Vadim Medvedev called for a new concept of socialism and gave the green light for borrowing concepts from the capitalist West when he stated: "In working out the socialist perspective and in formulating a modern concept of socialism we cannot ignore the experience of mankind as a whole, including the nonsocialist world." Medvedev called specifically for close study of Western social organizations, industrial production, and integration into the world economy. See his speech in *Pravda*, October 5, 1988.

borders, along with the conviction that ideological conformity was the best guarantee of political loyalty, locked it into an extremely rigid policy stance toward Eastern Europe. Bloc unity was imposed and maintained by cultivating a view of a Western ideological threat that also allowed Moscow to draw a sharp line as to which types of interactions with Western partners were a threat to Warsaw Pact security. As a result, Soviet rethinking on subjects as diverse as arms control, so-called "class" versus "human" interests, the reformability of capitalism and "militarism," or the pros and cons of 1992 and political-economic integration in Western Europe inevitably had implications for reform and bloc cohesion as it loosened the ideological and political straightjacket that Moscow once attempted to impose on the region and undercut previous Soviet definitions of security threats. Finally, the overall East-West climate now provided a far more hospitable environment for those reform forces in the ruling communist elites to push ahead with their own plans.[13]

In short, Soviet "new thinking" in foreign and security policy reinforced the conviction among ruling communist elites that muddling through was no longer a feasible strategy and that there was no alternative to launching a high-risk strategy of reform. There was a growing realization that Moscow was no longer willing or able to provide substantive political and economic assistance, and that it could not be counted upon to rescue any East European regime in a future crisis. The Soviet withdrawal from Afghanistan, Moscow's announced troop reductions in the region, along with statements by senior Soviet officials, above all Foreign Minister Shevardnadze, that the USSR's long-term goal was further reductions and the eventual elimination of Soviet troops in Eastern Europe, all underlined a single message: changes in Soviet policy were not only encouraging but in many ways compelling changes in the relationship between rulers and ruled in Eastern Europe.[14]

---

[13]As Hungarian Prime Minister Miklos Nemeth stated in early 1989 before a group of party activists: "This [i.e., reform] is something that is now primarily up to us. International conditions now favor the reforms, unlike in the 1970s. The Soviet Union is on the side of Hungarian reforms. The advanced capitalist countries have not only expressed their interest in the progress of the Hungarian reforms, but are also providing help." See Nemeth's speech, Budapest Television, 1905 GMT, January 14, 1989 (*FBIS-EEU-89-010*, January 17, 1989, pp. 28–29).

[14]Both points were laid out in a memorandum authored by Mieczyslaw Rakowski in 1987 and subsequently leaked to the Western press. See excerpts in *Der Spiegel*, No. 29, 1988, pp. 119–120.

THE EVOLUTION OF SOVIET POLICY:
A GORBACHEV DOCTRINE?

Speaking at the Warsaw Pact summit held in Bucharest in summer 1989, Soviet leader Gorbachev summarized what have become the dominant themes in official Soviet commentary on Eastern Europe under his aegis. There is no model for the building of socialism, he emphasized, and each communist party has to pursue its own strategy in line with its national conditions. Socialist pluralism, Gorbachev said, is not only a new *leitmotif* in domestic Soviet politics, but in Soviet–East European ties as well; each communist party enjoys total independence in its internal affairs. The model for the socialist community, according to the Soviet leader, is one of "unity in diversity, namely . . . a looser and more pluralistic communist alliance in which each country [is] free to pursue its own policies in accordance with national conditions while learning from the experience of its fraternal neighbors."[15]

Gorbachev's remarks reflected what at the time was the culmination of a significant transformation in Soviet attitudes toward Eastern Europe. Coming shortly before the wave of revolution swept across the region, it reflected what in many ways amounted to a Gorbachev Doctrine toward Eastern Europe. It was nevertheless a transformation that took place in a quiet and low-key fashion and in conjunction with the Soviet debate about reforms in domestic and foreign policy. While distancing himself from past Soviet policy toward the region, Gorbachev clearly sought to avoid exposing the sensitive area of Soviet–East European ties to the type of scrutiny and criticism that could undermine current leaderships in Eastern Europe.[16]

One should recall that Mikhail Gorbachev initially adopted a rather conservative stance on bloc unity immediately after becoming CPSU General Secretary. During his first year in power, Soviet policy appeared largely a continuation of the past, complemented by the fresh sense of dynamism and vigor interjected by a new and younger Soviet leader. In his maiden speech as General Secretary, for example, Gorbachev emphasized that the "first priority" of Soviet foreign policy

---

[15]See Gorbachev's remarks as reported by TASS (in English), July 7, 1989.

[16]Soviet policy toward Eastern Europe is one area in which *glasnost* and criticism of past policy was limited. One should point out that the debate on "blank spots" has thus far been focused primarily on each communist party dealing with its own history, as well as the role of Stalin and the history of the Comintern. There has been little open debate in the Soviet press over interparty relations or detailed discussion of past Soviet policy toward individual East European countries. In an interview in early 1989, Vitalii Korotich, editor of *Ogonek*, observed that Soviet journalists were still more hesitant to criticize Soviet foreign than domestic policy. See the interview in the *Journal of International Affairs*, Spring 1989, pp. 357–362.

would be "to protect and strengthen in all ways the fraternal friendship with our closest comrades-in-arms and allies, the countries of the great socialist community."[17] Speaking at a Central Committee plenum the next month, the new Soviet leader repeated the need for greater bloc cohesion.[18] Moscow's desire to shore up the longer-term cohesion of the bloc was also apparent in the official extension of the Warsaw Pact in April 1985, when Soviet officials pushed through a 30-year renewal (20 years plus an automatic 10-year renewal) and rejected suggestions voiced in Eastern Europe for a shorter renewal period.[19]

The appearance of an article in *Pravda* in June penned by O. Vladimirov, presumably a pseudonym for Oleg Rakhmanin, deputy chief of the Central Committee's Liaison Department, appeared to signal a conservative approach to Eastern Europe. In the strongest attack against the reformist position to date, he accused "anticommunist theoreticians and opportunists" of trying to "pose as advocates of some new kind of 'unity.'"[20] The fact that the article was written under a pseudonym, however, along with the fact that this Vladimirov line was immediately countered by other reformist voices such as Oleg T. Bogomolov, Director of the Institute for the Economics of the World Socialist System, suggested that the subject of future policy toward the bloc was still disputed within the Soviet elite.[21] Such discord was reminiscent of debates witnessed a few years earlier over how much leeway East European states enjoyed to pursue their national interests.[22]

There were nonetheless concerted official Soviet attempts to reverse the sense of disarray that had crept into bloc affairs in the early 1980s. In the course of 1985, for example, four separate gatherings of Warsaw Pact leaders were convened, and Gorbachev initiated a new tradition of

---

[17]*Pravda*, March 12, 1985.

[18]Gorbachev called for "the improvement and enrichment of cooperation among the fraternal socialist countries in every possible way, the development of comprehensive ties, the assurance of close collaboration in the political, economic, ideological, military, and other spheres, and efforts to organically combine the national and international interests of all members of the great socialist community." See his remarks printed in *Pravda*, April 23, 1985.

[19]See Vladimir Kusin, "Impending Renewal of the Warsaw Pact," *Radio Free Europe Research*, RAD BR/36 (Eastern Europe), April 22, 1985; and Vladimir Socor, "Warsaw Pact Summit Renews the Warsaw Treaty," *Radio Free Europe Research*, RAD BR/53 (Eastern Europe), June 19, 1985.

[20]O. Vladimirov, "Vedushchii faktor mirovogo revolyutsionnogo protsessa," *Pravda*, June 21, 1985.

[21]See Oleg T. Bogomolov, "Soglasovanie ekonomicheskikh interesov i politiki pri sotsializme, *Kommunist*, No. 10, July 1985, pp. 82–93.

[22]See Ronald D. Asmus, "The Dialectics of Détente and Discord," *ORBIS*, Winter 1985; A. Ross Johnson, *The Impact of Eastern Europe on Soviet Policy Toward Western Europe*, The RAND Corporation, R-3332-AF, March 1986; and Ernst Klux, "Contradictions in Soviet Socialism," *Problems of Communism*, November–December 1984.

regular consultations with his East European allies following major foreign policy pronouncements.[23] The same pattern of increased consultation and a greater emphasis on coordination was evident in the realm of intrabloc economic ties. Two sessions of the Council for Mutual Economic Assistance (CMEA) were held in 1985, the second of which produced the ambitious 15-year Comprehensive Program for Scientific and Technical Progress. The political significance that Gorbachev still attached to the CMEA as a cohesive economic bloc was highlighted by his observation that the comprehensive program was of "paramount importance" in ensuring "technological independence from and invulnerability to pressure and blackmail on the part of imperialism."[24]

Such calls were matched by warnings about the dangers of Western economic ties. Speaking in East Berlin in April 1986 at the 11th party congress of SED, the East German communist party, Gorbachev called for cooperation between the socialist states "to be raised to a still higher level, not just by a point or two, but, as mathematicians say, by a whole order."[25] The same message was conveyed several weeks later in Warsaw at the 10th congress of the Polish communist party, PUWP, where Gorbachev claimed that "there are traps laid down on the trading routes to the West," warned about the "pitfall" of "dependence" on the West, and called for more vigorous introduction of new forms of cooperation in CMEA.[26] In a speech delivered in late summer 1985 to the secretaries for economic affairs of the central committees of the East European countries, Gorbachev is also reported to have issued a harsh warning against the glitter of market reform. "Many of you see the solution to your problems in resorting to market mechanisms in place of central planning. Some of you look at the market as a lifesaver for your economies. But, comrades, you should not think about lifesavers but about the ship, and the ship is socialism."[27]

---

[23]See Ronald D. Asmus, "Warsaw Pact Meeting after Geneva," *Radio Free Europe Research*, RAD BR/135 (East-West), November 26, 1985.

[24]*Pravda*, December 18, 1985. Such comments were echoed by Nikolai Ryzhkov, who emphasized that better utilization of the economic potential of the CMEA was a key strategic objective for Moscow. According to Ryzhkov: "It must be admitted quite openly that the socialist countries are by no means adequately utilizing the potential of scientific and technical progress and the joint resolution of existing scientific and technical problems. That is why the comprehensive program for scientific and technical progress is acquiring strategic importance for us." *Izvestiya*, December 18, 1985. See also Vlad Sobell, "Mikhail Gorbachev Takes Charge of the CMEA," *Radio Free Europe Research*, RAD BR/146 (Eastern Europe), December 20, 1985.

[25]*Neues Deutschland*, April 21, 1986.

[26]TASS, June 30, 1986.

[27]Quoted in Seweryn Bialer and Joan Afferica, "The Genesis of Gorbachev's World," *Foreign Affairs*, Vol. 64, No. 3, p. 612.

Such statements came, of course, at a time when Gorbachev's own domestic reform program was circumscribed, the primary emphasis being put on economic modernization and restructuring as opposed to *glasnost* and democratization. The East European corollary to this initial phase of Gorbachev as a limited reformist consisted of renewed emphasis on bloc unity and integration within the confines of the existing framework. Just as Gorbachev limited his analysis of the USSR's woes to a concession that the problems resulted from erroneous policies and not endemic systemic weakness, his analysis of difficulties in Eastern Europe was also circumscribed and linked to past policy errors.[28] Similarly, just as Gorbachev's call for domestic reform had been modest and had stayed within the framework of predominant Soviet views on political and economic organization, the remedies he prescribed for the socialist bloc also remained within a framework of limited economic reform and enhanced intrabloc cooperation, with the result that countries like the GDR initially received Soviet praise but the efforts of countries such as Hungary to move toward market-oriented reform were still the subject of occasional veiled warnings.[29]

In short, this was Gorbachev Mark I, a new, young Soviet leader clearly in a hurry, the modernizer seeking to revitalize existing structures without necessarily altering them radically. There were few indications at this point that he was to become a radical reformer, the Gorbachev Mark II. His initial policy statements toward Eastern Europe seemed further proof that his reform agenda was limited in scope and that his primary concerns were greater economic efficiency and the maintenance of stability, both for the USSR and the bloc.[30] That

---

[28]Speaking at the 10th PUWP Congress in Warsaw, for example, Gorbachev described the Polish crisis of 1980–81 as "not a protest of workers against socialism" but an expression of popular dissatisfaction with "subjective distortions of the socialist system"—i.e., implying that Poland's socialist system was still essentially healthy. Gorbachev concluded that the primary lesson of the 1980–81 crisis was that "socialist gains" in Poland were irreversible and that any attempt "to wrench a country away from the socialist community" represented a threat to "the entire postwar settlement and, in the final analysis, peace"—a statement few would remember when communist rule collapsed peacefully at the ballot box a mere three years later. See Boghdan Nahaylo and Elizabeth Teague, "Gorbachev Addresses Tenth Congress of PUWP," *Radio Liberty Research*, RL 253/86, June 30, 1986.

[29]See Elizabeth Teague, "Pravda Cautions Hungary on Economic Ties with the West," *Radio Liberty Research*, RL 45/86, January 23, 1986.

[30]A report entitled "Eastern Europe: 40 Years after Yalta" issued by the London Institute for Strategic Studies in the spring of 1986 captured the dominant view in the West at the time when it related that Gorbachev "favored modernization over reform," that he seemed "totally innocent of any belief in democratization," and concluded: "In fact, Gorbachev has said little to suggest that he favors even 'reform': he might be prepared (or feel compelled) to tolerate it in Hungary, but he might feel threatened if it were adopted generally in Eastern Europe. It would seem to be the East German 'modernization strategy' that he favors most."

Soviet policy toward Eastern Europe was caught uneasily in a sort of limbo between an old desire to maintain bloc cohesion and a growing recognition that the old ways were increasingly unable to deliver efficiency and stability was reflected at the 27th Soviet Union party congress in February–March 1986. Gorbachev's lengthy speech barely touched upon Soviet–East European relations, and it provided little substance on Moscow's future approach to Eastern Europe.[31]

In retrospect, it is clear that Gorbachev's comments on Eastern Europe were brief because official Soviet policy was already undergoing reappraisal. The paucity of his remarks on Eastern Europe notwithstanding, his embrace of the need for "radical reforms" and his lengthy comments on the need for "new thinking" in foreign policy must have indicated to the Eastern European communist leaders in attendance that the winds of change were starting to blow and that reform was on the horizon.[32] Following the party congress, Gorbachev would move more assertively to push a reform agenda in both domestic and foreign policy. At the Central Committee plenum in June, Gorbachev criticized conservatives for resisting reform, and in a speech in Krasnodar in September, he first spoke of the "democratization" of Soviet society as his main priority.[33] In a closed-door meeting between himself and the USSR's leading diplomats, Gorbachev explicitly criticized the previous conduct of Soviet foreign policy, including that for Eastern Europe. The Soviet leader described past policy toward the region as paternalistic and prejudiced, and called for greater respect and recognition of the national needs and interests of the individual socialist countries.[34]

[31]No more than six paragraphs out of a five-and-a-half-hour speech were devoted to intrabloc relations. See Gorbachev's speech in *Pravda*, February 26, 1986.

[32]See Sarah M. Terry, "The Twenty-Seventh CPSU Congress and Eastern Europe," *Radio Liberty Research*, RL 136/86, March 25, 1986.

[33]See Elizabeth Teague, "Gorbachev Attacks Opponents of Reform," *Radio Liberty Research*, RL 232/86, June 18, 1986; and "Gorbachev's First Two Years in Power," *Radio Liberty Research*, RL 94/87, March 9, 1987.

[34]Gorbachev's comments were not published until over one year later. His remarks on Eastern Europe were summarized by a Foreign Ministry publication in the following fashion: "Reemphasis was made of the priority that questions of the relations with the socialist countries occupy in Soviet foreign policy. Attention was also directed to the need to build those relations on the basis of respect for their experience and dignity, the understanding of the national specifics, and trust in the search for national paths of development. In order to guarantee the new quality of the relations with the socialist countries, it is important to overcome the prejudice, complacency, and stagnation that continue to exist in the consciousness of several of our representatives. It should not be felt that we can teach all of them. No one has given us that right. On the contrary, as the most powerful country in the socialist community we must demonstrate modesty. Contacts with the socialist countries must be concrete and informal. It has proven possible to achieve this at the summit level and we must also try to achieve it at other levels.

Such shifts in tone were reinforced by shifts in personnel. In March 1986, Vadim Medvedev became head of the Central Committee department responsible for intrabloc affairs, replacing Konstantin Rusakov, longtime head of the Party's department for relations with ruling communist parties, who had retired several weeks before the 27th party congress. Several months later Rusakov's key deputy, Oleg Rakhmanin, the alleged author of the numerous hard-line articles on relations with Eastern Europe published under the name O. Vladimirov, was retired and replaced by the reformer Georgii Shakhnazarov.[35] In May, Gorbachev initiated a major personnel and organizational shakeup in the Soviet Foreign Ministry in an attempt to assert his personal control and the implementation of "new thinking."[36] In September 1988, Medvedev was promoted to full membership in the Politburo in charge of ideology. The amount of East European expertise in Gorbachev's immediate entourage increased further with the appointment of Vladimir Kryuchkov, a former expert on Hungary who had worked with Yurii Andropov in the Central Committee Department for Socialist Countries, to the Politburo post of chairman of the KGB, and the appointment of Nikolai Talyzin to the post of chief Soviet representative to the CMEA.[37]

In fall 1986, Gorbachev is reported to have officially announced the shift in Soviet policy to a CMEA summit in Moscow.[38] In the spring months of 1987, a Gorbachev Mark II emerged on the political stage as a radical reformer in Soviet domestic politics, but as an active proponent of a new vision of Soviet–East European relations under the guise of fraternal equality and "unity." Soviet leaders were more explicit than ever in stating that it was up to each country to decide its

---

It is necessary to involve our allies in a real manner in our common affairs—even if we are talking about the smallest countries—and to engage in preliminary coordination with them concerning the essence of foreign policy actions and to distribute the efforts of the fraternal countries in the foreign policy sphere." See "Report on 'Basic Theses' of speech by M. S. Gorbachev at USSR Ministry of Foreign Affairs, May 23, 1986," in *Vestnik Ministerstva Inostrannykh Del SSSR*, August 5, 1987, pp. 4–6 (*FBIS-SOV-87-170*, September 2, 1987).

[35]Shakhnazarov would subsequently be promoted to one of Gorbachev's immediate foreign policy advisors, reportedly responsible for Eastern Europe. He has been one of the most outspoken proponents of the "de-ideologization" of East-West relations in Europe. See his article in *Kommunist*, No. 3, 1989.

[36]See Alexander Rahr, "Winds of Change Hit Foreign Ministry," *Radio Liberty Research*, RL 274/86, July 16, 1986.

[37]For further details see Vladimir V. Kusin, "The Recent Soviet Personnel Changes and Eastern Europe," *Radio Free Europe Research*, RAD BR/202 (Eastern Europe), October 7, 1988.

[38]Soviet authors repeatedly refer to the November 1986 meeting as a turning point in Soviet–East European relations.

own reform needs.[39] Gorbachev himself used a series of visits to Eastern Europe in the course of 1987 and 1988 to publicize this new line. Speaking in Prague in April, he stated:

> We proceed above all from the premise that the entire system of political relations between the socialist countries can and should be built unswervingly on a foundation of equality and mutual responsibility. No one has rights to claim a special position in the socialist world. The independence of each party, its responsibility to its people, and the right to resolve questions of the country's development in a sovereign way—for us these are indisputable principles. At the same time, we are profoundly convinced that the successes of the socialist commonwealth are impossible without concern on the part of each party and country not only for its own interests but for the general interests, without a respectful attitude toward friends and allies and the mandatory consideration of their interests.[40]

The same themes were embraced by the Soviet leader in his book *Perestroika*, which appeared the same year.[41] The culmination of this shift in Soviet policy took place in Gorbachev's remarks delivered in November 1987 during the celebration of the 70th anniversary of the Bolshevik Revolution.

> The experience accumulated permits relations among the socialist countries to be better constructed on generally recognized principles. These are unconditional and total equality, the responsibility of the ruling party for affairs in its state, and for patriotic service to its people; concern for the general cause of socialism, respect for one another, a serious attitude toward what has been achieved and tried out by friends; voluntary and varied cooperation, and the strict observation of the principles of peaceful coexistence.

> The world of socialism now rises before us in all its national and social variation. This is good and useful. We have become convinced that unity does not mean being identical or uniform. We have also become convinced that socialism does not and cannot have a model against which all are compared. The criterion for its development at every stage and in every country is the totality and quality of the real successes which have reconstructed society in the interests of the working people.

---

[39]After the CPSU Central Committee plenum, Vadim Medvedev met with East European representatives in February and is reported to have stated that "every country lives under its own peculiar conditions and far be it from us to believe that the political conclusions arrived at by some ought to be automatically foisted on others." See the coverage of the meeting in the Czechoslovak party daily *Rude Pravo*, February 19, 1987.

[40]*Pravda*, April 11, 1987.

[41]Mikhail Gorbachev, *Perestroika: New Thinking for Our Country and the World*, Harper & Row, New York, 1987.

We also know what damage can be done by a weakening of the internationalist principles in mutual relations of socialist states, by deviation from the principles of mutual benefit and mutual aid, and by a lack of attention to the general interests of socialism in action on the world arena. It is with satisfaction that we state that recently our relations with the socialist states have acquired dynamism and are improving.[42]

Speaking one year later at a Foreign Ministry conference following the 19th All-Union Party Conference, Foreign Minister Shevardnadze also embraced the call for a restructuring of Soviet–East European relations.

The structure of our allied relations with the fraternal socialist countries took shape during the first postwar decade. Naturally, it mirrored the features of that period, specific notions of the nature of allied commitments and of the juridical procedures that formalized these commitments. In the period that followed much was done to consolidate the alliance of fraternal countries on the basis of equality and respect for sovereignty and independence. . . . In practical terms, however, it was far from always that coordinated political principles of mutual relations were implemented. A lack of collective thinking and decisionmaking, formalism, window-dressing and insufficient consideration of development specifics and an inability to understand them inflicted damage to the common cause.[43]

---

[42]See Gorbachev's anniversary speech, carried on Moscow Television and translated in *FBIS-SOV-87 212*, November 23, 1987, p. 60. The same line was backed by Vadim Medvedev, now Politburo member in charge of ideology, who confirmed that Moscow had revised its previous stance on national paths to socialism. See Medvedev's speech delivered at the conference "The Great October Revolution and the Modern World," *Pravda*, December 9, 1987, translated in *FBIS-SOV-87-287*, December 10, 1987, pp. 72–75. See also his subsequent interview in *Kommunist*, in which he explains the Kremlin's new line on national diversity in the following terms: "The correlation between basic laws and national features in building socialism is a problem of exceptional political and theoretical importance. This problem has its history. At one point, acknowledging national features was almost considered a deviation from Marxism-Leninism. Somewhat later, this problem began to be interpreted in the sense that national differences were inevitable and admissible in the early stages of building socialism, but that they would be subsequently surmounted, smoothed over and become part of the past. This is why most of the talk at that time was about the national features in the building of socialism rather than about socialism itself. In reality, national characteristics are not something alien to and conflicting with socialism. The acknowledgement, consideration, and utilization of the multiplicity of forms of national manifestations are the strengths of socialism, the confirmation of its universal nature, and an enrichment of the socialist idea itself." *Kommunist*, November 1988, translated in *JPRS-UKO-89-005*, March 2, 1989, pp. 1–12.

[43]See "The Report by Member of the Politburo of the CPSU Central Committee, Minister of Foreign Affairs of the USSR Eduard Shevardnadze at the Scientific and Practical Conference of the USSR Ministry of Foreign Affairs," *International Affairs*, October 1988, p. 22.

At the same conference, the message was delivered even more forcefully by Alexsander Kapto, promoted to first deputy head of the Central Committee Liaison Department in early 1988, when he stated:

> I will remind you that the question of restructuring relations with the socialist countries was raised pointedly and in a principled way and then substantiated in detail in Mikhail Gorbachev's Memorandum to the Politburo of the Central Committee and in his speeches at the working meeting of the fraternal parties in November 1986. . . . The elements of "paternalistic" relations, in which we, as it were, played the role of patron are gone. The need for strictly observing the equality principle, which was advanced before, has been reaffirmed in the spirit of new thinking by the conclusion that no party has a monopoly on the truth of socialism, and only the strengthening of socialism in practice can serve as criterion of this truth. It is no longer viewed as harmful to the unity of the socialist countries that there exist different ideas on how to build a socialist society and that individual socialist countries may have their specific national and state interests. In light of new thinking we have fully realized that the most reliable way to unity lies not in the mechanical unification of these countries, but in the persistent search for solutions based on a balance of their interests, and our common socialist foundation provides the most favorable conditions for this. The fact that disputes over whose socialism is better and more "correct" have been entirely stopped has proven most beneficial for our cooperation. The results are obvious: changes for the better have clearly taken place in the relations among socialist countries in the last two or three years.[44]

Such statements came at a time when Shevardnadze and the Foreign Ministry were beginning to articulate a more coherent world view that took into account Soviet domestic reforms, provided a rationale for pursuing rapprochement with the West, and started to challenge the previous monopoly of the Defense Ministry on key questions of military doctrine and arms control.[45] Shevardnadze also continued to publicly push the vision of the dissolution of the military blocs in Europe and the elimination of all foreign bases in line with his apparent belief that the Soviet Union could enjoy greater security at lower cost if the United States pulled back militarily from the borders of the USSR. The foreign minister appears to have believed—rather naively in retrospect—that such positions were compatible with the maintenance of socialism in Eastern Europe, albeit in a reformist guise. As late as

---

[44]See Alexsander Kapto, "Priority to Be Given to Our Relations with Socialist Countries," *International Affairs*, November 1988, p. 29.

[45]For further details see John Van Oudenaren, *The Role of Shevardnadze and the Ministry of Foreign Affairs in the Making of Soviet Defense and Arms Control Policy*, The RAND Corporation, R-3898-USDP, July 1990.

October 1989, Shevardnadze, in his foreign policy report to the Supreme Soviet, reiterated his call for the elimination of all foreign military bases by the year 2000.[46]

Looking back, it is clear that this period was only the lull before the storm. Initially, Soviet sanctioning of greater national autonomy in the bloc and a new emphasis on "unity in diversity" seemed to be a stroke of political genius by Gorbachev, for it satisfied his multiple and conflicting needs. First, it allowed him to pursue his own course of increasingly radical domestic reform while relieving the CPSU of the responsibility for day-to-day management of intrabloc affairs. Moreover, it was popular in Eastern Europe among very different constituencies: the regimes inclined toward reform, above all Poland and Hungary, immediately interpreted the new leeway as a green light for the pursuit of their own reform programs; more conservative regimes, on the other hand, sought to use it to avoid such steps, arguing that their national circumstances and needs were different from those of the Soviet Union. Moscow, meanwhile, showed itself quite willing to tolerate both interpretations in light of its overriding interest to maintain stability in the region. Gorbachev's own preferences were made clear in his treatment of leaders such as Poland's communist leader Wojciech Jaruzelski, for example, who was singled out for praise.[47] At the same time, Gorbachev was careful not to prematurely push any regimes in the direction of reform and change, as his behavior toward the more conservative communist leaderships in Prague and East Berlin demonstrated.[48]

Nothing illustrated Gorbachev's attempts to walk the tightrope between supporting reform and maintaining stability better than his ambivalence on the Brezhnev Doctrine. The changes in Soviet ideology and security policy supported by Gorbachev went a long way in undermining the original justifications of the Brezhnev Doctrine. Similarly, several statements by Gorbachev, above all the joint Soviet-Yugoslav statement issued following his visit to Belgrade in the spring of 1988, implicitly renounced the Brezhnev Doctrine insofar as it recognized different paths to socialism and renounced the use of force.

---

[46]*Pravda*, October 24, 1989.

[47]During Gorbachev's visit to Warsaw in the summer of 1988, for example, the Soviet leader stated that "although each party chooses its own path to a new quality of socialism . . . there is nevertheless a similarity of direction in the understanding of the need to renew socialist society." *Radio Warsaw*, July 11, 1988.

[48]Gorbachev's own views were best reflected in a remark made during the visit of Italian communist party leader Achille Occhetto to Moscow in the spring of 1989, when he stated: "Perestroika can certainly not be imposed but renewal is inevitable, and it brings with it the necessity to reassess many aspects of the history of each country and of each party." Quoted in *Corriere della Sera*, March 1, 1989.

While a growing list of individual Soviet scholars would explicitly renounce the Brezhnev Doctrine, the Soviet leader himself hesitated to take this step and attach his own name to a new Soviet policy toward Eastern Europe. As one Soviet academic expert on Eastern Europe noted in late summer 1989—just before the political earthquake hit Eastern Europe—the Brezhnev Doctrine was buried in all but name:

> That doctrine has already been buried. All that is lacking is the official death certificate. . . . The facts clearly show that Gorbachev is against the logic, the method, and the system that led to the tragic events of 1968. It is, however, equally clear that as leader of the Soviet Union he cannot put in danger that degree of solidarity and understanding that is indispensable between so-called fraternal countries. In practical terms Gorbachev cannot today allow himself to adopt a position that would then be rejected by the political leadership of an allied country. This is an objective condition and it is the reason why one cannot ask of Gorbachev more than he can and must do.[49]

FROM REFORM TO REVOLUTION

The guiding principle behind Gorbachev's East European policy was the belief that socialism was reformable both in the USSR and in Eastern Europe. The Soviet leader's policies were designed to facilitate the rise of reform communist leaderships who would pursue similar sets of policies tailored to their own national circumstances, i.e., East European equivalents of Gorbachev. Indeed, the belief that some vague version of reform socialism was viable in the region was a crucial element of Gorbachev's broader vision of Europe, which encompassed notions of a gradual rapprochement between the two halves of Europe, the transformation of the two alliances, and the creation of the Soviet version of a "common European home."

In retrospect, it is apparent that such calculations were badly flawed. Questions of just how convinced the Soviet leadership was of the reformability of socialism in Eastern Europe, whether there were differences within the leadership on this issue, and what type of information and intelligence it had as to the mood of the respective peoples in the region, may have to await the opening of Soviet internal archives. In any case, once Gorbachev had started his own country down the path of reform, he had precious few options toward Eastern

---

[49]Evgenii Ambartsumov, a well-known reformer and departmental head in the Institute for the Economics of the World Socialist System, quoted in *La Repubblica*, August 13–14, 1989.

Europe other than to counsel a cautious approach based on the same principles, while professing nonintervention.

The precipitous collapse of communism in Eastern Europe in the fall of 1989 took many observers by surprise in both East and West. It is nonetheless useful to recall that as late as early 1989 many prognoses of change for the region were based on the expectation of slow and gradual reform. By the end of 1988, Soviet leaders could easily have concluded that they had some grounds for satisfaction with regard to the evolution of a new approach to Soviet–East European relations. First and foremost, the CPSU was relieved of the responsibility of the micromanagement and supervision of domestic affairs in Eastern Europe at a time when Gorbachev increasingly had his hands full with his own agenda at home.

Second, Moscow's own reforms and its new flexibility and willingness to sanction greater autonomy for East European countries was universally hailed by the various national communist elites. In many ways, Gorbachev's stance managed to please communist elites with very different wants and needs. Reformers in Eastern Europe saw in Gorbachev's own reform program a green light for their own experimentation. More conservative regimes, on the other hand, immediately sought to use Soviet recognition of each party's independence and its sanction of different national paths to socialism to justify staying their own orthodox courses.[50] All throughout the region, there were signs that the Soviet leader's personal popularity even went some way toward starting to reduce traditional animosities between the peoples of Eastern Europe and the USSR.[51] Last, but certainly not least, Soviet

[50]One of the best examples of the latter can be found in a comment by East German ideologist Kurt Hager. Asked about the relevance of Gorbachev's Soviet reforms for the GDR, Hager dismissed their significance by replying that the fact that one's neighbor wallpapered his home didn't mean that one had to follow suit. See his interview with the West German weekly *Stern*, reprinted in *Neues Deutschland*, April 10, 1987. In Prague, Prime Minister Lubomir Strougal, leader of the moderates in the Czechoslovak communist party, commented on the efforts of conservatives to exploit Gorbachev's new line to solidify their own position: "While they used to consider the pool of common characteristics an absolute value, now for a change they try to make particularity an absolute principle. One might be forgiven for wondering if this attitude is not just an attempt to hide their reticence to change anything at all of the basis of our Czech experience." See *Rude Pravo*, March 3, 1987.

[51]Adam Michnik has been a leading proponent of the idea that the Polish opposition must reconsider its traditional anti-Soviet stance in light of the changes taking place in the USSR. According to Michnik: "All the previous attempts at reform also failed owing to the international context. This is the first time the international situation is so favorable. This opportunity should not be wasted. . . . The road we are entering on is important as a test case of the transition from totalitarian Stalinist barracks communism to parliamentary democracy. The changes in the USSR are so far-reaching that it is precisely the opposition that should reconsider its traditional anti-Soviet rhetoric. For such rhetoric is becoming barren and cannot answer the questions formulated by the changing reality." *Warsaw ITD*, No. 21, May 21, 1989 *(JPRS-EER-89-072).*

flexibility toward Eastern Europe also reinforced Gorbachev's improving image in the West, where a hands-off policy and greater tolerance of reform was widely seen as a test case of the sincerity of Gorbachev's "new thinking."

Meanwhile, the years 1987 and 1988 saw a much more aggressive and reformist Gorbachev at home and abroad. He was engaged in a series of battles against opponents at home and challenged by an ambitious internal and East-West agenda. With so many other priorities, the relatively tranquil developments in Eastern Europe in the first two years of Gorbachev's rule may very well have lulled the Soviet leadership into believing that its new approach to Eastern Europe would be relatively cost-free and, above all, could be steered in such a fashion to not do violence to basic Soviet interests. The Soviet leader duly traveled to the capitals of all the East European countries, preaching the new principles of unity in diversity, urging them to find their own national solutions to the problems they faced, to move toward greater pluralism and openness and to fill in the so-called "blank spots" in bilateral relations, namely those trouble spots from the past previously ignored or glossed over in official relations.

In short, Gorbachev may very well have thought that the nations of Eastern Europe would welcome Soviet abandonment of Brezhnev's heavy-handed policies and reciprocate with voluntary restraint and a more organic sense of mutual interest and cohesion on some new and more loosely defined socialist basis—the advantages of which seemed abundantly apparent to him. As events would show, his belief was astonishingly off the mark. The details of the fall of communism in Eastern Europe will be analyzed later on in this report. The question that concerns us here is what the Soviet reform concept toward Eastern Europe was in reality, and why and where it went wrong. In order to understand the former, we must first examine the impact of Soviet policy toward Eastern Europe in the region itself.

The crucial change in Soviet policy under Gorbachev has been the USSR's cessation of active, visible intervention in the internal affairs of these countries, once a hallmark of Soviet policy. For the first time in the postwar period, the primary limits to political change in Eastern Europe are not external but internal. Moscow's tolerance for reform, and its assertion that individual countries should seek individual solutions to national problems, led to a historical shift in the nexus of factors shaping the politics of the region. Throughout the postwar period it had been Soviet policy that set the guidelines and boundaries for permissible change in the region. Ironically, Moscow's claim to ideological uniformity had placed a good portion of the blame for the existing state of affairs on Soviet shoulders as opposed to those of the national communist elites, who were often seen as obtaining the best possible deal under the circumstances and unable to introduce real changes even if they wanted to. In countries such as Poland or Hungary in the 1970s, for example, the Gierek and Kadar regimes had skillfully exploited a sense that the rules of the game were set in Moscow and that it was therefore useless and counterproductive to try to push them for more or faster change, since that would only lead to Soviet opposition and possible intervention. In return for political passivity and subservience, the communist party offered a certain amount of economic security and consumer goods, or what became known as "goulash communism."

With the onset of Mikhail Gorbachev, however, there was an important psychological shift as the Soviet Union was seen, and increasingly so, not as an impediment but as a catalyst for change. Gorbachev's criticism of conditions in the USSR and his call for radical reform automatically legitimized criticism of the existing regimes and policies. Even if the Soviet Union was not directly telling recalcitrant regimes to change, the indirect effect of the Gorbachev example was to unleash pressures for change from within, as Soviet opposition to change seemed to dissipate. The exact limits of Moscow's tolerance remained undefined, but the awesome deterrent factor of its former hard-line disapproval now seemed diluted if not removed.[52] In short, as it became clear that Soviet power might no longer be a major factor, the political calculus in these countries changed dramatically; it was now the local party elites confronting their own societies, with Moscow seemingly on the sidelines.

Another crucial aspect of the Gorbachev factor was the fact that the Soviet leader has been important in Eastern Europe as a factor in delegitimizing past communist rule but not as a source of intellectual or political emulation. Gorbachev and other Soviet officials have always made it clear that while they do not have a clear blueprint for the future of reform, they do believe in some form of "reform socialism."[53] With regard to Eastern Europe, Gorbachev and other Soviet leaders have always emphasized that the problems currently confronting these countries should be attributed to the mistakes of past leaders (and the exploitation thereof by the West), and not the socialist system

---

[52]As Bronislaw Geremek summed it up: "Of course there are limits, which are not well-defined. The question of how far we can go without clashing with the USSR remains unanswered. Though dangerous, it is necessary to seek these limits in practice." Interview in *La Repubblica*, August 11, 1989 (*FBIS-EEU*, August 16, 1989).

[53]As Gorbachev stated during a press conference during his recent Paris visit: "To say that we have rejected socialism is simply misleading. If we can bring people back into the socialist system instead of alienating them, we can give socialism a second wind." As quoted in *New York Times*, July 6, 1989.

per se.[54] Even more radical reform scholars writing on Eastern Europe, while harshly criticizing past Soviet policy toward the region, have been careful not to go so far as to question the legitimacy of the initial communist seizure of power in those countries.[55]

But the forces of change did not seem to be interested in reforming the system along the lines suggested by Gorbachev. While the Soviet leader undoubtedly came to enjoy a certain popularity in Eastern Europe, such admiration did not translate into any desire to copy Gorbachev's notion of reform socialism. In vogue in the 1950s and 1960s, reform communism was long passé in much of Eastern Europe by the late 1980s. Even among leading communist reformers there was a clear recognition that the halfhearted efforts of the past were no longer sufficient.[56] Countries such as Hungary and Poland had been practicing their own national versions of socialist reform and *peres-*

---

[54]In *Perestroika*, for example, Gorbachev writes: "I want to note here that it was not socialism that was to blame for the difficulties and complexities of the socialist countries' development, but, chiefly, miscalculations by the ruling parties. And, of course, the West can also be "credited" with helping, through its constant and stubborn attempts to undermine the development of the socialist states, to trip them up." See *Perestroika*, p. 163. Similarly, speaking in Prague in April 1987, the Soviet leader stated: "Of course it is not the socialist system that is to blame, as our ideological opponents claim, but miscalculations among the leadership in the running of the country about which we have openly told the party and the people." See *Pravda*, April 11, 1987.

[55]See, for example, the argument in the paper presented by the Soviet delegation from the Institute for the Economics of the World Socialist System, which carefully skirts the issue of how these regimes came to power in the first place. "A new situation arose in Europe after World War II as a result of the defeat of the Axis powers and the downfall of the pro-fascist regimes in Eastern Europe, creating favorable conditions for a radical reorganization of relations between the Soviet Union and the East European states on the basis of neighborly and mutually beneficial cooperation. The course of events in Europe had been such that conservative bourgeois circles and the capitalist order were seriously discredited. At the same time, there was the unprecedented rise of a mass movement for social renewal, which had its origins in the context of wartime resistance. These two developments placed revolutionary transformations of the socio-economic system of the East European countries on the agenda. Clearly, the sympathy and support of the Soviet Union were with the mass movement; this led at first to the formation of the people's democracy regime, and then to the victory of the socialist system in the countries of Eastern Europe." *Problems of Communism*, May–August 1988, p. 61.

[56]In the words of the former Minister of Culture and leader of the Patriotic People's Front, Imre Pozsgay: "Since the mid-1960s Hungary has tried to implement a reform program. It was exactly the halfheartedness, the ambiguity of these reform efforts that later made us open up more and go even further. When I say that the reform efforts were implemented halfheartedly or ambiguously, this is not because the intentions of the reform were ambiguous or halfhearted. Rather, the conditions and the opportunities were limited. The limited opportunities provided by the surrounding international conditions made Hungarian reform politicians reconcile themselves to taking the first step only in the sphere of the economy in implementing these reforms. Today this kind of reform is being criticized very strongly in my country." See Pozsgay's speech, reprinted in *Frankfurter Rundschau*, January 13, 1989.

troika for over 20 years, and the result was what one Western observer has termed "catastroika."[57]

Throughout much of Eastern Europe, the noncommunist opposition had since gone on to develop new theories and strategies for social and political renewal increasingly modeled along Western lines.[58] For Gorbachev and his plans they felt a combination of admiration, sympathy, and deep skepticism about the reformability of communism. Polish trade union leader Lech Walesa captured this ambivalence in an interview with a Western newspaper:

> I wish Gorbachev and his reforms all the best. But we still don't know what communism in its final form will look like. In contrast, we know very well which political and economic models in Europe and in the world have passed the test of time, and it is to these models that we must turn as opposed to attempting to "reform" failed ideologies and concepts.[59]

Such sentiments underline two crucial differences between the USSR and Eastern Europe that help explain the dramatic events of fall 1989. First, whereas Gorbachev could look back in Soviet history and try to tie his own legitimacy to an ostensibly "healthy" pre-Stalinist communism, this option does not exist for regimes in which the coming to power of the communist party was inescapably intertwined with Stalin and his policies. Second, the countries of Eastern Europe have historically been far more integrated into Western political, economic, and cultural traditions. Despite 40 years of a divided Europe, the East's yearning to be integrated into the West has survived. Indeed, one of the most striking trends in the push for reform in Eastern Europe has been the clear desire for a return to the Western political, economic, and cultural community, a trend that has only been reinforced by the evident failure of the Soviet system.

It is of course rare for regimes to give up power voluntarily, and the communist elites in Eastern Europe were no exception. Responding to the internal critics who accused them of committing political suicide, leading reform communists in both Poland and Hungary insisted that they were simply abandoning a failed and discredited version of party rule and influence. They were certain that a renewed, reformed, and refurbished party would still end up being a dominant political force, above all when it became clear that the opposition parties were

---

[57]See Jacques Rupnik, "Bloc Busters," *The New Republic*, May 22, 1989.

[58]One good example of this evolution among opposition intellectuals in Eastern Europe is Adam Michnik's essay "A New Evolutionism" published in Adam Michnik, *Letters from Prison*, University of California Press, Berkeley, California, 1985.

[59]See Walesa's interview in *Die Welt*, April 24, 1989.

fragmented, unorganized, and without easy answers or solutions to the problems the country faced. Party reform leaders boldly maintained that the ruling party would retain its central role in society and that the reforms being introduced were a demonstration of strength and bold and decisive leadership, not weakness.[60]

And in general terms, such reformers clearly enjoyed Soviet support and sympathy. Soviet authors explicitly held up Hungary as an experiment they were keen to learn from, and there is some evidence to suggest that the USSR supported the final downfall of Janos Kadar and the elevation of Karoly Grosz to Secretary General of the Hungarian Socialist Workers' Party (HSWP).[61] In Warsaw and Budapest, party reform leaders argued that their countries were serving as a sort of laboratory for reform experiments from which other countries, including the Soviet Union, could benefit.[62] In the case of Poland, both Gorbachev and Jaruzelski went out of their way to underline their close personal and political relationship.[63]

---

[60]According to Secretary General of the Hungarian Socialist Workers' Party (HSWP) Karoly Grosz, "No political party voluntarily hands over power to another party, and we do not have the slightest intention of doing so. However, if we lose power we are to blame for it." *Nihon Kaizai Shimbun*, January 10, 1989. See also Jaruzelski's speech to party military activists in Bydgoszcz on February 27, where he insisted that "we are not a defeated party" and that the roundtable discussions between the government and the opposition were a symbol of the party's strength, not its weakness. Warning against anarchy, the Polish leader insisted that the reform process would not result in a nonsocialist Poland: "We will not be pushed off the path of socialism. The fact that I am stating this in this very place and at this very time should also be a warning. It is not a defense of old positions. On the contrary, it is a defense of our new development stage. It is action in the cause of the socialism of tomorrow." Warsaw Domestic Service (radio), 2111h, February 27, 1989. Asked in February whether the Polish United Workers' Party would give up power if voted out of office, the Politburo member in charge of ideology, Marian Orzechowski, said that it would, but that it could not since there was no successor to take over. *TT News Agency* (Sweden), February 14, 1989. On the same day, Solidarity leader Walesa told Polish miners: "If you had free elections, you'd choose people who do not know how to rule. You'd have chaos here like you never had before." Reuters, February 14, 1989.

[61]See Richard Kemeny, "Hungarian High Politics on the Eve of the Party Congress," *Radio Free Europe Research*, RAD BR/70 (Hungary), April 22, 1988.

[62]Interviewed in September 1988, Vadim Zagladin stated: "We know that our Hungarian friends support the idea and practice of restructuring and we highly appreciate this. All the more so because we have studied and also today we study your endeavors, and we have utilized them as well in our practice." Budapest Television Service, 1700 GMT, September 11, 1988. For a positive Soviet view of the Hungarian experience as a model for the USSR, see Oleg Rumyantsev, "Perestroika in Hungary," *International Affairs*, No. 9, pp. 50–56. Following the 19th CPSU All-Union Party Conference, Gorbachev praised the recent HSWP national conference as having been identical to the main thrust of *perestroika*. "Grosz's visit to Moscow," *Radio Free Europe Research*, Hungarian SR/12, Item 1, August 12, 1988.

[63]See Jaruzelski's interview in *Corriere della Sera*, in which he states: "We were, and still are, the experimental laboratory for the great reform. To use military terminology, I would say that Poland has performed a reconnaissance role, opening the way to the forces represented by Gorbachev's restructuring." *Corriere della Sera*, May 9, 1989.

The fact that Hungary and Poland would be the first to step onto the slippery slope of reform was certainly no accident. In many ways, Warsaw and Budapest were destined to be the trailblazers in exploring the new leeway for reform and experimentation now officially sanctioned by Moscow. Both countries had ruling communist parties with strong reform wings and traditions. Emboldened by Gorbachev, the reform wings in both parties managed to gain the upper hand in intra-party struggles and to launch themselves down the path of change. In both countries there was a basic recognition that past reforms limited to economic reorganization and selective grafting of capitalist elements onto a central planned economy had failed, and that what was needed was a market-based economy. It was also recognized that economic reform had to be matched by comprehensive political reforms, and that such reforms would force the communist party to give up its monopoly on power.[64]

The reform programs that emerged in Poland and Hungary represented a strategic gamble. The calculation was that a reformed communist party would be able to maintain some sizable plurality of votes in more open political competition. Moreover, the party—so it was believed—would be able to control the terms of that competition, at least initially, as well as the timetable, thereby ensuring a climate of gradualism that would give the regime a breathing space, the opposition a period of preparation, and Moscow an assurance that reform did not mean revolution. This, it was hoped, would pave the way for some new coalition government in which the communists would still play an important role while coopting important elements of the opposition, and in which they would reserve to themselves the responsibility for foreign and defense policy, thereby leaving the issue of the future of the Warsaw Pact largely in communist hands.

The long-term goals of these reformers, to the degree that they were clearly articulated, pointed to a mixed economy with a strong state sector and welfare state, along with a parliamentary system led by reformed communist and socialist or social-democrat parties—all wrapped up in some loose form of socialism. The countries often held out as models were the Scandinavian social-democrat-led welfare

---

[64]According to Imre Pozsgay: "The political reform cannot be a consolation prize to the people for a lack of economic reforms and economic performance. The two things should be encouraged and carried out simultaneously." See Poszgay's interview in *Magyar Hirlap*, December 31, 1988. As Rakowski put it in an interview with *Der Spiegel*: "You can no longer fool people in our country by using [concessions] as safety valves. You could say that in 1980–81 the Poles very rapidly passed through a nationwide political academy." See *Der Spiegel*, May 1988.

states.[65] Many East European reformers looked toward the West European left as a model, either the social democrats or the eurocommunist parties such as Italy's PCI.[66] In all, they wanted the process to be controlled and gradual—to give themselves time to adjust to more political competition as well as to give Moscow time to adjust to the diminution of the role of East European communist parties. While proclaiming their willingness to abandon their monopoly on power, leading officials in both Poland and Hungary spoke of a transition lasting a period of several years, during which the communist party would remain firmly in control of the reform process.[67]

For a communist party, it was a step into unknown waters.[68] In retrospect, it is clear that it was also a first step down a very slippery slope toward unmitigated political defeat. Reform was a process that proved impossible for the communist regimes in Eastern Europe to keep either gradual, controlled, or limited. Economically, it was clear

---

[65]According to Politburo member and architect of the Hungarian 1968 reform Rezso Nyers: "What I personally have in mind is a socialist society which could synthesize the practices of communism and social democracy. From social democracy we would borrow the parliamentary democracy, market economy, the autonomy of trade unions, and notion of self-government, and from the communist ideology the spirit of collectivism freed from any Utopia, the struggle for social equality, and a bold approach to transformation." MTI 1906h (radio service), March 1, 1989. See also Rezso Nyers, "Erfahrungen Ungarns aus vier Jahrzehnten," Probleme des Friedens und des Sozialismus, August 1988, pp. 1022–1130.

[66]In an interview with Nepszabadsag, Imre Pozsgay suggested that the HSWP should discard Marxism-Leninism, just like the West German SPD discarded its old socialist dogmas at the Bad Godesberg party congress of 1959. In this way, according to Pozsgay, "the SPD again became a force capable of forming a government" and the HWSP was capable of the same. At the same time Pozsgay emphasized the need for the party to discard conservatives, whom he described as "advocates of the flat earth theory who continue to preach the leading role of the party after it has become clear that this party led the country into an impasse." See Nepszabadsag, September 28, 1989. The PCI has been rehabilitated by Soviet scholars, who now acknowledge that its past criticism of the USSR was correct. See Kevin Devlin, "Kommunist Rehabilitates Berlinguer: 'We Were Wrong,'" Radio Free Europe Research, RAD BR/18 (World Communist Movement), February 6, 1989.

[67]In an article published in Pravda on October 19, 1988, Marian Orzechowski, Central Committee secretary in charge of ideology, responded to the concerns of "our friends abroad" worried that "recent events in Poland, including the idea of a roundtable, could cause certain doubts and even concern" over whether the Polish communists knew what they were doing. Orzechowski claimed that the party was developing a new model of socialism free of Stalinist distortions, and he assured Soviet readers that the Polish communist party had everything under control, that the initiative in Polish politics remained "unalterably in our hands. The party completely controls the situation."

[68]During the roundtable discussions in Poland, one high-ranking Polish party leader is reported to have remarked to an opposition representative: "You know, all the textbooks tell us how difficult it is to seize power. But no one has described how difficult it is to relinquish power." As quoted in Timothy Garton Ash, "Revolution: The Springtime of Two Nations," The New York Review of Books, June 15, 1989.

from the outset that transition from a Polish or Hungarian economy to
something akin to Austria's or Sweden's was only a fantasy. The same
was true in the political realm, where a little bit of pluralism and
democracy turned out to be like being a little bit pregnant. As the
regimes started to relax the existing political controls, they released a
groundswell of public discontent and pressures for faster and more radical change. The limits initially imposed by the communist reform
leaders from above were rapidly overtaken by the momentum and pressures from below.

The magnitude of the credibility gap facing the ruling communist
regimes became increasingly apparent. This in turn strengthened the
demands for faster and wider reform from more radical reformers,
eager to distance themselves from hard-liners and to demonstrate that
the parties had indeed broken once and for all from the Stalinist past.
The early plans for staged and gradual transition were overtaken by a
surge of popular pressure from below for more radical changes.

The plight of the communist reformers was magnified by what can
only be characterized as major strategic and tactical errors. This is
especially clear in the case of Poland, where the Jaruzelski regime
badly miscalculated the depth of societal estrangement, the latent
popularity of Solidarity, and the quickness with which the union could
recover as an organization and mount an effective electoral campaign.[69]
At the roundtable talks in early 1989, the regime proposed rules for the
coming June parliamentary elections that can be explained only as a
total misreading of public opinion. Apparently assuming that they still
enjoyed significant support in some circles, the communists themselves
imposed the requirement that candidates running for the party's
guaranteed seats still had to win 50 percent of the popular vote, a standard that only one candidate met. The result was the political humiliation of the communists in the Polish elections.[70] Less than a year
after it had been reinstated, Solidarity was forming the government.

In the case of Hungary, the process was slower but the direction
comparable and the outcome similar. Having committed in principle to
the concept of political pluralism, the communist authorities were compelled to make one change after another and ultimately failed in their
attempts to shed the past and acquire new democratic credentials.

---

[69]Former Jaruzelski aide Stanislaw Kwiatkowski, head of the Public Opinion
Research Center, for example, wrote in the liberal intellectual weekly *Polityka* in March
that the majority of Poles favored the political system of real socialism, that they feared
the radicalism of Solidarity and Walesa, and that a significant section of Polish society
therefore took an inimical view of the opposition. See his article "Opinions on the Opposition," *Polityka*, March 4, 1989.

[70]Jaruzelski subsequently told the Western press that "if the Solidarity label had been
stuck to a horse's head, the horse would have been elected." *Le Figaro*, June 14, 1989.

Asked in mid-1989 whether the Hungarian communist party leadership had ever anticipated having to give up its claim to a leading role in society so quickly, Rezso Nyers, Politburo member and architect of the Hungarian 1968 reform, replied that it had not.

> Frankly we were not prepared for the appearance [of this question]. In 1986, for example, we had no inkling at all that the question was going to be raised. To all appearances the following factors had come into play. The Hungarian economy was in a critical condition, mainly as a result of foreign debt, a state budget deficit, and an obsolete industrial production structure whose potential was almost exhausted and more typical of the early rather than the late twentieth century. One reason why the economy was in such a state was the patent bankruptcy of the investment policy and the corresponding ideology which had failed to react in time to changes in scientific-technical progress. The conditions of *glasnost* are also making their mark on political processes. Once, in the Kadar era, the level of *glasnost* was higher [in Hungary] than in the Soviet Union under Brezhnev. Then came the Gorbachev era with its democratization and *glasnost*, which for Hungary provided a powerful stimulus for the democratization of social-political life. I call this effect, which was perhaps more powerful in our country than in others, the 'Gorbachev effect.'[71]

Such reform attempts were harshly attacked by more conservative communist elites in Bulgaria, Czechoslovakia, the GDR, and Romania as amounting to political suicide. And although their pronouncements on the danger of reform may have been correct from their own parochial viewpoints, they lacked any alternatives other than to temporize on the need for change and introduce half-measures, a strategy that ultimately proved self-defeating: the combination of rising expectations for change with small and in many cases inconsequential steps toward liberalization only created a classic prerevolutionary situation. Opposed to the overall reform strategy being implemented by Gorbachev in the USSR but lacking any real alternative, the conservative regimes in Eastern Europe were reduced to the position of trying to wait the Soviet leader out, hoping that trends in Soviet politics would either lead to his downfall or compel him to desist. Writing in early 1989, a Swedish commentator accurately described the drama that was being played out in East Germany, traditionally the most loyal of the USSR's East European allies:

> Fear of change seems so deeply rooted in the GDR that the only prospects for change that can be permitted amount to little more than a refinement and perfecting of that which already exists. The fact remains that it is Brezhnev's ideas that still represent the

---

[71]See Nyers's interview in *Izvestiya*, July 23, 1989.

overriding ideology underpinning East German policy. . . . But the
East German leaders too feel increasingly insecure. Official reactions
to Soviet "new thinking" would not be so overly sensitive if the self-
satisfied arrogance shown by the East German leadership were not
mixed with a great many anxieties. And the reports about the mood
of the people which are supplied to the elderly gentlemen in the
Politburo by the security police only strengthen their conviction that
the stability of the GDR is threatened and that the best form of protection is to resist change for as long as possible. The result, however, is apathy which slowly but surely is spreading and which in
time will become more aggressive. Young people have no prospects
and they can no longer bear being treated like children. They simply
see their lives stretching as far as retirement but containing no challenges. In the GDR people are dying of boredom.

At the same time Erich Honecker is playing a game of political chess
with Gorbachev and he knows that he is in a weaker position. He
simply does not have the players to win the game. He continues the
game, however, knowing that he has one slight advantage, namely
that Gorbachev is simultaneously playing against many other
opponents and it is here that Honecker sees his chance. He hopes
that time is on his side and that Gorbachev will run out of time
before he can outplay Honecker. For the latter this would mean that
he had won the game without having to introduce basic change in the
GDR.[72]

But Honecker lost his game. Gorbachev's warning, delivered during
an October 1989 trip to East Berlin, that "history punished those who
came late" turned out to be profoundly accurate in a fashion that not
even the Soviet leader could have anticipated. Within weeks the men
who had run the SED and ruled the GDR for decades were swept out
of power and put under house arrest. Shortly thereafter the political
avalanche buried communist conservatives in Prague, and before year's
end the Ceausescu regime fell in a bloody revolt. Whether it could or
would have been otherwise if changes had been made earlier is one of
those academic questions that are as tantalizing as they are unanswer-
able. One might note the remarks of one communist politician on the
subject, Mieczyslaw Rakowski, first secretary of the Polish United
Workers' Party, who in his heyday enjoyed the reputation of a reform
communist in the West and ended up as a primary victim of the collapse of communism in Poland. Asked whether in retrospect the Polish communist party had made a mistake by proposing the roundtable
and agreeing to legalize the opposition, Rakowski replied:

---

[72]Editorial in *Svenska Dagbladet*, January 22, 1989.

I am deeply convinced and I assert that sooner or later, and probably sooner, matters would have evolved to the point of some sort of spontaneous events taking place in Warsaw similar to those that took place in Berlin and Prague. Knowing the temperament of my fellow countrymen, we may have had 'two Pragues' or 'three Berlins' in Warsaw. In my opinion we selected the only correct path. This was and is the path of peaceful change under the control of all responsible political forces of the country during a time of transition from a system of single-party rule to a system of parliamentary democracy.

This created a paradoxical situation. Although the PUWP selected the only correct path, it was also the path off of the political stage. Who was it that decreed such a harsh sentence? Several books could be written on the subject. Leave that for the historians. In the meantime, we must be satisfied with the view that this was the sentence passed by history. Or, to put it more accurately, by the political and economic failures of real socialism. We were unable to cast off the shackles imposed by Stalin. . . . All of us were seduced by absolute uncontrollable power. . . . Obviously I would be the last to ascribe my failures and mistakes to the Soviet Union. There nonetheless remains no doubt that in the past decades our party has been heavily influenced by the programs and plans of the CPSU. Such is the truth which cannot be denied.[73]

---

[73]See Rakowski's interview entitled "The Goal is Democratic Socialism" in *Pravda*, January 24, 1990.

II. POLAND AND HUNGARY

The events of 1956 caused Poland and Hungary to be paired in the minds of many East Europeans as well as Western observers. The Hungarian Revolution of that year and the occurrences in Poland known collectively as the "Polish October" took place almost simultaneously. Both were the result of the interaction of similar causes: Soviet domination, its very fact and its severity; repression by Stalin's local minions at all levels of public life; humiliation; national economic misery; fading expectations of improvement after Stalin's death; weakness, disunity, and loss of confidence among the Polish and Hungarian communist leaderships; an often subconscious, popular notion that communist rule might be transient; and hopes for Western support. These factors, which affected both countries in varying degrees, helped produce the first great challenges to communist, as well as Soviet, rule in Eastern Europe.[1] In 1989, over 30 years later, Poland and Hungary would again challenge communist rule, this time successfully. But this second convergence in the paths of the two countries had happened only recently. For many years after 1956, developments in both countries took quite different directions. As late as, say, 1985, few would have predicted the role that both were soon to reassume.

The immediate results of the Hungarian Revolution and the Polish October seemed clear at the time, although this view proved to be delusive. In Hungary the popular defeat looked decisive and permanent. After Soviet power crushed the revolution, repression continued for at least two years and seemed likely to persist. In Poland, on the other hand, the coalition of reform communists with a militant society seemed to have won a stable victory. United under Wladyslaw Gomulka, who was restored to the leadership by popular demand and with (nervous) Soviet acquiescence, Poland seemed set to evolve toward a status which, if still undetermined, held the promise of both national dignity and domestic progress. But in the event, the future brought the reverse of what was expected for each country: Hungarian despair gave way to hope; Polish hope soon lapsed into despair.

Gomulka lost little time in demolishing the liberal pedestal on which most Poles had placed him. Within two years he had "closed down" the Polish October by rescinding all the reforms to which it had given rise. Poland then settled into a continuum of disappointment and

---

[1]In 1948 Yugoslavia had thrown off Soviet control, but communist rule remained—more rigid than ever—through the mid-1950s.

decline, punctuated by upheavals in 1968, 1970, 1976, 1980, and 1981. The bloodiest of these, in December 1970, cost up to 50 lives, by the official count. It also cost Gomulka his party leadership, which was then assumed by Edward Gierek. Gierek brought with him from Silesia a modernizing, managerial reputation that, however deserved it may have been at the provincial level, rapidly evaporated on the national scene. After a deceptive flurry of reforming energy, Gierek's leadership became complacent, self-deluding, corrupt, lethargic, and incompetent. A rash of workers' strikes in 1976 against food price increases, the cause of Gomulka's fall in 1970, marked the beginning of the end of his regime. This eventually occurred in September 1980, just weeks after his delegates had been forced to sign into existence the first free trade union in the history of communist rule: Solidarity.

The apparent contrast with Hungary could not have been greater. Hungary's leader after 1956, Janos Kadar, began his rule with the stigma of having betrayed the revolution. But while Gomulka saw his task as cooling, then closing, Poland's reform process, Kadar saw his as seeking well-being, reconciliation, relaxation, and economic recovery through reform. And each leader was backed in his policy by Khrushchev, who was as anxious to check the momentum in Poland as he was to revive the morale in Hungary. Both Gomulka and Kadar were firm Leninists, dedicated to the twin tenets of party supremacy and democratic centralism. But, unlike Gomulka, Kadar was to reveal a political dexterity, flexibility, and receptiveness, allied to an attractive public persona, that helped to bring about a remarkable change in Hungarian life. His success in conciliation was dramatically shown in 1964, eight years after the revolution and only four years after repression ended and revival began. When Khrushchev was ousted in October of that year, many Hungarians were obviously fearful that the same might happen to Kadar.[2] As for Gomulka, most Poles cared little by that time whether he stayed or went.

Kadar's policies were based on what some observers have called the "unwritten social compact" between his regime—above all himself—and the majority of Hungarians.[3] In 1956 the Hungarian nation, though eventually defeated, had once again asserted itself and its historic right to be reckoned with. Once its active resistance had been put down by

---

[2]For a description of Kadar's appeal see Charles Gati, "The Kadar Mystique," *Problems of Communism*, May–June 1974.

[3]See J. F. Brown, *Eastern Europe and Communist Rule*, Duke University Press, Durham, North Carolina, 1988, pp. 200–208; Charles Gati, "Reforming Communist Systems: Lessons from the Hungarian Experience," in William E. Griffith (ed.), *Central and Eastern Europe: The Opening Curtain*, Westview Press, Boulder, Colorado, 1989, pp. 218–241.

Soviet military power, it was Kadar's task to lead Hungarians through the phases of passive resistance and noncooperation that followed, toward those of acceptance, then cooperation, and eventually support. And even if the support was not active, it was enough. "He who is not against us is with us" became his slogan.[4] What he offered was a system of rule which, while thoroughly Leninist, was tempered by humanity. If not respecting the individual, it at least left him alone. What Kadar promised was a perceptible, continuing increase in the material standard of living, and this promise he kept. The Hungarian people accepted their part of the bargain—1956 never again—at first with resignation but then more readily, some even enthusiastically. Theirs was hardly a noble role—as so many of their intellectuals, keepers of the nation's conscience, kept telling them—but after the trauma of the revolution, it was not without dignity. It was not only much better than they had expected; as it developed, many Hungarians began to feel that at least some of the goals of 1956 were being recovered.

But just as important as Kadar's political leadership skills within Hungary itself was his ability to "manage" the Kremlin. With Khrushchev this task was relatively easy, once the Soviet leader's erratic ebullience ceased to disconcert or intimidate. Khrushchev was as eager for Kadar to succeed as Kadar was himself. The Hungarian Revolution might well have cost Khrushchev his position. He was then still only "first among equals," and many of his peers resented not only his grab for power but also what they considered his reckless reformism, typified by his onslaught against Stalin at the 20th CPSU congress in March 1956. The upheavals in Poland and Hungary the following autumn could be traced in part back to Khrushchev's secret speech—many Soviet communists and East European hard-liners considered it *totally* responsible for the troubles—and it was clearly in Khrushchev's interests to see the postrevolutionary reconstruction in Hungary proceed quickly and smoothly. The choice of the new Hungarian leadership was, therefore, crucial not only for Hungary but for Khrushchev's political survival, as well as for the Soviet Union's international credibility.

The situation made Kadar more than the Soviet puppet he was at first dismissed as being. It gave him considerable leverage with his Soviet protectors, and while Kadar's relationship to Khrushchev was one of dependence, it was not one of total subjection. In fact, a good working relationship developed, fed by a growing mutual respect and even friendship. What was most important for Hungary's future was

---

[4]Kadar first publicized this slogan in 1961; see *Nepszabadsag*, December 10, 1961.

the conviction of both leaders that the wounds of the revolution must be healed quickly and that the country that had so nearly been communism's East European graveyard should soon become its showcase. The ensuing policy became known as "Kadarism," and in the climate of the 1960s it stood out for its boldness and its success. This gave the Kadar leadership increasing self-confidence as its East European, and even its international, standing grew.

Kadar safely negotiated the transition from Khrushchev to Brezhnev. By October 1964 he had become a pillar of stability in Eastern Europe, safe and successful, and thoroughly compatible therefore with the new Soviet leadership's predilections. He was left to expand his policies of domestic conciliation and to prepare for the introduction in January 1968 of the New Economic Mechanism (NEM), the process meant to deepen and widen the Kadarist course. The evenness of Kadar's relations with Brezhnev, however, was to be disturbed by the consequences of the Prague Spring, one of the catalysts of East European communist history comparing in importance to the Hungarian Revolution itself. Kadar's own reaction to the reforms in Czechoslovakia was one of caution, but it also contained understanding and probably some sympathy. But in August 1968, however sympathetic he may have been, his loyalty to the Soviet Union and bloc unity came first. He joined first in the Soviet-orchestrated warnings against the Prague Spring and then in the Soviet-led invasion that ended it.[5]

But his support for the invasion, and for the Brezhnev Doctrine justifying it, was not given unconditionally. After the events of August 1968, at a time when even the use of the word "reform" was inhibited in the Soviet bloc, the NEM went forward. Hungary became the only country in the entire Soviet bloc where reform was tolerated and sustained. It brought Kadar much notice and a growing prestige.

Gomulka's relations with the Kremlin soon disappointed the initial hopes Poles had placed in him after October 1956. He had been swept back to power on a wave of national feeling. It was hoped that, as far as geopolitical considerations allowed, he would adopt the model set by Tito's Yugoslavia. In the event, he followed a course not of "national communism" but of "national distinctiveness." It was less heroic, more realistic, and more suited to his own personal inclinations. (It was quite different, at any rate, from the conformism of contemporaries like Novotny, Zhivkov, and even Ulbricht). For example, throughout

---

[5]It should be mentioned that Alexander Dubcek, the deposed leader of the Prague Spring, over 20 years later criticized Kadar severely for not having stood out against the invasion, arguing that had he done so, Brezhnev might have called it off. Series of interviews with Hungarian television during April 1989, see *Radio Free Europe Research*, Czechoslovak SR/10, Item 3, "Dubcek's Interview in Hungary," May 5, 1989.

1957 he openly resisted the suffix "headed by the Soviet Union," which became almost obligatory when referring to the "socialist camp." He refused to join in the Soviet-orchestrated denunciations of the Hungarian Revolution, Imre Nagy, and the "revisionist" Yugoslav party program of 1958 as enthusiastically as Moscow would have liked. By shrewdly preserving (although hardly protecting) those two unique Polish institutions, the Roman Catholic Church and the private peasantry, he was also furthering the "national distinctiveness" goal. He did his best to suppress the "spontaneity" that was the essence of the Polish October but did not systematically persecute those who had embodied it. Polish cultural life remained relatively free and quite dynamic, there was much private freedom of speech, and the Polish media remained the liveliest in Eastern Europe, with the spasmodic exception of the Yugoslav.[6]

Gomulka was able to keep Poland's national distinctiveness for four reasons:

- His own stubbornness and determination, though often a negative, destructive characteristic, helped repel recurring pressures for conformity from Moscow, Poland's other East European allies, and within his own party.
- If faced with sufficient determination, Khrushchev, for his part, was ready to tolerate limited diversity in the interests of legitimacy and viability. As for Brezhnev, he paid little attention to domestic East European matters until the onset of the Prague Spring. By that time Gomulka himself had become alarmed at developments in Czechoslovakia, and he was a willing Soviet ally against the Czechoslovak reform.
- The emerging Sino-Soviet dispute unleashed centrifugal forces that the Soviets considered far more dangerous than any Polish unorthodoxies.
- Gomulka never claimed any universal application for his Polish unorthodoxies. This was in definite contrast with Tito, whose Yugoslav revisionism was considered a threat by Moscow precisely because of his ecumenical pretensions.

Gomulka's grip on Polish politics began to weaken in the second half of the 1960s. His personal dogmatism became more evident as his political pragmatism waned. In March 1968 during mass repressions against students and liberal intellectuals, many of whom were Jewish, he virtually lost control to the party's national-populist faction. It was

---

[6]On Gomulka's "distinctiveness" see Zbigniew Brzezinski, *The Soviet Bloc: Unity and Discord*, Harvard University Press, Cambridge, Massachusetts, 1967, pp. 338–356.

probably only the overriding need for bloc stability after the Czechoslovak trauma later that year that saved him from removal after the "March events." But his final, most disastrous political mistake—the imposition of steep price increases on basic foodstuffs just before Christmas 1970—led to riots along the Baltic seacoast, then to his quick removal and replacement with Edward Gierek.

But just before Gomulka's final act of folly, Poland had signed its historic treaty with the Federal Republic of Germany "normalizing" relations between the two countries and involving de facto West German recognition of Poland's postwar Western frontier on the Oder-Neisse. This had been preceded by an 18-month period of busy European diplomacy in which Poland had achieved international prominence and respect. It had acted, of course, with both the approval and the support of the Soviet Union but also very much in its own national interests. The agreement with West Germany, therefore, was in some ways the crowning achievement of the policy of "national distinctiveness," which now acquired a truly international dimension. Poland was communist. Poland was a Soviet satellite. But Poland was different.

Although these retrospective considerations in no way rehabilitate Gomulka, they could make a total assessment of his legacy less negative. His suppression of the October reforms relegated Poland to a backwardness from which it might never recover, and it is for this that he must mainly be judged. Still, he left institutions, practices, and principles intact that provided the backdrop for Poland's two-stage revolution in the 1980s. He deliberately destroyed the Polish October, but in doing so he unwittingly helped facilitate the eventual rise of Solidarity.

HUNGARY: THE KADARIST PRELUDE

Despite his having joined in the invasion of Czechoslovakia, Kadar's international reputation stood high at the beginning of the 1970s. (It is ironic now to recall that at this time no East European leader's reputation was higher than Ceausescu's. He had openly defied the Soviets over Czechoslovakia, was expanding his relations with the West, and even at home had been showing some signs of liberalization.) NEM, the New Economic Mechanism, had made what looked like an auspicious beginning, and in a generally gloomy Soviet and East European setting Hungary stood out as both reformist and relaxed. Its compliance with Moscow on the invasion was excused at home on the grounds of force majeure and the memories of 1956.

Kadar's reputation continued to grow for at least another ten years. Despite the difficulties that both the Hungarian economy and the attempts to reform it were to encounter in the 1970s, Hungary continued to be the only East European country that was reforming at all, and one of the few to enjoy a climate of political and psychological relaxation. Above all, the general standard of living kept rising, a fact readily attested to by the increasing flow of Western visitors.

But despite its early success, the NEM revealed not only its own inconsistencies but also the basic weakness of the Leninist system. As early as 1972, just four years after introducing NEM, the regime began restricting even the limited application of the market mechanism originally planned. At the same time, three forces converged (or colluded) to check further progress of the reform.

The first was the conservative faction inside the Hungarian party. Kadar had been successful in neutralizing the small neo-Stalinist group that had entered the newly constituted Hungarian Socialist Workers' Party after the 1956 revolution. But the NEM roused more widespread opposition as many party members who had genuinely supported the strategy of reconciliation could not make their peace with the implications of the NEM.[7]

The second force consisted of a large number of industrial workers who nursed a grievance. At the turn of the 1970s Hungary benefited from the global economic boom. This was more responsible for domestic prosperity than the NEM, but it was to the latter that the regime propaganda gave the credit. Whatever their source, however, the fruits of success mainly went to the official and managerial classes and to the farmers. Little of it went to the workers, and the workers were resenting it.

Obviously, this proletarian restlessness was grist to the party conservatives' mill. But the third force now opposing reform provided yet more grist: the Soviet Union itself. Kadar may have deflected Soviet opposition when the reform was introduced in 1968, but he had not disarmed it. It was only to be expected that the Brezhnev leadership, bent on ideological counterreformation, would revise its original permissiveness toward the NEM. Beginning in 1972, pressure was exerted on Budapest to slow down the reform and modify it, and Budapest complied. The regime also became less tolerant of political and cultural dissent. Conspicuous champions of reform were dropped, not only Premier Jeno Fock but also Rezso Nyers, the "father of the NEM." Nyers, however, was to re-emerge in the late 1980s as one of the leaders of Hungary's second (peaceful) revolution.

---

[7]For the shelving of the NEM and its political consequences, see Brown, *Eastern Europe and Communist Rule*, pp. 210–214.

Just as the NEM was being shelved, an economic disaster was looming that helped radically change the whole course of East European development. The first OPEC oil price explosion of 1973, though it affected the Western industrialized states almost immediately, took well over a year before it began to affect Eastern Europe, which was partly insulated by its protective economic ties with the Soviet Union. But the Soviets could not be expected to continue their liberal pricing policy for energy exports to Eastern Europe when world oil prices were rocketing. In 1975, therefore, they altered their fixed-price scale to a more flexible one that reflected the movement of world prices more quickly. The result was that the Soviet price of oil to Eastern Europe doubled between 1974 and 1976 and quadrupled between 1976 and 1983. Even with these increases, though, it still remained well below the world price until the mid-1980s, when the world price rapidly dropped.[8]

But favorable comparisons with world prices held little relevance and no comfort for Hungary, Poland, or any other East European country, all of which (except Romania) were almost totally dependent on Soviet oil. They were now faced with a massive readjustment that not one was capable of making. For several years Hungary seemed to be coping better than most, better certainly than Poland, whose economy, after a spuriously brilliant showing in the first half of the 1970s, went into a rapid decline that had momentous social and political repercussions. Hungary's success was due partly to the relative flexibility of its economic system but mainly to the regime's ability to maintain the political consensus that had been forming since the 1960s. This was a product of Kadar's own political skills and his ability to project continuing economic success long after the serious weaknesses of the economy had been recognized by those in the know or by the few interested in finding out. Thus Eastern Europe's "consumerism," conceived by the Kremlin as a strategy of accommodation after the trauma of Czechoslovakia, and artificially kept going by the increasing—and eventually ruinous—resort to Western credits, held up better and longer in Hungary than anywhere else.[9]

But the preservation of the political consensus was not just due to well-filled shops and what they signified. It derived from the still strong memory of 1956 itself. This made not only for a prudent calm, but even for a national eagerness, amounting often to neurosis, to enjoy the good days while they lasted—because Hungarian history,

---

[8]See John M. Kramer, "Soviet-CEMA Energy Ties," *Problems of Communism*, July–August 1985.

[9]See Laura d'Andrea Tyson, *Economic Adjustment in Eastern Europe*, The RAND Corporation, R-3146-AF, September 1984.

recent and bygone, taught that they might not last long. It was this buoyancy that helped keep Kadarism afloat. But when, in the early 1980s, the good days did come to an end, the euphoric high sank to a correspondingly bitter low, and the hunt for a scapegoat was on.

The scapegoat was Kadar. As Kadarism failed, its eponym fell from grace. His reputation could not survive the unraveling of the social compact: once he failed to deliver, he was vulnerable. But his fall went deeper than that. By the turn of the 1980s a new generation was emerging for whom the revolution was history, not living memory; for them the social compact was a scrap of (nonexistent) paper. Many of its articulate members attacked Kadar for manipulating the revolution and their elders for being intimidated by its memory.

This sentiment began to grow at a time when Kadar was losing his political touch. His physical health was deteriorating and his mental grasp was weakening. But even more significant was his inability to adapt to, or even understand, the new complexities and demands of the situation. By the 1980s, economic reform, as many Hungarian economists were now telling him, no longer meant deciding which bits of capitalism to tack onto socialism but which bits of socialism to keep after the introduction of capitalism.[10] He had come to accept that economic and political reforms were a tandem, even that political reform might have to go in front. But he could not face the political imperative of the 1980s: the dismantling of Leninism. Pluralism was to be accepted, even encouraged, but only within the framework of party supremacy. He had always believed in inner-party democracy, but even more in democratic centralism. He simply could not countenance the party's genuinely *sharing* power. Parliamentary democracy and the multiparty system were for the other side.

Kadar had outlived his usefulness and his relevance. He was the pilot waiting to be dropped. It is true that a good 10 years before his dismissal Hungary had resumed the economic reform that had been shelved in 1972, introducing bold departures toward the market and capitalist practices. But he really understood none of them, and in any event they could not cope with the seriousness of Hungary's crisis. Now there was mounting pressure for what must have sounded to him like the "counterrevolution" of over 30 years before. Thus it was more than the ghost of Imre Nagy that returned finally to break Kadar's health and spirit. The heresies that had caused him to desert, disown, and betray Nagy in 1956 would now return to mark his own demise.

---

[10]Perhaps the most prominent of these was Janos Kornai. See, for example, his article "The Hungarian Reform Process: Visions, Hopes, and Reality," *Journal of Economic Literature*, No. 24, December 1986.

POLAND: GIEREK, SOLIDARITY, JARUZELSKI

Between 1956 and 1968 the so-called "Iron Triangle" or "Northern Tier" of socialist states in Eastern Europe—the GDR, Czechoslovakia, and Poland—had experienced a period of strong leadership stability. Walter Ulbricht had been the East German party leader since the foundation of the GDR in 1949, Antonin Novotny the Czechoslovak party leader since 1953, and Gomulka the Polish party leader since 1956. But in less than three years, between January 1968 and May 1971, all three had been pushed from power. (In Czechoslovakia there were two changes of party leader during that period.) Novotny went in January 1968, Gomulka in December 1970, and Ulbricht in May 1971. The first two were dismissed for solely domestic reasons, and Ulbricht went because he stood in the way of Soviet détente with the Federal Republic of Germany. Novotny was succeeded by Dubcek, who was himself succeeded by Gustav Husak in April 1969 following an eight-month void after the Soviet-led invasion in August 1968. Gierek succeeded Gomulka and Erich Honecker succeeded Ulbricht. Little in the way of reform was expected from Honecker, but many observers speculated that Husak, a victim of Stalinism and a man who had originally associated himself with the Prague Spring, and who was initially compared with Janos Kadar, might eventually introduce his own version of "Kadarism." In the event Husak turned out to be no Kadar, the only (slim) consolation being that he was no Stalinist either.

As for Gierek, he bounced into power on promises of reform and revitalization. So much so that during the first four years of his rule, he seemed to be not just adopting Kadarism but broadening and deepening it. In fact, whereas the early 1970s were for Hungary a period of retrenchment, even retreat, Poland was in a ferment of activity and promise.[11] But the trailblazing was largely confined to rhetoric. The second half of the 1970s saw Poland settle into stagnation and then move toward collapse. At the same time, the goodwill with which many Poles had greeted Gierek evaporated. Gierek's regime will probably be remembered in history for two things: First, it signed the agreement that brought Solidarity, the first free trade union in a communist state, into being. Second, it was the first communist regime to have the immensity of its corruption exposed publicly. Not that it was the first corrupt communist regime, just the first to have some of its books opened—during the Solidarity period 1980–81. This, in the event, turned out to be just a curtain raiser for the much bigger exposé of the Brezhnev regime, which was to follow after 1985 in the Soviet Union.

---

[11]See Brown, *Eastern Europe and Communist Rule*, pp. 171–181.

Gierek's regime did not just end in discredit. It ended with the party's morale, authority, and organization shattered. The party limped on after Gierek's removal in September 1980 under Stanislaw Kania. His hapless rule was at least partly vindicated by his honesty: he seemed ready to try to work with Solidarity. (Later he was frank in his disclosures about Soviet pressure and threats to invade.) Kania's replacement in October 1981 by Jaruzelski, already prime minister, was in retrospect one of the final preparations for the declaration of martial law in December. Solidarity had already appeared to be superseding the party in some aspects of its public role. Now the military, backed by the police and those sections of the technocracy prepared to cooperate with the new order, was superseding the party in everything except the rituals of power.[12]

The party, in short, was being replaced. This, again, was unprecedented. Right from the beginning of military rule after the declaration of emergency in December 1981, Jaruzelski emphasized that his main aim was to bring the party back to center stage, with the army retiring first to the wings and then to the barracks. But whatever appearances of revival the party may have shown were fraudulent. The PUWP was basically no stronger at the end of 1988 than it was at the end of 1981. In hindsight, it would probably have been wiser for the PUWP to have been dissolved when the military took over and a new communist party founded, much leaner than the over three million it had numbered before the rise of Solidarity. (The reorganization of the Hungarian party after the revolution in 1956 could have served as an example.) Jaruzelski did throw overboard some of the accumulated ballast of inefficiency and corruption, but the party remained a body without coherence or profile, with most of its members unconvinced of the need for basic change.

This too was unprecedented. No other communist party had ever remained so impotent for so long, a factor that must also be taken into account when explaining the Polish response to Gorbachev's *perestroika*. The contrast with Hungary is clear. There, the party, despite the steady loss of reputation and confidence caused by its failures of the 1980s, did remain the *only* institutional entity with any coherence until the end of 1988, when new political movements emerged. In Poland there were actually *three* such entities: the military, Solidarity, and the Roman Catholic Church—but *not* the party. There was no organized worker challenge in Hungary, and none of the Hungarian churches had any real strength. Neither had the military, politically or

---

[12]Many books have been written on the rise of Solidarity. See, especially, Abraham Brumberg (ed.), *Poland: Genesis of a Revolution*, Random House, New York, 1983; and Timothy Garton Ash, *The Polish Revolution: Solidarity*, Scribners, New York, 1984.

professionally. The initial challenge to Kadar came from dissident intellectuals, first outside and then inside the ruling establishment. But the real threat to him came from within the party itself when its reform wing solidly took shape. In Poland there were many party members who saw the need for reform; some of the important ones were to emerge strongly at the roundtable talks in early 1989 when they made some common ground with the Solidarity representatives. But they did not form a wing or group, with an agreed platform, as the Hungarians did. In this they were both a reflection and a product of the decimation of the Polish party over the previous decade.

When Gorbachev first praised Jaruzelski publicly at the 10th PUWP congress in July 1986, he was, therefore, endorsing the leader of a most unorthodox, controversial regime, a leader in effect with little party and no popular following and whose position rested directly and blatantly on military strength. Any Soviet leader would have had to recognize the service Jaruzelski had rendered the Soviet Union. He had averted, with remarkable ease, potentially the worst crisis in East European communist history. He had saved communism in Poland from extinction. But relieved though the Soviets were, they also had reservations, at least until Gorbachev took power in March 1985. In saving communism Jaruzelski had not restored communist rule but had imposed military rule. His coup had been directed against Solidarity, but it was not aimed at restoring the system that had preceded it—the Brezhnevite system. This was why Gorbachev liked him and what they had in common: in his own way Jaruzelski was a radical, like Gorbachev.

As soon as he had become prime minister in February 1981 Jaruzelski had strongly supported the concept of *odnowa* (renewal), which a few reformers, particularly at the lower level, saw as the only means of avoiding collapse. For most party officials, though, *odnowa* was at best a handy pose till the situation changed. After December, therefore, when catastrophe had been avoided, they considered it high time to return to apparat rule. The Soviet leadership believed this too—from Brezhnev to Chernenko. But Jaruzelski disappointed them. His goal was to revive the party, but it would be a different party, with a different attitude to power and to those it ruled. This alone made him a radical in terms of the ethos personified by Brezhnev and Gierek. What he felt most strongly about was clean government, with power being seen not as a mark of superiority but a pledge of service.[13] He

---

[13]Roger Boyes in *The Times* (London), December 18, 1989, wrote: "Martial law had two functions: to crush Solidarity and any direct competition to the communist party, and to allow General Jaruzelski to outflank the antireformist old guard of the state apparatus."

also insisted, much as Gomulka had done, that though Soviet hegemony was not to be questioned, Poland's special character and situation had to be taken into account.

This kind of radicalism in no way made Jaruzelski a "liberal," an overturner of institutions or systems. He was a military communist (a special breed whose East European variety might need deeper historical analysis), inclining toward centralization and strict procedures. Not for several years did he accept the need for systematic reforms in politics and the economy, and then he went about promoting them with the same austere single-mindedness he had shown throughout his entire career. But during the 1980s his regime was not dissimilar—ideology apart—to traditional military dictatorships bent on regulation, modernization, centralization, efficiency, and the fight against corruption. Much closer to home, there were similarities with the prewar Polish dictatorship of Marshal Jozef Pilsudski, of whom Jaruzelski has always been a strong admirer.

Immediately after 1981 the Polish situation seemed suited to such centralized prescription. Essentially it was not dissimilar to the conditions holding in the Soviet Union when Gorbachev took over in March 1985; and initially, Gorbachev too seemed to be the reorganizer, the modernizer, the efficient manager. This phase for him lasted about 18 months, an educative period in which he learned the immensity of the task before him. Then he realized that *revolutionary* solutions were necessary, and the new Gorbachev emerged in early 1987.

Although he took longer than Gorbachev, Jaruzelski did come to realize the inevitability of systemic change. But he unfortunately lacked Gorbachev's flair, even genius, for embracing the political imperative of the moment. Jaruzelski, the soldier, could never shed his unbending rigidity. He never embraced systemic reform, but dutifully submitted to it. Nor did he ever really understand its nature and ramifications, and was thus unprepared for its consequences. He lacked the political touch that not only Gorbachev showed in plenty, but also Tito and Kadar, even Gierek for a few tawdry years. In the end, he became the military commander blundering with his company into a minefield. At the close of the 1980s, Poland, despite Jaruzelski's best intentions, was in an even worse state than at the beginning of the decade.

Once physical order had been restored after December 1981, Jaruzelski single-mindedly set about attempting to neutralize Solidarity. Organizationally this was done in a few weeks. But he was never able to break the popular identification with it, although in 1986 and 1987 it seemed to outsiders that he was fairly close to doing so. He first tried to appease a sullenly hostile society by offering it *participation* in public life, a typical military-in-politics gesture. When this offer was rejected, he indicated that he would settle for an *acceptance* of his power, however grudging. The spirit of this policy was reflected in a passage in a speech he made to the party Central Committee in May 1983:

> We must carefully study views that differ from ours but are characterized by a sense of responsibility for Poland. . . . We have enough real foes who are passionate and stubborn. That is why we do not want to regard as adversaries those who are not adversaries in fact.[14]

There was similarity of sentiment here—although, typically, it was less felicitously expressed—with Kadar's clarion call of reconciliation of 1961: "He who is not against us is with us."[15] But the Poles were never won over.

The implacability of the Polish population was ultimately responsible for Jaruzelski's failure to achieve reconciliation. But some elements in his regime were lukewarm, others downright hostile, to the notion of making any attempt at all. His regime, in fact, was a model of disunity. Although his success in 1981 made his leadership unchallenged, it did not make him necessarily all-powerful in policy formulation, not to mention implementation. He still had to contend with those who opposed his whole policy approach and looked askance at the basis of his power.[16]

At one level, it was the military dimension that many party officials opposed. Even though it was precisely the military that had saved them, they feared the possibility of Bonapartism and its attendant dangers. But many were carry-overs from the Gierek regime and feared something more immediate than any Bonapartist specter: the loss of their privileges, even their jobs. And their fears were not without reason, as it turned out. Martial law did not mean automatic security of tenure. While not questioning the principle of the *nomenklatura* system, Jaruzelski was intent on purifying it. One observer estimated that between 1981 and 1986, 80 percent of the posts in the party apparatus were filled by new cadres. Many of those purged were, of course, deemed unreliable because of ties or sympathies with Solidarity. But many others were the incompetent, corrupt, and primitive ballast that Jaruzelski despised as much as Solidarity had. These were the ones who were soon to find that the present savior could be just as dangerous as the previous threat.[17]

---

[14]*Trybuna Ludu*, June 1, 1983.

[15]See footnote 4.

[16]For a brief review of Jaurzelski's role in the 1980s, see J. F. Brown, *Poland Since Martial Law*, The RAND Corporation, N-2822-RC, December 1988.

[17]See the article by Boyes in the *Times* (London), cited earlier.

Within the party leadership under Jaruzelski, serious factionalism persisted from the imposition of martial law until at least the 10th PUWP congress in July 1986. It centered on both personalities and policies. There were two main discernible groups: one of "hard-liners" and another that looked "liberal" by comparison. In between was a number of floaters, mostly opportunists uncommitted to either side until one appeared to be winning.

For a few years it was the hard-liners who seemed to have the initiative. There were differences among them, but they were united by an implacable attitude toward the Polish public for having supported Solidarity and a vague desire to return to what they called "orthodox Leninism." The generally recognized leader of this group was Stefan Olszowski, an able political figure with good connections in Moscow who had come to the fore in the late years of Gomulka.

The liberals around Jaruzelski were mainly well-educated communist officials. They regarded economic reform as a prime necessity, with marketization and enterprise independence as its main ingredients. Politically they favored some concessions to former Solidarity supporters and the appeasement of society generally. Some also accepted the notion of political pluralism, but they insisted, at least for several years, that it be safely tucked under the party umbrella. Mieczyslaw F. Rakowski steadily emerged as their leader. But Rakowski had become a very controversial figure owing to his acrimonious negotiations with Solidarity representatives in 1981, when a mutual antipathy developed that persisted to the end of the communist regime.[18] Rakowski also became the Polish intellectuals' best-hated figure. Still, within the parameters of Polish politics for most of the 1980s, Rakowski was a liberal. In fact, his fortunes and those of Olszowski roughly served as weather vanes for the political winds of the period. When Olszowski was in, Rakowski was out; when Rakowski came back, Olszowski left. It was to be Rakowski and his reform group who steered the regime toward the overture to Solidarity in the summer of 1988 and took part in the roundtable talks in the first half of 1989.

Another group must be considered in this review of the elements in Jaruzelski's regime: the security apparatus, beyond politics but pervading them. Many of its members were totally unreconciled to the aftermath of December 1981. What they wanted was repression; Stalinist-type terror held few fears for them, since they would be the ones who administered it. They were bewildered by Jaruzelski's course, especially his mildness toward his opponents. This was not the sort of

---

[18]For more on Rakowski, who in July 1989 became the Polish communist party leader, see Brown, *Poland Since Martial Law*, p. 31.

normalcy they had looked forward to. Many particularly resented his correctness toward the church, for which some had always harbored a violent animosity. In view of this attitude and their freedom from legal restraint, the October 1984 murder of Father Jerzy Popieluszko, the militant pro-Solidarity priest, was virtually waiting to happen. In killing him they were venting both their hatred for the church and their anger at Jaruzelski. And there are grounds for thinking that their selective murders of popular priests—much more cleverly carried out—continued through the 1980s.[19] Many of the old security apparatus continued in place, perhaps chastened but not changed, presenting a serious problem for the new democratic government after August 1989.

Very briefly, then, this was the Jaruzelski regime, its situation, components, and divisions. But to try to explain Poland in the 1980s through its ruling elite and institutions would be fruitless and misleading. The fact is that except for a period of about a year, September 1986 to November 1987, when it appeared it might be taking the initiative, the Jaruzelski regime was not directing Polish society but responding to it. And even though observers recognized this, they continued to misjudge the tenacity and resilience of Solidarity and its ability to survive as a political force. Solidarity simply refused to go under. There were several reasons why it did not: its ability to form an underground network soon after it was suppressed; Walesa's charisma and realism—a legend, leader, and symbol all in one;[20] the ability of Solidarity's advisors; the militancy of the younger workers; the deteriorating economic situation; the regime's own political ineptitude; and the Gorbachev factor. These conditions helped Solidarity to endure, revive, and then come back to center stage, and they will be discussed later on. But even they do not totally explain what happened.

Ultimately the explanation lies in the Polish temperament. A catastrophe like martial law can elicit a devastating public reaction against the leaders of the cause that has been so repressed; yesterday's heroes become today's scapegoats. (Czechoslovakia after 1968 was a case in point: for nearly 20 years, most Czechoslovaks in their despondency turned their backs on the leaders of the Prague Spring.) But Poland was different. The nation did not turn against Solidarity or its leaders. Its level of *active* support did fall off noticeably. Workers became less responsive to underground Solidarity's occasional calls for militancy

---

[19]See "Third Priest Dies in Unexplained Circumstances," *Radio Free Europe Research*, Polish SR/13, Item 8, August 22, 1989.

[20]Of the millions of words written about Walesa, John Lloyd's contribution in *The Financial Times* (London), August 19, 1989, is among the most relevant, titled: "Lech Walesa—A Shrewd Grasp for the Substance of Power."

(always nonviolent), and they were selective about taking its advice and often niggardly in their financial support. Other opposition groups began to proliferate that rather dimmed Solidarity's appeal. Many Poles, too, settled into "organic work," the Jaruzelski era having some similarity with the conditions under the partitions in the nineteenth century, when the practice of "working for tomorrow" began. Some members of the older generation, weary of a lifetime of turmoil, just settled for peace and quiet. These signs were unmistakable, and they contributed to a widespread view that, except as a symbol, Solidarity might be passé. But for a nation with a history like the Poles, those symbols that are identified with national aspirations are not just supportive but inspirational. After martial law, Solidarity did not become the casket of Poland's defeat but the vessel of its hopes. What had begun as a trade union became a national cause, with strong intellectual support, tempered by struggle and betrayal. It was more than something to hold onto; it was something not to let go.

Without the Roman Catholic Church, though, Solidarity might still have gone under. The church's relationship with the union had not been without a shadow. Cardinal Wyszynski had hardly greeted its foundation with enthusiasm. As for Cardinal Glemp, though he later strongly defended its members, initially he appeared to greet its suppression with relief. Nor has he ever hidden his reservations about some of Solidarity's (nonbelieving or Jewish) intellectual advisors. But most of the bishops and the mass of the priesthood supported Solidarity, a few with rather more valor than discretion. It was the blessing of Pope John Paul II that made the final difference. His election in 1978 stirred the wave of national assurance that gave birth to Solidarity and then sustained it. And it was his third visit as Pope to his native land, in June 1987, during which he called openly for the relegalization of Solidarity, that hastened its full return to public life.

HUNGARY: THE COLLAPSE OF KADARISM

While Poland was still the desert that martial law had created, Hungary, by contrast, presented the picture of an oasis of calm, high public morale, good government, and material prosperity. Kadar seemed to have the same political touch he had shown since 1956. But in retrospect the great Hungarian decline, leading to Kadar's fall in May 1988, had already begun by the turn of the 1980s, ironically at about the same time that Gierek, whose early successes had led to spurious comparisons with Kadar, was forced from power in September 1980. The beginnings of the decline were quietly noted by many regime officials, one of whom was Imre Pozsgay. A former minister of culture whose growing rebelliousness led to his "rustication" as leader of the politically harmless Patriotic People's Front, Pozsgay used this unpromising position as a base to build the reform wing of the Hungarian Socialist Workers' Party. The decline could also be measured by the growing number of extra-establishment dissidents, who were to be the basis of the eventual opposition. But it took until the middle of the 1980s for the *public* mood to change. It took even longer for outsiders to grasp that an epoch was ending.

The catalyst for the change was inflation. In the 1970s price hikes became as familiar in Hungary as they were in Poland. But the finesse with which Kadar handled them was taken as an example of his adroitness, so unlike the calamitous blundering of Poland's Gomulka and Gierek. Kadar could also bank on his continuing political credibility; the social compact was still holding. Higher prices were explained as the down payment to the NEM for the good times coming. But by 1985 the good times for most Hungarians were further away, not closer. Slowly, at first, but then torrentially, the grievances poured out. Charles Gati has summed up the six interrelated factors that led to the public's disenchantment.[21]

The economic factor. Inflation was the main force here, and its effects quickly discredited the reform process as a whole. The response to inflation—spending, borrowing, panic buying—further jeopardized the reform's chances of success. The fears of unemployment and about social benefits, poor as they were, compounded the malaise. The confidence necessary for the reform to work was undermined: confidence in Kadar eroded with astonishing swiftness.

The social factor. A chasm had been developing between rich and poor in a society still mostly attached to the principle of equality, or at least the appearance of it. After the liberalization of private ownership in 1982, conspicuous consumption had come back to Hungary—for the very few. Private entrepreneurs started flaunting their wealth. (The *nomenklatura* nobility were modest by comparison.) At the other end of the social scale was a huge, glaring increase in poverty. Many workers had to take one or two extra jobs to keep up. Most pensioners were in a desperate condition, with practically no one taking effective pity on them. This situation was exacerbating social problems like suicide (always alarmingly high even in precommunist Hungary), divorce, and alcoholism. Drugs were making inroads in the younger generation. NEM and the regime behind it were getting blamed for these social ills.

---

[21]These points are based almost exclusively on Gati, "Reforming Communist Systems . . . ," in Griffith (ed.), *Central and Eastern Europe: The Opening Curtain*, pp. 230–234.

The generational factor. By the 1980s the post-1956 generation began setting the pace of public life. Its criteria were not set by the revolution and its aftermath—at least, it did not think they were. It was unaffected by the social compact of 1956. Many young Hungarians rejected it openly, believing it to be simply the cover for inertia, doublethink, doubletalk, and corruption. Kadar personified for them a foul compromise that had worsened with time.

The oppositional factor. It was among the disillusioned young that opposition flourished. Hungary's dissidents began to surface after 1968. At the start, the most vocal of them were left-wing sociologists and philosophers who accused the regime of perverting Marxist ideals. The most prominent were Andras Hegedus, an erstwhile "whiz kid" of the 1950s Rakosi regime, prime minister of Hungary at 33 when the revolution started and now recycled into a scholar and reform sociologist, and Gyorgy Konrad and Miklos Harasti, both able writers who came to reject socialism and helped inspire the reform movement of the 1980s. Subsequently, the nucleus of dissent enlarged, with several *samizdat* publications to give it expression. As it developed, the movement could be divided into four groups: urbanists, populists, liberals, and economists. All four drew on honorable Hungarian traditions. The liberals and the economists often collaborated and were sometimes indistinguishable. The urbanists and the populists, on the other hand, were quite distinctive, sometimes hostile, rarely collaborating. They provided the cutting edge of the opposition in the 1980s. Roughly speaking, the urbanists, some of whom were Jewish, were international in outlook and favored quick, radical change. The populists were very Hungarian. They stressed the minorities abroad issue but domestically they stood for a gradualist, incremental approach toward liberal Christian democracy. The Kadar regime at first shrugged off the dissidents, taking them seriously only after it was too late. Dissent grew as the situation worsened. Disaffection among the young became particularly evident. Eventually the dissidents, now graduated to the status of "opposition," developed a mutuality of interests with party reformers, and the road toward change was open.

The Gorbachev factor. Gorbachev did not initiate reform in Hungary. He may even have cribbed some ideas from the Hungarian experience. By the end of 1989, in terms of what was on or near the statute books, reform in Hungary—economic, political, social, and cultural—already went some way beyond what was only being contemplated in the Soviet Union. Still, Gorbachev did make an impact on Hungary, on the public at large as well as on the governing process. By identifying with reform itself he broke through many of the inhibitions that still clouded and slowed its course in Hungary. He also helped undermine the continuing opposition to it. In doing so he broke Kadar's grip on power. For the first time in 30 years, Kadar could not manage the man in the Kremlin. He was more than out of touch with Gorbachev; he was incompatible with him. When this was realized in Hungary itself, and it didn't take long, Kadar's last line of political defense—his line to Moscow—was breached. But Gorbachev went out of his way to hasten Kadar's fall, with protocol slights, diplomatic snubs, and other signals by which communist elites communicate disdain for each other. Kadar must have known the game was up, but he did not realize just when.

The Romanian factor. The steady policy of assimilation of the two-million-strong Hungarian minority in Romania pursued by Ceausescu's regime became a crucial public issue in Hungary in the 1980s. It grew not only as the pressure in Romania grew, but also as the domestic situation in Hungary worsened. The darkening mood caused by the latter served to raise the indignation over the former. To disinterested observers the indignation, which was justified, often ballooned to a fixation on a "Romanian threat," which was not. But what counted was that Romania became a potent political issue in Hungary in the 1980s, as it had been in the 1920s and 1930s, regularly fueled by the provocative truculence of the Bucharest regime. It was politically exploited by both sides in Budapest. The opposition first argued that the regime's reticence on the subject showed a pusillanimous lack of patriotism. Then the regime, increasingly beset by difficulties at home, soon realized that Romania was good politics. Transylvania was back on the Hungarian agenda.

One more factor might be added to Charles Gati's list of six: **the Austrian factor.** While Romania was returning to the status of inveterate enemy, Austria was becoming the irresistible attraction. Through travel and television, Austria became the yardstick by which the Hungarian condition was measured, and this only added to the rising dissatisfaction. But the Austrian impact was not solely materialistic: it was nostalgic, emotional, political, and intellectual, with a touch of sheer snobbery to go with it. It encompassed respect, admiration, envy, and plain wishful thinking. Its appeal was both historical and current. The Vienna link, not much liked by many Hungarians before 1918, seemed like paradise compared with the Moscow link since 1948. (Otto Habsburg was feted during a visit to Budapest in the spring of 1989; some Hungarians later wanted him to run for president.) More to the point is that modern Austria is free, neutral, democratic, economically prosperous, and socially caring. By one of the miracles of East-West relations, it secured independence in 1955. When Hungary tried the same thing one year later it was crushed by Soviet troops.

This is the key to the Hungarian preoccupation with Austria. Austria is the great "might-have-been" for the Hungarians, a nation wistful about its past and morbid about its present. *Tu, felix Austria!*

These, then, were the main factors that caused the Kadarite consensus to collapse. The consensus had been built between 1960 and 1970 and firmly maintained between 1970 and 1980. Then it began to weaken, and between 1985 and May 1988 it collapsed. Now there was the need to build a new one, not on the public's acquiescence, but on its active participation. In both Hungary and Poland, whatever regime-society consensus had existed before had depended on the economic situation. When there was prosperity there was passive, depoliticized consensus. But when prosperity waned, as it did in Poland in the second half of the 1970s and in Hungary a few years later, the consensus fell apart. What reformers in both countries now aimed for was an active consensus, modeled after the Western example, based on a notion of a civil society not nearly so predicated on material prosperity.

POLAND: JARUZELSKI'S FAILURE

In Poland under Jaruzelski, the issue was not one of prosperity but of encroaching destitution. In 1987, some six years after the imposition of martial law, one observer described the situation as follows:

> Poland has one of the lowest growth rates in Eastern Europe, about 3 percent. Spare parts for industrial machines, as well as cars, trucks, and freight trains, are virtually unobtainable, and they stand idly rusting away. Sixty-two percent of industrial capacity is not being used. Ryszard Bugaj, the economist, . . . puts the rate of inflation at nearly 20 percent. State investment is growing at 4.5 percent annually, but since consumption increases at little more than 2 percent a year, the average Pole's living standard hasn't improved at all. Housing construction is practically at a standstill—which means that young couples, even those with children, are forced to live in cramped quarters with their parents, a situation breeding domestic tension and divorce. Polish products, once fairly common on the industrial market, are now so shoddy that no one wants to buy them.[22]

After 1983 there were considerable improvements in the gross social product and in the balance of trade; in 1985, however, national income per head was still 20 percent lower than in 1979.[23] In the first year

---

[22]Abraham Brumberg, "New Deal for Poland," *The New York Review of Books,* January 15, 1987.

[23]Bernard Margueritte cites these figures in his excellent "Polen 1986: Realitäten und Perspektiven," *Europa-Archiv,* Vol. 20, 1986.

after martial law the Polish people had experienced a drop in living standards not seen since World War II. In time, goods did become somewhat less scarce and the shopping queues shorter. But this was due to the series of large price increases that eventually, in 1988, shattered the social calm. The regime did, however, have one stroke of luck: agriculture, overwhelmingly private, produced well for a number of years, owing to a rational policy and kind weather.

Looming over the economic situation and all attempts to better it was Poland's massive hard currency debt. In 1989 it stood at about $38 billion. (In 1970 it had stood at $1 billion.) About 40 percent of the debt was owed to West Germany and the United States, and 40 percent to four other main creditors—France, Britain, Austria, and Italy.[24] Relatively, Poland's debt may always have been low in per capita terms, compared, for example, with that of Israel, several Latin American countries, and even Hungary.[25] But that was cold comfort for both the Polish economy and the Polish population. Polish hard currency exports recovered gradually during the 1980s but could not cover interest payments, let alone capital repayments. In addition, the Soviet Union, an unexacting economic partner for 30 years, began to show signs of business rigor.

As if all this were not enough, two ominous new factors had now emerged. The first undermined one of communism's basic claims to legitimacy: that it could, far better than capitalism, ensure its citizens not just the basic material essentials of life, but also, however modestly, essential social services like medical care, job security, child care, and education. (Housing, once on the list, was quietly dropped long ago as the years of waiting went into double figures.) But it was now obvious that in Poland, as well as in other parts of Eastern Europe, the assumptions were no longer valid, the promises could not be kept. The second disturbing factor was the ecological threat. In some parts of Poland, especially in Silesia, the threat had already become disastrous reality before either the regime or many citizens could bring themselves to recognize that it even existed. Now it was feared that, while time might be needed for other problems, time was running out for this one. Yet the resources required to solve it would be immense. Where could they be found, and from what other pressing priorities should they be diverted?[26]

---

[24]Wlodzimierz Rydzkowski and Krystyna Zoladkiewicz, "Poland's International Debt: Prospects for Repayment," *East European Quarterly*, June 1989, p. 217.

[25]Ibid. p. 218.

[26]See Brown, *Eastern Europe and Communist Rule*, pp. 384–414.

For all of Poland's problems, urgent measures were needed. All sides, official, semiofficial, and oppositional, were agreed on this. The martial law regime had inherited, and rejected, a model of reform—the Reformed Economic System (RES)—worked out by Solidarity's economic advisors. Its characteristics were:[27]

- Enterprise independence, based on the "3 S's" principle; self-administration, self-management, and self-financing.
- Greater flexibility in pricing and the encouragement of competition, even to the point of allowing for bankruptcies. Domestic markets would be thrown open to foreign competition.
- Central planning to be indicative, not directional. Financial instruments to be used to steer enterprises toward the required performance.
- The introduction of "economic *glasnost*"—widespread use of the media, trade unions, professional bodies, the Sejm (parliament), and other institutions to publicize and debate economic questions and influence the planning center in its choice of economic decisions.

The RES would have gone into operation at the beginning of 1982 if martial law had not intervened. Had it been implemented then, it could have put Poland in the forefront of economic reform. But at the end of the 1980s, although it would still have been revolutionary in, say, Romania, it had a distinctly mildewed look compared with reform models in Hungary, Poland itself, and even the Soviet Union. However much capitalism was being added, the RES still had a socialist frame.

In 1982, however, it was too progressive for the Jaruzelski regime. (The 3 S's were retained, though, and they at least kept alive the principles of enterprise autonomy and internal democracy.) Whatever his common sense might have told him, Jaruzelski was by instinct and by training a centralizer, and Poland's anarchic condition at the beginning of the 1980s must only have strengthened his inclinations. Even as late as the 10th party congress in June 1986 he outlined an economic program—the so-called "attestation" proposals—that involved more centralization and government control than ever.[28] Had those proposals been implemented, even the 3 S's would probably have been scrapped. But in the event, the intention was less important than the widespread resentment it aroused. Nor was the resentment just from

---

[27]Ibid. pp. 119–120.

[28]On these "attestation" proposals and the opposition to them, see Brown, *Poland Since Martial Law*, pp. 14–15.

opposition circles. It also came from elements inside the ruling establishment: members of the Sejm, meetings of the usually predictable PRON (Patriotic Movement for National Rebirth, set up by Jaruzelski as a "popular" front organization), workers' self-management groups (an institutionalized expression of the 3 S's), the media, and the legal trade unions that had officially replaced Solidarity and hence occasionally had to show some backbone. In fact, the opposition became so strong that Jaruzelski withdrew his proposals and ordered his advisors back to the drawing board.

This episode did not receive the attention it deserved. It was notable on two counts: First, even regime bodies showed surprising vigor in opposing Jaruzelski. Official political life was beginning to respond to the resilience of the opposition and the popular defiance on which it was based. Second, Jaruzelski demonstrated an intriguing combination of rigidity, uncertainty, and readiness to change. It explains the inconsistency in his political behavior much more convincingly than the interpretation often given: sheer bad faith and duplicity. It accounts for his sudden conversion in the second half of 1988 to "socialist liberalism," his proposal of the roundtable talks, his agreement to partly free elections in June 1989, and his acceptance of their results. His single-minded dedication to centralism was now replaced by what seemed an equally single-minded dedication to liberalism. But had he changed enough? Much of Poland's future might depend on the answer.

Jaruzelski's retreat on the "attestation" proposals was the first, and least, of the three retreats he made between 1986 and 1988, each more consequential than the last. The second was in November 1987, immediately after the referendum rejecting his political and economic reform proposal. The third was the decision in summer 1988 to talk with Solidarity. The period between the first retreat and the second—July 1986 to November 1987—was the watershed of the Jaruzelski regime. It saw his eventually unsuccessful effort to build a national consensus through a reform program of his own. When that effort was defeated—and this became clear only in the summer of 1988—the reform initiative passed to the opposition. Then Jaruzelski's retreat was turned into the rout of communism in Poland.

Jaruzelski's reform effort was serious, and most Poles were unprepared for it. It followed a period of repression in the first half of 1986, when for a time it seemed that even Walesa might be arrested.[29] Then, at the 10th party congress in June came the "attestation" proposals, very much in tune with the prevailing rigidity. After the

---

[29]Ibid. p. 9.

congress, however, the strategy changed toward conciliation. There were two reasons for the change. First, the opposition had obviously not been intimidated by the repression of the first half of the year, and second, as already mentioned, several components of the regime's own support system had rebelled against attestation. But even more important was the Gorbachev factor.

The Soviet leader attended the 10th party congress. He had been in power for over 15 months and was already well along in his evolution from reorganizer to radical reformer, now understanding more fully the extent of the Soviet Union's own problems. He must also have realized that Jaruzelski was backing Poland further into the dead end it had been in since the beginning of the decade. But he was also convinced that Jaruzelski was the only man to lead Poland out of the dead end and on toward revitalization. Poland without him would be in more danger than Poland with him; Gorbachev continued to hold firmly to this view. Hence the Soviet leader played a dual role at the Polish party congress: demonstrative supporter of Jaruzelski and, at the same time, strong counselor for change.

Jaruzelski lost no time warming to his task. The total amnesty he announced in September 1986 was a political and psychological masterstroke that, for the first time since December 1981, gained him the national initiative. There had been partial amnesties in 1983 and 1986 that satisfied nobody. There was also one before the 10th party congress, but it was hedged around with tantalizingly vague conditions. But the September 1986 decree was what it said it was: a full amnesty. And it was plainly successful. It caused some shift in public opinion toward participating in public activities, and it was favorably received by the church leadership, removing previous obstacles to negotiation. It was also a serious blow to a divided opposition, which now became even more divided over how to respond to the regime's initiative. It put some shine on the regime's tarnished image in the West, paving the way for the American decision in February 1987 to lift the economic sanctions imposed five years earlier. Most important, it softened the attitude of the Vatican. Pope John Paul II received Jaruzelski during the latter's state visit to Italy in January 1987.[30]

That papal audience would turn out to be a mixed blessing for Poland's communist regime. Whatever its immediate advantages, ultimately it served to hasten the demise of Polish communism because it led to the Pope's third visit to Poland in June 1987. Just as on his 1979 visit he had given Poles the confidence to stand up to a faltering regime, in 1987 he would renew that confidence and help channel it

---

[30]On the effects of the amnesty, see Abraham Brumberg, "Poland: The New Opposition," *The New York Review of Books*, February 18, 1988.

toward a specific national goal. For the moment, however, it seemed to be Jaruzelski who had the confidence. Toward the end of 1986 he established the Social-Consultative Council, designed to be a body of notables to advise on the broader issues of public life. Most of Poland's notables remained chary but some respected figures did join, and the church made no objection to lay Catholics cooperating.

As the regime gained ground, the opposition seemed to be in disarray. The issue of the amnesty only illustrated its organizational, political, and generational divisions. Solidarity itself was now competing with several other groups that were recruiting support and attracting publicity.[31] It was still the largest group and its reputation was unchallenged, but it had steadily been losing active support and nobody ever saw it regaining its old powers. Some observers were already writing it off, even those still aware of the bedrock of popular opposition to the Jaruzelski regime. What no one could foresee was the chance confluence of events that within a year would give Solidarity back its national mandate. The Pope's visit was probably the most crucial, certainly the most spectacular, of these events. But its impact was not immediate, and for the moment it was the regime that was trying to exploit its apparent advantage. It hoped that the good will arising from the September amnesty and the momentum it was gaining would ease the acceptance of the basic economic reform it was now contemplating. Everybody knew that if the reform were to be effective it would have to be painful. The regime's task was to acquire the minimum popular legitimacy necessary for the pain to be tolerated. Then, if reform worked, the economic upturn would broaden that legitimacy into unassailable support.

For much of 1987 the regime's economic and political planners worked on new blueprints for reform. The plans that resulted showed signs of both inner and outer direction. The economic reforms were influenced by the old 1982 reform proposals, and the political proposals, vague as some of them were, reflected the thinking of the more liberal members of Jaruzelski's entourage and went some way toward meeting the ideas of the opposition. And the Gorbachev factor was also evident. The new Soviet leader had begun his domestic reform offensive at the beginning of 1987, and in both Poland and Hungary the impulse for change consequently quickened. The difference between the two countries was that whereas the Kadar leadership was complacent about its achievements and did not grasp the significance, or realize the dangers, of the new situation, the Jaruzelski leadership,

---

[31]Some of the more important segments of the opposition are mentioned in Brown, *Poland Since Martial Law*, pp. 18–23.

with no achievements to be complacent about, was desperately anxious to follow and adapt. The Polish leadership was at least responsive to the new *Zeitgeist*, while the Hungarian was not.

The binding public referendum on the new proposals, held at the end of November 1987, demonstrated Jaruzelski's willingness to experiment. In retrospect it can be considered the prelude to the much bolder move the following summer, when the regime offered talks to Solidarity. The aims were basically the same: to seek the public's support and get it to commit itself to change on regime terms. That aim failed because as much as the public might want change, it did not want it on regime terms.

In the referendum the voters were asked to decide on two propositions: a "full government program for economic recovery" and a "Polish model" for "democratizing political life aimed at strengthening self-government, extending the rights of citizens and increasing their participation" in public life. In the event, the operation took on the aspect of fiasco. Both propositions were rejected—but mainly on a technicality. A majority of all *eligible* voters had to approve, and although about two-thirds of those who voted did say yes, this amounted to only about 45 percent of all eligible voters. About one-third of the electorate stayed home. To complicate matters further, many voters had been baffled by an unnecessarily complicated voting procedure that somehow symbolized the doom-laden destiny of the whole venture.[32]

Many Poles, inclined by history to a conspiratorial *my* (us) versus *oni* (them) view of the world, concluded that the regime had actually wanted rejection so that it could now claim popular backing for a do-nothing policy. But it remains very doubtful whether Jaruzelski would have engineered a deception that also involved such personal humiliation. His mistake lay in exposing himself to a judgment that went beyond specific questions to the broader issue of public confidence in his leadership. This issue could not be taken out of the whole attitudinal context in which the referendum was held. Taking an economic cure was one thing; giving Jaruzelski a blank check was quite another.

The referendum illustrated the weakness not only of the regime's broader political conception, but of its managerial and procedural skills as well—the same combination that was to bring on the electoral disaster some 18 months later in June 1989. The referendum in November 1987 was not just poorly conceived, it was badly handled. Yet Solidarity, which had called for a boycott of the referendum, had little cause for satisfaction. Over two-thirds of the electorate defied that call (which was taken then as a further sign of Solidarity's diminishing

---

[32]The referendum is well analyzed in Brumberg, "Poland: The New Opposition."

pull), and over two-fifths actually supported the regime's proposals. If the referendum did nothing else, it confirmed the divisions then existing in Polish society. Unofficial opinion polls in 1987 were indicating that about 25 percent of the population supported the regime to some degree, with the same percentage actively supporting the opposition. The remaining 50 percent tended to float between the two viewpoints. Only later did a decisive part of this 50 percent tip toward the opposition.[33]

After the referendum the regime announced that regardless of the result, it would have to introduce steep price increases on basic commodities at the beginning of 1988. These were the price increases that started the chain of events leading to the rout of not only the regime but the communist system. Strikes for higher pay followed within a month. With no clear instructions from the center, and acting autonomously under the rubric of the 3 S's, many factory managers opted for social peace at any price and gave the workers what they wanted. Dangerous precedents were set. Preserving social peace sowed the seeds of future social unrest.

The social unrest that began in April 1988 marked the beginning of the next historic round between state and society in Poland.[34] The strikes, which affected only a few of the major industrial concerns throughout the country, were both economic and political—they asked for higher pay but also for the relegalization of Solidarity. They petered out in early May amid disappointment and recriminations. The strikes did not spread and, though some strikers went back to work with bigger paychecks (though not much bigger purchasing power), their demands on Solidarity were rejected out of hand. Nevertheless, these strikes were important. They set off a process that eventually changed the political face of Poland.

Still, Solidarity seemed to come out of this episode with its reputation hardly enhanced. Its internal generational conflicts had surfaced again, vitiating the effectiveness of strikes that had been badly organized anyway. The strikes had been started mainly by young militants

[33]The most thorough study of Polish attitudes, putting them in their historical perspective, is by Hans-Henning Hahn, "Zur Dichotomie von Gesellschaft und Staat in Polen—Genese und Aktualität eines Grundmusters der politischen Mentalität," *Berichte des Bundesinstituts für ost-wissenschaftliche und internationale Studien* (Köln, 20–1989).

[34]For the developments in Poland (as well as in Hungary and Czechoslovakia) from the beginning of 1988, the analyses of Tim Garton Ash published in *The New York Review of Books* are the best. See "The Empire in Decay," September 29, 1988; "Reform or Revolution," October 27, 1988; "Revolution: The Springtime of Two Nations," June 15, 1989; and "Revolution in Hungary and Poland," August 17, 1989. These and other essays were collected in 1989 in Timothy Garton Ash, *The Uses of Adversity*, Granta, London, 1989.

who, like some of their forerunners in 1981, had chafed under Walesa's caution. Walesa himself had thought the strikes premature, supporting them only for the sake of a unity that did not really exist. So some observers were yet again writing Solidarity off. Others, not prepared to go that far, argued that its whole existence, purpose, and strategy needed redefining. Actually, the divisions that were affecting Solidarity, though serious, were typical of any organization of its kind. What was remarkable about Solidarity was its resilience in surviving them, and this was due in no small part to Walesa. He rode the rapids with skill and nerve, though every ride seemed more hazardous than the last.

It was in response to a new wave of strikes beginning in August 1988 that the Jaruzelski leadership made its offer of talks with Walesa with a view to legalizing Solidarity. It was a sensational reversal of policy, and it marked the real breakthrough for the historic developments to come. Four interacting reasons can best explain it:

- The regime realized that although it might defeat the strikes, the victory would be costly and tenuous. The strikes were always in danger of spreading and becoming an unsustainable national disaster.
- The regime sought to deepen the divisions among the opposition by a dramatic conciliatory offer, the actual substance of which could be scaled up or down as circumstances dictated.
- The regime's own divisions had resulted in a decisive victory for the liberals, who convinced Jaruzelski that the impasse stretching back to 1981 was now degenerating into simmering civil war. The process might be halted by a sweeping gesture that would at the same time return the political initiative to the regime.
- Gorbachev visited Poland again in July 1988, between, as it happened, the two strike waves. Jaruzelski must have discussed the advisability of such a move with the Soviet leader, who must have concurred. In doing so Gorbachev was adding his own unwitting twist to the unraveling of communist rule in Poland.

The regime's offer, and its acceptance by Solidarity, began the last stage in the process of unraveling. It caused a minor upheaval inside its own leadership, resulting in the withdrawal of those who could not resign themselves to the defeat it involved. Zbigniew Messner, prime minister since October 1985, resigned, as did Zbigniew Szalajda, one of the acknowledged leaders of the hard-line faction. The ascendancy was now with those "liberals" who had long favored contacts with the "moderate" elements of the opposition. They also supported some degree of institutionalized political and trade union pluralism. This group included the Politburo members Josef Czyrek, Wladyslaw Baka, the regime's most respected economic official, Stanislaw Ciosek, president of the ill-fated PRON, Kazimierz Barcikowski, Czeslaw Kiszczak, and, of course, Rakowski. Typically, Jaruzelski apparently took some convincing of the wisdom of this course, but once won over he pursued it single-mindedly.

Similarly, among the opposition support had been growing since the general amnesty of September 1986 for contacts with what were considered the "moderate" elements on the regime side. Since the beginning of 1988 the lead had been taken by Bronislaw Geremek, a medieval historian turned Walesa's intellectual equerry, later one of the giants of Poland's democratic revival.[35] Geremek had insisted on the relegalization of Solidarity as a precondition for talks; hence his overtures had up to now been rejected by the regime. Times were changing, however, and the dividing line between the moderates on both sides was beginning to soften, even blur. It was this process that eventually made the roundtable possible. And it was the roundtable that agreed on the historic elections of June 1989.

Walesa's role during this period once again confirmed the importance of personality in politics. In 1980–81 he was principal founder and leader of Solidarity. During the period of repression and illegality his real importance lay in his role of national, even international, symbol. And in the second half of 1988 he reemerged as popular leader and hero, vindicated, wiser, and politically mature. Ironically enough, the regime's dramatic offer to negotiate in August 1988 had actually pulled him back from the edge of what could have been a steep decline. Solidarity's divided, ineffectual showing during the spring strikes, coming at the end of a long period of stagnation of the movement's fortunes, had cast doubt on its relevance. But history gave Walesa a second chance, and in taking it he showed not just resilience but also a touch of greatness.

Nothing secured his triumphant return more than his debate on television with the leader of the regime trade unions, Alfred Miodowicz, self-anointed tribune of the plebs, telegenic, and no mean performer in the medium. Walesa ran all over him, and on that one night in November 1988 he more than made up for the ground lost in the years

---

[35] A good deal of credit should go to Geremek for holding the Solidarity side together during the roundtable talks with the regime, for drafting Solidarity's position, and for the whole success of the opposition during 1988–89. For good insight into his thinking, see his interview with Veronique Soule in *Liberation* (Paris), August 22, 1989.

before.[36] He followed this with a celebrity visit to Paris. Internationally as well as nationally, his name was again a household word.

But Walesa's return testified not just to his abilities or to the power of television. It also illustrated yet again the regime's political ineptitude. Offering to negotiate with Walesa was one thing; making him a star before the negotiations had even started was quite another. The television debate was probably a brainstorm of Rakowski, who had succeeded Messner as prime minister the previous September. His appointment had been greeted with dismay by Solidarity and practically the entire Polish intelligentsia. His hubris of 1981 was still unexpiatable in their eyes. Now, the TV debate idea was probably a case—not the first—of Rakowski being too clever by half. Allowing Walesa to go on television (as well as to Paris) would, he probably thought, demonstrate his own no-hard-feelings magnanimity as well as attest to his oft-disputed liberalism. But once on the small screen, Walesa, whom Rakowski had always despised, would be bested by Miodowicz and would, therefore, die of overexposure. In the event, Walesa was not the one who died.

HUNGARY: THE LIBERAL VICTORY

In both Poland and Hungary the situation in the spring of 1988 was tense and expectant. The end of an era in both countries was felt to be approaching, one that had lasted in Poland over six years, and in Hungary nearly thirty-two. In Poland the breakthrough came in August with the regime's offer of talks. In Hungary it had come the previous May with the ousting of Janos Kadar from the party leadership.

But though Kadar's ouster was a historic event, it was only a partial breakthrough, which led to democratization, Eastern-style. There was a delay, a period of transition, before the real breakthrough occurred toward democracy, Western-style. This period of transition is associated with the name of Karoly Grosz, who had become Hungarian prime minister in June 1987. Grosz was never a reformer, although with reform becoming more de rigueur every day he tried hard to look like one. He was more the early Gorbachev type of modern political manager, with a touch of populism and more than a touch of opportunism.

When Grosz replaced Kadar, after a carefully planned conspiracy among allies who later became adversaries, he seemed very much

---

[36]See *Radio Free Europe Research*, Polish SR/19, Item 1, "Walesa Victorious in Television Debate," December 16, 1988.

Hungary's man of the moment.[37] He combined for a time both the party leadership and the premiership, a fashion that went out with Khrushchev but had been revived by Jaruzelski during Poland's crisis. Its revival now in Hungary was strong evidence of the official and popular anxiety over Hungary's condition. It also tended to impute almost savior-like qualities to Grosz himself.

Unfortunately, Grosz had no recipe for salvation. The surge for reform following Kadar's downfall made him irrelevant and isolated. As a politician he was ready for both the market and pluralism, but he remained at heart a party official who balked at capitalism and Western-style parliamentarianism. As the reform gathered pace, he tried to slow it. He stood for party supremacy, modified but still basic. But the party, in the words of one eminent Hungarian, was like the man being chased by the wolf, shedding his clothes step by step to avoid being caught, until he is stark naked. Most Hungarians, of course, relished the sight. Grosz, however, did not, especially when it became clear that the man most immediately concerned was himself, and that he was not going to get his clothes back. As Imre Pozsgay, Rezso Nyers, and Miklos Nemeth (the new prime minister and once considered Grosz's minion) moved further toward dismantling the old system, Grosz became an embarrassing obstacle. The immense national sentiment evoked by the reburial and rehabilitation of Imre Nagy in spring 1989 accelerated his decline. In June 1989, 13 months after he gained the party leadership, he was effectively stripped of it.

The changes in the party leadership in June 1989 involved the creation of a four-man Presidium composed of Pozsgay, Nyers, Nemeth, and Grosz.[38] (They also involved the creation of a new Political-Executive Committee of 21 members. The abolition of the Central Committee was also announced.) Nyers was named party chairman, an honorary post that had been created for Kadar when he was ousted in May the previous year. But there was nothing honorary about the post Nyers now assumed. He became the real leader of the party and was recognized as senior in the new quadrumvirate. An erstwhile member of the Social Democrat party who "merged" with the communists in 1948, Nyers in the 1980s had capitalized on his intimate association with the NEM in the 1960s and then his eclipse in the 1970s when reform was shelved. His reputation, therefore, was vindicated now that comprehensive reform was seen as the only alternative to disaster. Aged 65, he had returned to the Politburo in May 1988, some 13 years

---

[37]See George Schoepflin, Rudolf Tokes, and Ivan Volgyes, "Leadership Change and Crisis in Hungary," *Problems of Communism*, September–October 1988.

[38]For the significance of this move, see Alfred Reisch, "Hungary in Transition: A Commentary," *Radio Free Europe Research*, Hungarian SR/12, Item 7, July 27, 1989.

after he had been dismissed from it.[39] Nemeth, at 41, was a promising politician who had ditched his patron, Grosz, and embraced reform. His inclusion in the four-man Presidium derived from his post as prime minister. But the leading spirit of reform was Pozsgay. From his position with the Patriotic People's Front, Pozsgay had created a veritable power base. As the party as well as Kadar lost credit in the 1980s, the search began for both institutional and personal alternatives. Pozsgay's answer was that Hungary need look no further than to Western-style social democracy for either. By 1989 he had become basically a social democrat and was almost ready to admit as much. The Hungarian Socialist Workers' Party, he argued, should and could evolve toward social democracy: the multiparty system, parliamentary democracy, a constitutional state, a mix of public and private property, and capitalist practice tempered by the welfare state. Capable, canny under his frankness, personable, and courageous, he was well liked and admired by intellectuals and reformers.[40]

But among much of the party apparatus, where the conservative strength lay, Pozsgay was public enemy number one, much more feared and hated than Nyers, for example. By 1989 the authority of the apparatus had lost much of its credibility. That was because it had lost control of many of the levers and the channels of power. But it had not become impotent. Like the Polish apparatus, it still retained large reserves of power through the *nomenklatura* and its control over provincial administration. In both countries the apparatus would keep that control until there were free local elections and a determined assault on the *nomenklatura*. In the present circumstances, although the apparatus could endanger reform outright in neither country, it could still delay it, even partially block its implementation, and exploit the many ways of discrediting its viability. In Hungary the apparatus therefore remained a threat that any reformer with political sense and responsibility had to take into account. That was why Grosz, irrelevant, reduced, even humiliated, was still not totally disabled. As long as the apparatus could obstruct, and as long as it identified with Grosz—which it now did, even if *faute de mieux*—then Grosz could not be discarded. Hence he retained the post of party secretary-general, with the near certainty (subsequently borne out) that he would lose it at the next party congress in October 1989. (In August he was already hinting at his retirement.) Grosz could also not be discarded as long as there was some hope of maintaining party unity. But as the acrimony

---

[39]On Nyers, see Henry Kamm, "Budapest Encore: Old Socialist Elected," *The New York Times*, October 10, 1989.

[40]One of the best insights into Pozsgay's thinking is contained in an interview he gave to *Marxism Today* (London), March 1989.

increased there was a growing expectation of a split. Many on both sides of the ideological fence regarded it as inevitable.

For the present, however, reform sentiment in Hungary was such that it was making headway even in some sections of the party grassroots, among the "reform circles," which were at the farthest end of the spectrum from the conservative apparatus. The reform circles had begun as a youthful radical faction but were now a growing political movement.[41] (Observers compared them with the 1981-vintage reform groups in the Polish party, which demanded internal party democracy based on a horizontal instead of vertical organizational structure, rejecting democratic centralism.) Most members of the reform circles liked Pozsgay but wanted to go even further and faster. The HSWP, they agreed, must become a new, grassroots party with a new name (suggesting socialism but not communism), controlled by the rank and file and not by the apparatus. Their main difference from Pozsgay and most reformers in positions of authority was over methods. They rejected the need for tactical caution, insisting that the party conservatives were no longer a threat; in their view, patience was no virtue but a self-defeating vice, and discretion just an excuse for faint-heartedness. These reform circles were seen by many Hungarians, and not just opponents of reform, as latter-day Jacobins, embarrassing, not assisting, the cause they espoused.

There was much in common between many in the reform circles, nominal party members though they were, and intellectuals in some of the main opposition groups, such as the Alliance of Free Democrats, led mainly by "urbanist" intellectuals, and particularly the youthful and radical Federation of Young Democrats (FIDESZ). The newest group on the scene was the Democratic League of Independent Trade Unions, composed of several branch unions that had separated from the official trade union organization. But the main opposition group, in terms of ascertainable membership and following, continued to be the populist Hungarian Democratic Forum, with its "Hungarian-ness" reflected, *inter alia*, in its militancy on the question of Hungarian minorities abroad and above all in its robust provincialism.

Adding to both the profusion and confusion of the Hungarian political landscape was the reappearance of former parties that had disappeared under Rakosi in the late 1940s. The most notable probably were the Smallholders, the strongest party before the communist repression; the Peasant Party; the Social Democrats; and the Independence Party. It remained to be seen what impact they would have. At

---

[41]The "reform circles" played a very important role in radicalizing the Hungarian party. See *Radio Free Europe Research*, Hungarian SR/15, Item 1, "HSWP Reform Circles Call for a New, Radically Reformed Party To Be Set Up," October 4, 1989.

least one of them, the Social Democrats, was gravely weakened by generational conflicts among its leaders. It was more likely that some of the newer groups would solidify into real, formal, political parties and gain most of the oppositional support. The Hungarian Democratic Forum, for example, competed against the communist party in four parliamentary by-elections in July 1989 and won three of them.

There was one largely unknown factor remaining on the Hungarian scene, clearly distinguishing it from Poland's and lending a quite different character to its reform politics: the attitude of the working class. Whereas in post-1956 Poland worker militancy had usually been the main driving political force, in Hungary the workers had been largely quiescent since the revolution of that year. It is true that toward the end of the 1970s, when inflation started to hurt, scattered strikes had become a very common occurrence, but the Kadar regime had managed to contain them. Many workers were becoming increasingly dissatisfied, but as long as a second or even a third job could still put the prizes of consumerism within their reach, they stayed on the treadmill. And as late as the second half of 1989, when the condition of most workers had seriously deteriorated and their prospects looked even worse, they still hesitated over the reform option. Not that they necessarily opposed it—many had, in one way or another, been initiated into the capitalist ethos through their second or third jobs. But how much they would support systemic economic reform, especially when it began to bite, was still a matter of conjecture and debate.

It was this absence of worker committment to Hungarian reform that for some observers gave the whole process an air of inconsequentiality, a lack of knuckle that could be fatal if resistance to it stiffened. For the moment, reform in Hungary did indeed recall 1848, "the revolution of the intellectuals." But however intellectually exciting the movement might be, reform would not go far without worker support. Conversely, the main danger to reform in Hungary could lie in this worker noncommitment turning to antagonism as the pains of economic reform became more acute for the many while its rewards became more conspicuous for the few. In this respect, Poland was already becoming for some Hungarians a deterrent rather than an inspiration. If anything, Czechoslovakia in 1968 offered the best analogy to the situation in Hungary. The Prague Spring had blossomed from the same combination of regime reformers and opposition intellectuals. The Czech working class was slow to respond; only when the invaders were already there did it realize what it might have lost. The Hungarian workers have never been as content as their Czech counterparts, but they might think they still had something to lose.

Neither have they ever been as numerous, solid, or prickly as the Poles. But they could still make or break reform in Hungary. Reformers could not assume too readily that the workers were bound to be on their side. Most of the tens of thousands who lined the streets for Janos Kadar's funeral in July 1989 were workers, a gesture not without political significance. Some reform intellectuals, however, scarcely hid their belief that life would be much simpler without the workers and its improvement much easier to achieve. That was a safe enough notion in the universities and the think tanks. On the streets it could be risky.

Some Hungarian intellectuals had, in fact, long tried to contact and cultivate the workers, mindful of the revolution in 1956 and of their belief in the common fate binding all Hungarians. Intellectuals who later formed the Hungarian Democratic Forum were especially notable in this. They made the attempt during the 1970s, but it was part of the Kadar regime's divide-and-rule strategy to prevent this. In the 1980s it became easier, but some of the Democratic Forum's leaders would be the first to admit that more could have been done and that many intellectuals could find neither the time nor the inclination to make the effort.[42] If the Democratic Forum could develop its worker contacts this could, combined with its position on the minority issue and its generally gradualist approach, stand it in good stead for the next year's general elections. It could help it finally breach the dwindling communist working-class strongholds.

POLAND: THE PEACEFUL REVOLUTION

In the second half of 1989, general elections in Hungary were still several months away. The Poles, however, were still trying to pick up the pieces of their own election, held in June, the culmination of the extraordinary political process that had begun with the regime after talks that produced the roundtable.

The basic change in politics, habits, and psychology that produced the roundtable is hard to comprehend. The leaderships of both sides—regime and Solidarity—had been under great pressure from many of their supporters not to negotiate at all. For the party apparatus, for example, with its many representatives in the Central Committee, the negotiations were more than a reversal of the policy of the last seven years: they were a betrayal of the whole principle of communist rule. For their part, many members and supporters of

---

[42]Private conversation with Sandor Csoori, one of the leaders of the Hungarian Democratic Forum, November 1988.

Solidarity regarded negotiation with "communists" as immoral and a betrayal of Poland itself. Many workers bridled at the thought of Solidarity negotiating with the people who had suppressed and persecuted them since 1981. They were led by some of Solidarity's leaders from that time, household names and heroes like Walesa's old deputy Andrzej Gwiazda, Marian Jurczyk from Szczecin, Jan Rulewski from Bydgoszcz, and Seweryn Jaworski from Warsaw. Many young people too, well educated and less so, opposed negotiations, their implacability often alarming their seniors, who had been through 1981, 1970, 1956, the communist takeover, and even World War II. With opposition so fierce, the Solidarity leaders, both the trade unionists and their intellectual advisers, more than ever needed the support of the church, not just from their own bishops but from the bishop of Rome. Without it Solidarity might never have advanced to the roundtable, or might never have taken its historic opportunity.

However difficult it was for Solidarity to come to the negotiating table, it was even more difficult for the regime. No matter how profound the moral objections of many of Solidarity's followers, the political reality was that the movement had won a big victory simply by being offered talks. For the first time in communist history, for the first time in Poland since well before World War II, there was the prospect of a *legal* opposition, and beyond that, a democratic government. The latter seemed still only a faint hope at the end of 1988, but Walesa and those around him realized that a primal shift was taking place in the communist system. What looked impossible today might be possible tomorrow, all the more so because the shift this time had begun at the system's center—the Soviet Union—not on its periphery.

But politics in Poland was still a zero-sum game: if Solidarity was gaining, the regime must be losing. This simple fact was not lost on many communists. And in terms of both Leninist political theory and established political practice, what the regime was losing was nothing less than its right to rule. In view of this, therefore, what was surprising was that the regime's decision to negotiate came to be accepted at all, however grudgingly. In any case, it led to two of the most turbulent Central Committee sessions (in December 1988 and January 1989) since Gomulka's fall in December 1970, sessions that heard threats from Jaruzelski, Rakowski, and others to resign. But after weighing the apocalyptic alternative, the opponents settled for trying to save something rather than risk losing everything.[43] In doing so the Polish Central Committee at least showed a certain realism. Many of

---

[43]For the historic importance of the December 1988 plenum, see Jan B. de Weydenthal, "Striving for Change in Poland," *Radio Free Europe Research*, RAD BR/245 (Poland), December 27, 1988.

its members had always mistrusted Jaruzelski, but they stuck by him now. In 1989 Jaruzelski was as indispensable in failure as he had been in success eight years earlier.

The roundtable talks in the first quarter of 1989 made history. They demonstrated that Poles *could* negotiate, and they gave fascinating glimpses into the Polish national character. But the Polish public, unlike foreign observers, maintained no sustained interest in them, in spite of the publicity on television. After the initial excitement, many Poles found them too long, tedious, and sometimes even irrelevant. What was most relevant to them was the deteriorating economic situation. The seriousness of this brooked no diversion.

The significance of the public's attitude was not lost on the clearer-sighted members of either the regime or the opposition. They saw it as a harbinger of wide and perilous public frustration with both the law's delay and the complexities of democratic procedure, particularly when a solution to the basic problems of physical existence seemed further off than ever. Of these problems, the most crippling was likely to be inflation. (Yugoslavia's case was already worrying many thoughtful Poles.) Inflation could not only destroy existing democracies, it could prevent new ones from being formed.[44] It was already emerging as the greatest single danger to a new society in Eastern Europe. The public, therefore, expected important and speedy results from the roundtable, and its impatience no doubt spurred the participants to come up with compromise and eventual agreement.

The roundtable's most important result was the agreement to hold Sejm (parliamentary) elections the following June under a *Proporz* arrangement for the distribution of seats. Sixty-five percent of the seats in the Sejm were allotted to the "ruling coalition"—communist party, Peasant party, Democratic party, and proregime Catholic groups—while 35 percent could be contested by Solidarity. In the newly created Senate (re-created, if precommunist history were considered) the one hundred seats were to be freely contested. The newly created (re-created) presidency was to have broad powers, especially over defense and foreign policy.[45]

The roundtable, however difficult, marked the high point of political consensus in Poland for many years to come. The discussions, though often lapsing into seemingly interminable bickering, could be seen as part of the energetic striving toward a civil society—the same process

---

[44]Judging from the movement of prices, there was already a well-founded fear that prices during 1989 as a whole would rise even faster than they had in 1988, when the retail price index rose by 159 percent from January to November. See *Polityka*, December 31, 1988.

[45]See Jan B. de Weydenthal, "Politics in Poland After the Round-Table Agreement," *Radio Free Europe Research*, RAD BR/67 (Poland), April 26, 1989.

that was taking place in Hungary, Slovenia, and, very slowly, in the Soviet Union. As the discussions continued, the growing commonality over means, if not ends, dulled the sharp edges separating the two sides and made compromise possible. General Czeslaw Kiszczak and Walesa, the leaders of the two delegations, set the example of moderation and revealed themselves as effective negotiators. Walesa, in particular, lionized by the world press, only enhanced his already towering reputation. Kiszczak, the epitome of the civilized state security man, interior minister, police chief, and erstwhile stalker of Solidarity, emerged as receptive and moderate, contributing much to the eventual success of the talks.

But the regime side would certainly not have been so ready to compromise had it had even the faintest inkling of what would happen at the polls. No one expected such shocking results, certainly not Solidarity. In the June elections the Polish regime's claims to govern were annihilated, despite its 65 percent advantage in the lower parliamentary house. This fixed percentage of seats had been designed to ensure gradualism in the pace of reform, a breathing space for the regime, and a period of preparation for the opposition, as well as to give Moscow the assurance that reform did not mean revolution. But what happened *was* a revolution, peaceful and parliamentary. It went much further, though, than anybody expected, or wanted. Walesa and his Solidarity advisers had all along been thinking that, all being well, a Solidarity-led government could be formed in the early 1990s, say in four years' time.[46] But what had been expected to take four years took less than four weeks. By August, Poland had a Solidarity-led government with one of its chief advisers, Tadeusz Mazowiecki (Catholic intellectual, friend of the Pope, "old-fashioned" Pole), as prime minister.[47]

In retrospect, perhaps the regime's humiliation in the elections made both the decisiveness and the speed of what happened inevitable. Of the 50 regime candidates, only one, who ran unopposed on the "national" ticket, got the required 50 percent of votes to be elected. The rest were simply, literally, crossed off the ballot by an electorate intoxicated with its freedom to say "No." In the newly created 100-member Senate, which had no fixed allotment of seats between the two sides, the regime coalition got one seat. In the lower house (Sejm) it got only the 65 percent of seats it had been guaranteed. (It had contested 100 percent of them, but every one of its candidates who faced competition failed miserably.)

---

[46]See John Lloyd, "Walesa Points the Way Forward," *The Financial Times*, August 18, 1989.

[47]The best press portrait is by Sylvie Kauffman, "Tadeusz Mazowiecki: la fermeté et la prudence," *Le Monde*, August 21–22, 1989.

But it was the regime's continuing ineptitude after this colossal defeat that shattered everybody's time frames and calculations. Still assuming that its lead in any new government was assured, based on its certainty that Jaruzelski would be the new president and the fact of its built-in 65 percent advantage, the communist leadership tried to salvage as much as it could. But its crudeness in doing so only hastened the revolution. It should have been chastened by Jaruzelski's hairsbreadth election to president—by one vote—in parliament. It was not Solidarity that nearly upset him, in fact, but a revolt among members of the communists' satellite parties and groupings: the United Peasant Party, the Democratic Party, and a small traditionally proregime grouping of Catholics. Together they took 27 percent of the coalition's built-in majority, leaving the communist party itself only 38 percent of the Sejm's 460 seats. The satellite parties, having so recently felt the winds of change at the elections and seeing communist domination shattered, now decided to think, act, and juggle for themselves.[48] Hence Jaruzelski's demeaning one-vote victory.

In its subsequent actions the regime leadership, without sensitivity itself, insisted on affronting everybody else's sensitivities. Jaruzelski, elected president, had to give up his communist party leadership; it went to Rakowski, recently prime minister, the intellectuals' bête noire and the workers' old enemy. Jaruzelski then asked General Kiszczak to form a government, the same Kiszczak who, despite the good impression he had made recently, had been (as the minister of interior and police chief) one of the main props of martial law. This was all too much for almost everybody. It was certainly too much for many United Peasant and Democratic party members. Also too much for Walesa, who began negotiating with the numerous rebels in both these parties.[49] The result was Poland's first democratic government since well before World War II—a government dedicated to democracy, market capitalism, social welfare, and a foreign policy that took into account both the Polish raison d'état and geopolitical considerations.

As for the communist party, it was still represented in the government, but only thanks to Soviet power, not any strength of its own. Rakowski, and especially a younger group of modernists now coming to the top, sought to understand the lessons of not only the recent

---

[48]The "independence" of Poland's satellite parties turned out to be catching. Subsequent developments in both the GDR and Czechoslovakia showed that some of the satellite parties there, like the East German Liberal Democrats and the Czech Socialists, were ready to jump on the reform bandwagon when there was no other choice.

[49]For a brilliant historical survey of the Polish opposition's progress to power, see Bernard Guetta, "La longue marche de l'opposition polonaise," Le Monde, August 24, 1989. See also the first eight items of Radio Free Europe Research, Polish SR/12, September 1989.

disaster but of the mistakes of the past 40 years. There was talk of a party split and of renaming the party. There would certainly be big changes, but it was doubtful whether the communist party could be a real political force in Poland for many years, if ever. Only a vicious reaction in the Soviet Union leading to a resurrection of the Brezhnev Doctrine could bring it back to anywhere near its old position.

HUNGARY: THE RISE OF CIVIL SOCIETY

While Poland was approaching the goal of a civil society more directly through the legalization of an independent opposition and eventual elections, in Hungary the reformers were trying a more round-about way to "constitutionalize" public life. It was reformers within the regime itself who took the lead in changing certain basic laws. In 1988 the minister of justice, Kalman Kulcsar, an internationally known sociologist, called for a complete revision of the country's constitution. His aim, and that of others who saw that this was the crux of the whole issue, was to make Hungary's new constitution a "*real* document genuinely transcending and enfolding" the political power of the communist party, which should now accept the superior power of the constitution.[50] Basic civil rights should also be anchored in the constitution, such as the presumption of innocence and the ban on retroactive legal regulation. The new constitution should also abolish the "discretionary quality of Hungarian life in which fine-sounding . . . principles are undermined by *ad hoc* powers given to administrative organs in excess of their proper competence."[51]

In politics the constitutional state meant parliamentary supremacy over state power. Parliament, therefore, should now become a vigorous actor, even a troublesome one, in session for much longer periods than before. The powers of the presidential council to enact legislation were to be curtailed. Above all, the principle of competitive politics should replace that of one-party rule. The communist party would take its place in the new multiparty system, but any future ascendancy it might enjoy would be through the ballot box and not by right or political theory. Other parties, legally recognized and independent, would now have no less, and no more, right than the communist party to compete for power.

The goal for both Poland and Hungary was the same. But they had come via different routes, in different stages. Poland formed its first free trade union, Solidarity, in 1980, and it quickly burgeoned into an

---

[50]George Schoepflin et al., "Leadership Change and Crisis in Hungary," p. 43.
[51]Ibid.

independent national movement in 1981. Suppressed in December of that year it turned into an underground opposition, becoming a national symbol. In April 1989 it reemerged as a recognized opposition, legalized by the same regime that had originally suppressed it. It then competed in the elections of June 1989, which, despite their limitations, put Solidarity in power. This was the Polish way, from socialism to the civil society. In contrast, the Hungarian way was more like "the long march through the institutions," the strategy Enrico Berlinguer designed for the Italian communists. Naturally the Hungarian and the Italian environments were quite different, but the framework in Hungary that Kadar had provided was spacious enough to allow political expression, which duly appeared, gathered strength, and increased rapidly after his downfall. Reformers in Hungary could therefore hope to transform the system from the inside, despite the constant danger of splitting the party; in Poland, the only recourse had been to confront it from the outside.

On their way to future equity both societies also had to repair past iniquities, and the very act of doing this—the emotions it aroused—lent strength and conviction to their efforts. In Poland, it was the journey back and eventual triumph of Solidarity. In Hungary it was even more profound and poignant: the rehabilitation and the reburial of Imre Nagy, symbolizing the vindication of the 1956 revolution. In both countries these were issues that transcended present politics. They concerned that indefinable but, to East Europeans, unmistakable entity: the soul of the nation.

After the reburial of Imre Nagy on June 16, 1989, Hungary's own roundtable conference, which had opened just two days before, could begin in earnest. Designed to further the whole reform process, it was obviously modeled on the Polish example but was an altogether more complex affair. The opposition delegation, which became known as the "opposition roundtable," was a veritable mosaic of groupings united only by a general desire for change. A roll call of its nine members gives some idea of the variety that made coherent action almost impossible: (1) Social Democratic Party, (2) Federation of Young Democrats (FIDESZ), (3) Independent Smallholders Party, (4) Democratic League of Independent Trade Unions, (5) Hungarian Democratic Forum, (6) Christian Democratic People's Party, (7) Alliance of Free Democrats, (8) Hungarian People's Party, and (9) The Endre Bajcsy-Zsilinsky Friendship Society, a progressive environmentalist group. These groups covered a wide range of Hungarian aspirations for a better life, while not necessarily giving the most businesslike impression around the conference table.

The conference also included a third grouping—delegates from a number of vaguely proregime or conservative organizations ranging from old classic transmission belts like the official council of trade unions (SZOT) and the Patriotic People's Front, through mildly Stalinist holdouts and unrepentant Kadarites, to the National Council of Women. There were seven in all, united at least in the cover name they chose for themselves: "The Silent Majority." They were sometimes dismissed derisively as "Leninism's Last Line of Defense," but some of them claimed that outside Budapest they were a force to be reckoned with.

As a demonstration of the pluralistic profusion that had swept over Hungarian public life, the roundtable was certainly impressive. But it was there to build a *modus operandi* to bring democracy to Hungary, a practical task for which it did not seem ideally equipped. Neither the regime (party) side nor the opposition was well-led; neither had its Kiszczak or its Walesa. Grosz had opened the conference for the regime, and the position of main spokesman was then taken by Gyorgy Fejti, a Central Committee secretary. But just over a month after the talks opened both were demoted. Although this reflected a victory for the more progressive faction of the party, it did little to improve the regime's overall showing in the negotiations. The opposition's main spokesman was Imre Konya, one of the leaders of the Hungarian Democratic Forum but chosen mainly on the strength of his membership in the Independent Lawyer's Forum. Konya was much respected but had yet to make his reputation as a public figure. Apart from questions of broad leadership, the opposition groups also had to contend with factionalism: the occasional inability of the Social Democratic Party to field a delegation because of divisions within its ranks was the most extreme example of the opposition's incoherence, but for many Hungarians it was not atypical. There was a commonness of purpose but too little unity on how to achieve it.

The regime's strategy was to try to keep the discussion on economic topics. For one thing, they presented a better chance for agreement. Both sides (though not most of "The Silent Majority") accepted marketization and privatization. Even so, there was disagreement on the extent to which those principles should be taken, not only between the two sides, but also within the ranks of each. For example, two important sets of proposals to the HSWP Central Committee—one submitted by a team headed by Ivan T. Berend, chairman of the Academy of Science, and the other by a team headed by Csaba Csaki, a well-respected economist—differed considerably in boldness and on several specific recommendations.[52] On the opposition side there were thoroughgoing capitalist converts, as well as Austrian-style social democrats. But if some of the differences were quite sharp, they were not incompatible, at least not enough to hold up the proceedings.

But the regime did not prefer economics simply because it provided a better chance of agreement. It was watching the public, too. The economic situation was still deteriorating. Remedy was getting more urgent than ever. And like its Polish counterpart, the Hungarian regime did not want to be seen by the public as the sole prescriber and purveyor of whatever bitter medicine was necessary. The opposition must also share the odium. At the very beginning of the conference Grosz put it nicely: "Even if it was not so in the past, the responsibility for the future is joint."[53]

But however pressing the economic question, the opposition rightly insisted on the primacy, or at least the equality, of politics as an issue to be fully discussed and resolved. For the regime, this meant facing the reality of the power it had enjoyed for over 40 years and the degree to which it was prepared to give it up; hence it was a painful, as well as divisive, issue. Naturally the regime wanted to avoid politics as much as possible—the less said about such questions, or the less they were debated, the better. The opposition, therefore, was finding itself confronted by an agenda it could not approve. In substance, procedure, and atmosphere, the Hungarian roundtable was soon in deep turmoil, as the Polish one had been in its early stages.

At the beginning of August the talks temporarily broke down amid a welter of mutual recriminations. The opposition charged the regime with refusing to allow full enough discussion on vital issues, while the regime accused the opposition of assuming that the present organs of government—now staffed mainly by officials who genuinely supported change—had no legitimacy and therefore no right to initiate change without their advice and consent.

Roughly, the contentious issues fell into five interconnected categories: ideological, institutional, personal, administrative, and political-military. The ideological wrangle, as the opposition insisted, had serious implications. It centered on the regime's desire to insert into the new constitution a formulation affirming the leading role of the working class in society. This would replace the old shibboleth about the leading role of the communist party, which both sides agreed

---

[52]The recommendations of the Berend committee were published in *Figyelo*, May 4, 1989. They included a big reduction in CMEA trade, aggressive reprivatization of economic assets, and free transfer and sale of land. The more conservative proposals of the Csaki committee appeared in *Tarszadalmi Szemle*, special edition, April 1989.

[53]Radio Budapest, June 14, 1989.

had to be dropped. The opposition saw the new formulation as an attempt to retain a communist essence in the new constitution.[54]

One of the most complex issues concerned the presidency. Both sides agreed on investing it with strong powers, like the new Polish presidency. But where they disagreed sharply, and where the opposition feared being outmaneuvered, was over how and when the new president should be chosen. The regime wanted it done by popular vote before the parliamentary election. The opposition saw this as a ruse to get Imre Pozsgay elected. Despite the growing anticommunist mood, he was still probably the most popular politician in Hungary—certainly the best known. And he wanted the job, a fact of which the opposition was well aware. To them he was a respected politician whose striving for reform had made their own efforts that much easier. But as long as he remained a member of the Hungarian Socialist Workers' Party, no matter how penitent it was now becoming or whatever it might evolve into, he still stood for an interest many considered alien to the Hungarian nation and inimical to themselves. They wanted the new president to be chosen by a newly elected parliament, which would also certainly contain an anticommunist majority. The regime side, for its part, thought it was sitting pretty on this issue—probably only this issue. In electoral terms, Pozsgay was running miles ahead of his party; once installed in the presidency, the reasoning went, much as he might relish the role of *vox populi*, he would still be in a position to do something for his old comrades, collectively or even individually. Besides, recalling Jaruzelski's cliff-hanger of an election to Poland's presidency, would it not be fitting for a more orderly nation like Hungary to do things somewhat differently?[55]

As for Pozsgay, he was desperately anxious to avoid becoming the center of a controversy like this. It could only hurt his chances of election and his own image as being above the battle. To be detested (as he was) by many of his fellow communists was a huge electoral asset these days, but to be suspected by the population of being used by the party to further its own political ends was a liability even he might not survive. His position was difficult. He was very anxious for the roundtable talks to succeed, so much so that he sometimes made the lives of the regime negotiators more difficult by sounding too conciliatory. He seemed rather slow to learn that you can't please all of the people all of time.

---

[54]Associated Press (Budapest), August 12, 1989. See also discussion on Radio Budapest Domestic Service, August 5, 1989, *FBIS-EEU-89-150*, August 7, 1989.

[55]See Tibor Fenyi, "Wohin kipt Ungarns 'runder Tisch'? Machtfülle für den Staatspräsidenten als Kernfrage der Verhandlungen," *Die Presse* (Vienna), August 28, 1989.

The "nitty-gritty" of reform lay in the fourth category: the administrative. The Poles had been able to defer this issue somewhat because of the halfway character of their parliamentary elections in June 1989. The Hungarians, set for multiparty elections without conditions, could not. Access to the media was one important question here; it caused some squabbling but turned out to be solvable. Ultimately the most difficult issue would be the *nomenklatura*, which all communist systems in dissolution would have to shed. In both Hungary and Poland the *nomenklatura* had been pared down over the years. The Hungarian regime, for example, claimed in May 1989 that its "list of cadres" had been reduced from 1700 state and economic posts in 1973 to 452 and was due to be reduced to about 150.[56] The *nomenklatura* had always presented problems of definition and composition, and this "list of cadres" was obviously specious, although in recent years the behemoth had been shrinking. This did not mean, however, that it would disappear without a struggle. It was the hard core that would fight most tenaciously of all.

But that was for the future. One of the pressing problems now was what the opposition considered the ill-gotten gains—wealth, assets—the party had accumulated over the last 40 years. Now the party, once the champion of collectivism, invoked the principle of "what's mine's my own." The opposition, on the other hand, took time off from hailing the advent of capitalism and adopted the classic socialist slogan of "share the wealth." It felt most strongly about the assets of the old "bourgeois" parties, sequestered by the communists in the late 1940s. These parties had now revived and wanted restitution. The communists argued that they had acquired these assets lawfully. Their opponents pointed to the difference between "lawful" and "legalistic," observing also that if the party was not willing to share its wealth, how could anyone believe it would ever share its power? So the quarrel went on and the Hungarian public looked on, with admiration withheld. It was withheld even more when the opposition gleefully revealed that the party had been salting away many of its assets in a company imaginatively called "Next 2000."[57]

Another pressing problem concerned the continuance of party organizations (cells) in the factories. The ubiquity of these organizations, not only in industry but in every facet of public life, had been an essential feature of communist rule everywhere; it was one of the basics of its existence, at the heart of Leninism. To challenge their presence was, in its way, just as serious a threat to communist rule (or survival)

[56]See *Radio Free Europe Research*, Hungarian SR/56, Item 2, May 30, 1989. On July 14, 1989, Radio Budapest reported that the party Central Committee had decided to reduce the *nomenklatura* authority of itself and the Politburo from 1200 positions to 435.

[57]See Henry Kamm, "Hungarian Party in Money Scandal," *The New York Times*, September 7, 1989.

as denying the party its predominance in the ruling institutions at the center. Both sides realized this, and the issue looked like it was becoming an intractable one.

Finally, there was the category that cast its shadow over the whole compass of reform in Hungary, and in Eastern Europe as a whole: the civil-military-Soviet interaction. On this cluster of issues the regime preferred to remain as tight-lipped as possible, ostensibly because of its extreme sensitivity. In reality, the Soviet connection was the communists' last best hope for survival, the surest chance of containing, and eventually turning back, the advances of reform. Specifically, the regime was insisting that there could be no "depoliticization" of the armed forces, that whatever changes the multiparty system might bring, the party's leading role in the military must be preserved.[58] The opposition was not united on this issue. Some accepted its sensitiveness and wanted it lowered on or even dropped from the conference agenda. Others insisted that Hungary could neither be free nor democratic until the question was resolved. It was another case of Hungary's opposition being divided between the strategies of shortcut and gradualism.

As most Hungarians and foreign observers had expected, the Hungarian roundtable talks eventually ended in compromise. They began in the middle of June and ended in the middle of September. The agreement included:[59]

- The election of the president. This most controversial issue ended in a regime victory. The new president, invested with strong but as-yet unspecified powers, was to be elected by direct, nationwide vote, and *before* the free parliamentary elections.
- The timing of parliamentary elections, to be held not later than 90 days after the presidential election.
- A new electoral law closely based on the West German system, involving both direct election and proportional representation.
- An overhaul of the legal system, including the criminal code, to conform with the "accepted norms of human and political rights."

---

[58]This was a much discussed issue, and it was characteristic of the atmosphere of *glasnost* that had developed in Hungary that, despite the subject's sensitivity, the discussions were widely reported. See, for example, the interview with Major-General Janos Seboek, army officer and a National Assembly deputy, Radio Budapest Domestic Service, June 10, 1989, *FBIS-EEU-89-113*, June 14, 1989.

[59]The following is based mainly on Judy Dempsey, "Fudging in Hungarian Poll Deal," *The Financial Times*, September 20, 1989.

- The total depolitization of the armed forces, meaning the disbanding of (communist) party committees and the end of political (communist) training. The Workers' Militia, the armed detachment of the party that many reformers feared as potential regime "shock troops," was to be brought under the direct control of the army.

On this last issue the opposition had clearly won its point, because the regime had fought hard for the retention of party influence in the military. For its part, the regime had for the moment won on the retention of political activity in the factories. It clearly had to give up its monopoly in this regard—other political parties and groups could also now begin activities in the factories—but this it was ready to do, believing that its strongest support would rest in the large industrial concerns.

But while the regime and the opposition were hammering out these broad but obviously vulnerable agreements on the country's future, both Hungary's government and its party were each in the process of making history. In September, the Hungarian government permitted several thousand East German citizens, vacationers in Eastern Europe who did not want to return to the GDR, to cross over into Austria on their way to the Federal Republic of Germany. It was the most significant foreign policy decision any Hungarian communist government had made since Imre Nagy's fateful declaration of neutrality in 1956, (the vital difference, of course, being that this decision presumably had Soviet approval). By permitting this massive exodus of East Germans, the Hungarians were not just spurning their alliance obligations. They were even going beyond an assertion of neutrality. They were declaring their preference for the West in a crisis involving a front-line ally. For the communist world, this was a first.[60]

In early October it was the party's turn. At its party congress the Hungarian Socialist Workers' Party dissolved itself and became the Hungarian Socialist Party. After the revolution in 1956, Janos Kadar had formed the Hungarian Socialist Workers' Party to replace the old communist party, which had disintegrated during the revolution. That action had been a symbolic and organizational shift from Stalinism to Leninism. Now, 33 years later, the party, by an overwhelming majority of the delegates represented, was disavowing Leninism and acclaiming democratic socialism on the West European model. It was too drastic a move for some. Karoly Grosz, for example, declared his unwillingness to belong to the new creation, and a new Leninist party was being

---

[60]See A. O., "Ungarns Entscheidung," *Neue Zürcher Zeitung*, September 13, 1989, Fernausgabe Nr. 211.

formed. But the momentum was with the name-changing reformers. Eyes were now on the forthcoming free election. The new party, as the Hungarian Socialist Party, led by Rezso Nyers, considered it would now stand a better chance of avoiding a total humiliation like the one suffered by the Polish United Workers' Party the previous June.[61] The more optimistic were still hoping for enough votes to win a role in the future government.

Such optimism was sounding more and more forced. By the end of 1989 the popular mood in Hungary had turned sharply against communism, whatever its form, however human and purified it may have become. This mood seriously threatened the assumptions and calculations that Hungarian political life had been based on only a few months before: that reform communism, and some of its leaders, had considerable public support; that an orderly transition to democracy required the participation of the reform communists; that however permissive the Soviet Union may have become in Eastern Europe, there were still, as the democratization process in Poland was apparently indicating, lines that should not be crossed. But anticommunism only increased as the inhibitions about Soviet power diminished. Anyone associated with the past regime became suspect, and so did any democratic forces prepared to deal with them.

The principal victim of this change of mood appeared to be Pozsgay. He was the man who tried to please everybody, and it was proving politically suicidal to please too many members of the old Hungarian Socialist Workers' Party in the effort to hold it together. Although Pozsgay would almost certainly have wanted to abolish party organizations in the factories and in the armed forces, to dispense with the party's great wealth, and to abolish the Workers' Militia, he had found himself hedging on these issues to try to preserve a party unity that was collapsing anyway. In the event, what had seemed to him to be good politics turned into a serious defeat when the Hungarian parliament, correctly sensing the political mood, voted to abolish the party presence in the economy and to disband completely the Workers' Militia.

Thus the roundtable agreement that Pozsgay had worked so hard to bring about began to unravel almost as soon as it was signed. Three of the more uncompromising groups had refused to sign the agreement anyway.[62] They were the Alliance of Free Democrats, FIDESZ, and the independent trade union organization, and it was the Free

---

[61]Charles T. Powers, "Reformers Win First Vote for New Hungary Party," *Los Angeles Times*, October 8, 1989.

[62]Dempsey, "Fudging in Hungarian Poll Deal."

Democrats and FIDESZ who went on to inflict on Pozsgay a decisive political defeat. They had refused to sign the roundtable agreement specifically because they objected to the provision on the election of the new president—that the office would be invested with strong powers and that the officeholder would be elected by direct, nationwide vote *before* the parliamentary elections. The dissenters argued that in the present context, this system of election would be undemocratic because it would heavily favor Pozsgay, the declared candidate. The parliamentary elections would be a more accurate reflection of the general popular will, and it would therefore be more democratic if the new parliament elected the president.

The Free Democrats and FIDESZ were not prepared to agree to what they saw as a partially stage-managed transition to democracy, as had been attempted in Poland. To forestall it, they took advantage of a constitutional provision allowing a referendum to be held on the mode of the presidential election, upon presentation of a petition with the required number of signatures. Accordingly, the dissenters circulated a petition asking for the nationwide presidential election system to be set aside. About 200,000 signatures, twice the number required, were obtained with surprising ease. That ease had looked ominous for Pozsgay; the result of the referendum looked decidedly more ominous. The communist-turned-socialist party, as well as the Hungarian Democratic Forum, had advocated a boycott of the referendum, a move tending to strengthen the public suspicion of collusion between the two. But about 58 percent of eligible voters did vote, and the Free Democrats and FIDESZ won the point, if only by the narrowest of margins. The presidential vote would now take place *after* the parliamentary elections.

Pozsgay's star was therefore on the wane, and the political situation looked more uncertain than ever. About 35 parties and groups were contesting the general election, now set for March 1990, but practically none of them spoke with a unified voice in the heady political free-for-all. Factions were emerging even in the major political groupings like the socialists, the Hungarian Democratic Forum, and the Alliance of Free Democrats, as well as the burgeoning independent smallholders. But what was sure was that anticommunism would dominate the election. In the event, the socialists (former communists) got just over 10 percent of the vote in the election, and Pozsgay failed to win direct election. The victory went to the Hungarian Democratic Forum, the serious party most associated with Hungary's national traditions.

POLAND AND HUNGARY: THE SHORT-TERM OUTLOOK

By the end of 1989, Poland and Hungary had made progress toward both a civil society and national sovereignty that no one would have thought even conceivable just one year before. After free elections, Poland had a democratically led government with an overwhelming majority. Hungary was moving toward free elections in which the communists-turned-socialists looked set for a serious defeat, despite their efforts at self-regeneration. The progress of either country toward national sovereignty was necessarily limited, however, on account of the Soviet connection. Both remained perforce in the Warsaw Pact, in CMEA, and in close bilateral relationship with the Soviet Union. But the Soviet relationship was transforming as well. The Warsaw Pact was being emasculated, CMEA was moribund, and the whole context of bilateral relations was changing. At the same time, both were widening and deepening their relations with the West and curtailing their relations with most of the smaller Warsaw Pact allies. Hungary had dramatically ruptured its relations with the GDR, hitherto its most important non-Soviet ally. With Romania, because of the minorities issue, its relations were flamboyantly antagonistic.

But the progress each country had made with its domestic reformation was the most significant measure of its assertion of national sovereignty. For both, the demolition of Leninism, the thoroughgoing adoption of Western-style parliamentary democracy, and the progressive introduction of capitalism simply erased the ideological underpinnings of the Soviet alliance. From now on, whatever that alliance became, it was in no sense ideological. There was still some mutual economic interest, but in the main the 40-year Soviet alliance had been reduced to one of circumstance. This had not been due solely to the exertions of the Poles and the Hungarians; much was owed to the permissiveness of Gorbachev, and the combination of intention, constraint, and loss of control that produced it.

There is no doubt that the developments in both countries, like many in his own, had gone further than Gorbachev expected or wanted. But while he remained in power, they were not going to be stopped. He was now accepting the East European revolution and trying to turn it to his advantage. Within the two countries themselves there seemed to be no possibility of reversal. The Polish communist party was in complete disarray, while its Hungarian counterpart was frantically trying to sail with the wind. In both countries the armed forces were no longer undying defenders of the status quo: they too were busy regrooming and refurbishing. The security services were being neutered. In Poland the ZOMOs were being disbanded, and in

Hungary the Workers' Militia, the strong arm of the party in the factories and the streets, was first placed under government control and then doomed to disbandment.

Indeed, the sole prospect of reversal now seemed to lie in largely self-induced catastrophe. To begin with, the huge victories the democratic forces had achieved had been due as much to the colossal ineptitude of their communist opponents as to their own efforts. Now they had to prove not just that they were better, but that they could govern better. And despite the massive popular repudiation of communist rule in both countries, many citizens had not yet come out openly for the democratic forces. In Poland, 38 percent of the electorate did not vote in the June elections. Preliminary surveys indicated that about half the nonvoters did not like the agreements and compromises made with the communists. (This included many former supporters of Solidarity.) The other half was just apathetic. In Hungary, it was the political and especially the voting intentions of the workers and peasants that were still uncertain. Neither the regime nor the opposition could take them for granted, and both would be currying their favor in the period before the election. Voter turnout in the parliamentary by-elections during the fall had been poor, and both sides feared a low turnout in the forthcoming general election.

The futures of both countries would be decided largely on economic results. And here the prospects were daunting. Although Hungary was generally considered "economically better off" than Poland, both were faced by four huge, interacting, problems:

- The command economic system was approaching collapse. In this respect Hungary was less badly off than Poland: it had at least been trying to reform, however halfheartedly, for a number of years. Regarding the introduction of capitalism, the dilemma for both was that nowhere, either in practice or theory, were there examples or models from which they could draw. They were making history largely on their own.
- Both had a crippling hard currency debt. Poland's was about $38 billion, Hungary's about $18 billion. In per capita terms, Hungary's was much bigger than Poland's.
- The welfare, health, and social services systems in both countries were beyond repair. They would deteriorate with increasing rapidity because they would be very low in the allocation priority order for many years to come.
- Parts of both countries were already engulfed by environmental disaster. If in, say, the next 15 years nothing were done to halt the destruction, many other aspects of public policy would become academic, even irrelevant.

Even to begin tackling these problems would need a large degree of unity among the democratic forces that had found themselves so suddenly in power. The prospects for this seemed by no means hopeless, but not assured either. In Hungary the roundtable discussions had revealed serious divisions among the opposition, and the election campaign would deepen them. In Poland, there had been an impressive show of unity among the three forces that produced the democratic victory: the workers and the intellectuals (both under the Solidarity umbrella), and the church. Now, however, there were signs of serious division, both organizational and ideological. Should Solidarity be primarily a political party or a trade union, or could it be both? This was the serious organizational debate. Ideologically, there were already splits between Solidarity's social democratic wing, with free-thinking tendencies, and its liberal-capitalist wing, with Catholic convictions. These divisions could deepen and fester as the economic situation grew more serious. Worse still, if the remedies applied began to hurt seriously, many workers in both countries—but especially in Poland— might become destructively militant. The ensuing political danger of an alliance of convenience between workers and sections of the former communist power structure, which now seems very remote, might become less remote. The West's response to the situation will be crucial. Whether it likes it or not, the West has now become one of the principal actors in Eastern Europe, and this role has its responsibilities.

III. THE GERMAN DEMOCRATIC REPUBLIC

While Poland and Hungary were destined to be the trailblazers of reform in Eastern Europe, the ruling communist elites in the GDR and Czechoslovakia each had their own specific reasons for rejecting experimentation. Not only was each led by a man who was clearly a product of the Brezhnev era, each also had its own specific dilemma and fear of reform. In the Czechoslovak case, the Husak-Jakes leadership was dominated by orthodox and conservative forces installed with Moscow's support after the 1968 Soviet-led invasion. For them the Prague Spring remained a menacing trauma.

In the GDR, the communist (SED) leadership faced its own unique dilemma, one that stemmed from the partition of Germany after World War II. From the outset, the SED regime's very legitimacy was intertwined with its efforts to inculcate a sense of national identity based on socialist ideology. Whereas other East European regimes could experiment with elements of capitalist economics or Western notions of political pluralism, the SED could see such moves only as dangerously diluting the differences between East and West Germany and eroding the single justification for the existence of a second German state. The basic East German response to *perestroika*, therefore, was conditioned by the way it saw itself in the perspective of German history and in relation to that other Germany, the Federal Republic. This reason for East Berlin's glacial response to Gorbachev had been diagnosed right at the beginning by Western observers, but it took until August 1989, not long before the East German people took matters into their own hands, before it was officially admitted. As Otto Reinhold, rector of the SED Central Committee's Academy of Social Sciences, candidly put it in an interview, socialism was the GDR's raison d'être: "What right to exist would a capitalist GDR have alongside a capitalist Federal Republic? In other words, what justification would there be for two German states once ideology no longer separated them?"[1]

Reinhold was thus admitting to the basic reason for East German reluctance. Previous official propaganda had maintained that the GDR had no need for systemic reform. Its leaders argued that its economy, give or take a few faults here or there, was doing very well, and they could point with some justice to how badly the economic situation was

---

[1]Radio GDR II, August 19, 1989.

in réforming countries like Poland and Hungary. (For several years now the faltering New Economic Mechanism in Hungary had drawn a hail of patronizing comments in both the East German and Czechoslovak media.)[2] East German complacence, even hubris, on the subject was clearly demonstrated as early as May 1986 at the SED party congress when Honecker, in the presence of Gorbachev himself, politely but firmly rejected the Soviet leader's reform policies. The GDR was doing well enough without them, was his unmistakable message.[3]

There are many examples of official East German "formulations of rejection" regarding Gorbachev's *perestroika*, but the best known was that of the regime's long-time top ideologist, Politburo member and Central Committee secretary Kurt Hager. Asked about the relevance of Soviet reforms for the GDR, Hager dismissively said that the fact that your neighbor wallpapered his house did not mean that you had to do the same.[4] (Hager's riposte, it might be added, was not just a classic piece of nose-thumbing at *perestroika*; it was also a case of the GDR following the letter—but not the spirit—of Gorbachev's policy of more independence for the East European states.)

To give its defiance an ideological and nationalist coating, the East German leadership launched a campaign to develop and justify its past policies as a national communist strategy, reviving the old slogan of "socialism in the colors of the GDR." While tolerating a budding reform debate among party intellectuals, the SED's main efforts were directed at explaining to the mass of the population why the sort of dramatic change taking place elsewhere in the region was inappropriate for the GDR. Successive party officials claimed that the SED had avoided the serious mistakes committed by ruling communist parties elsewhere and pointed to the GDR's past superior economic performance as proof of the correctness of its policies. In addition, party ideologues continued to pound the fact that the reforms being carried out in the USSR, Hungary, and Poland had thus far produced very little except inflation, unemployment, and new social tensions.

Last but certainly not least, SED officials repeatedly pointed out that the GDR's sensitive geostrategic position and the "relentless offensive" of the West German media made the margin of error for reform in the GDR extremely narrow. Calls for reform in the GDR

---

[2]On adverse comments about the situation in Poland and Hungary see, for example, Otto Reinhold in *Einheit* (No. 1 (1989)), p. 54; also Harry Nick in *Neues Deutschland*, March 25/26, 1989.

[3]See B. V. Flow and Ronald D. Asmus, "The 11th SED Congress," *Radio Free Europe Research*, RAD BR/63 (German Democratic Republic), April 30, 1986.

[4]*Stern* (Hamburg) April 8, 1987; reprinted in *Neues Deutschland*, April 10, 1987.

were increasingly deflected by the argument that change would jeopardize stability in the GDR and was therefore in no one's interest. Speaking at the 7th Central Committee plenum in December 1988, SED General Secretary Erich Honecker criticized the West German media for insisting that the GDR introduce reforms, noting how ironic it was that those "for whom our policies were always 'too Russian' were now recommending that we follow the Soviet example." This advice, Honecker continued, was "equivalent to demanding that we deviate from our course and march into anarchy."[5] Moscow understood, according to Otto Reinhold, that the key foreign policy task of the GDR was to ensure "stability and to make sure that a second Tbilisi does not erupt in Rostock."[6]

This mixture of defiance, complacence, and basic fear continued right up to the fall of Honecker in October 1989. It put the GDR with Romania in the unenviable category of the two East European Warsaw Pact states least responsive to *perestroika*. (Even Czechoslovakia, on account of a comprehensive, if fairly orthodox, economic reform plan, and Bulgaria, by virtue of a grandiose, though hardly implemented, reform program, were somewhat more responsive.) The GDR's attitude was soon to prove massively counterproductive, antagonizing the population to the point of open, though nonviolent, rebellion. It was not so much reform, but the regime's refusal to countenance reform, that led to the situation in which the GDR itself seemed headed toward extinction.

THE INTERNATIONAL IMPORTANCE OF THE GDR

Because of its apparent stability (and hence international obscurity) for nearly 30 years—from the building of the Berlin Wall in August 1961 to the opening of the borders in November 1989—it was easy to overlook the unique role the German Democratic Republic played in the post–World War II European security system. The state appeared so stable that not only its existence but also its permanence were taken for granted. Only when its future began to be questioned after the momentous events of the fall of 1989 did international attention concentrate on the role the GDR had played, and on what a Europe without it might be like.

The importance to the Soviet Union of the GDR's existence was obvious:

---

[5]Speech at 7th SED plenum, December 1988, *Neues Deutschland*, December 2, 1988.
[6]Quoted in *Der Tagesspiegel* (West Berlin), May 24, 1989.

> It was the division of Germany after World War II and then the (almost literal) cementing of that division by the creation of the GDR that constituted the single best Russian historical gain from World War II: the emasculation of German power. Thus one of the most basic historic security ambitions of Russia had been satisfied.[7]

After the building of the Wall in 1961 the GDR was to emerge as the strongest East European economic power, and it even made claims (although most of them turned out to be spurious) to be a world economic power. But the international importance of the GDR lay not so much in what it was—considerable though that turned out to be— but in the reinforcing of Soviet power that its very existence signified.

The benefits deriving from the GDR's existence were, however, never considered by the international community as accruing solely to the Soviet Union. By the rest of Europe—East and West—and by many people in the United States and Canada, the GDR was seen as an unattractive but effective means of preserving a status quo that could, if disturbed, have serious international repercussions. The GDR, therefore, continued as one of the great paradoxes of contemporary international relations. It was both the creation and the protectorate of the Soviet Union. As such, and on account of the frequent repressiveness of its regime, with its scant respect for human rights, it was often the object of universal disdain. Yet for what it signified in terms of European and world stability it was largely viewed, if not with satisfaction, then at least with relief. For over 40 years it enabled the world to avoid thinking about the power of a unified Germany. The world was grateful for it, including the West Germans. Most of the citizens of the Federal Republic, despite their paying lip service to reunification, and despite the fact that the goal of German unity was enshrined in their constitution, were content to relegate this issue to the dim, distant future. No one suspected that in 1989 the dim, distant future would become a matter of a year or two at the very most.

It was the unique usefulness of the GDR to the Soviet Union that made it Moscow's most important East European satellite. Poland, of course, is much larger, with well over twice the East German population, and there has never been any doubt about the importance Moscow attached to its immediate Western neighbor. But the character and function of the GDR made Soviet control over Poland all the more essential. Poland was the communications link with the GDR and the Soviet front-line position in Central Europe, the military link with the nearly 400,000 Soviet troops stationed in the GDR, and the economic

---

[7]James F. Brown, *Eastern Europe and Communist Rule*, Duke University Press, Durham, North Carolina, 1988, p. 32.

link ensuring the vital Soviet supplies of energy and raw materials to the East German economy. The East German sensitivity to this economic lifeline to the Soviet Union was shown in its neurotic reaction to the emergence of Solidarity in Poland in 1980–81. The record contains several East German statements expressing concern about supplies being interrupted because of the "anarchy" in Poland. But East German concerns went even deeper than this. The leadership realized the danger of being sandwiched between a democratic Federal Republic to its West and a democratizing Poland to its East.[8] When Solidarity was driven underground at the end of 1981 it seemed that the danger to the GDR had passed for good. But it was to return eight years later in much sharper form. Communist rule collapsed in Poland and democracy became a reality, with the permission this time of the Soviet Union itself. In historical perspective, this emerges as the basic reason for the collapse of the GDR just a few months later.

ECONOMIC MIRACLE AND ECONOMIC DIFFICULTIES

No one could have predicted that the collapse would come so quickly. In fact, for many years—at least since the middle of the 1970s—the GDR did appear to be the emerging prosperous socialist state its leaders never tired of claiming it was. Since the demise of the Honecker regime, however, what many had suspected has been revealed: that the success was not nearly as great as claimed and, in any case, that it had always had its darker and potentially fatal aspects. Günter Mittag, for many years the "overlord" of the East German economy, and who was given much of the credit for the regime's economic successes, later became the object of almost as much public opprobrium as Honecker himself as the man primarily responsible for East Germany's economic plight.[9] Still, whatever the reservations and deceptions, East German economic progress after the building of the Wall in 1961 was impressive, especially if one remembers the blight of World War II and the Soviet demands for war reparations in the early years after it, plus the loss of 2.5 to 3 million of its citizens to the West before the building of the Wall.

By the end of the 1960s the GDR had replaced Czechoslovakia and Poland as the Soviet Union's most important economic partner, and

---

[8]See James F. Brown, *Soviet Relations with the Northern Tier in East Europe*, EAI Paper No. 9, European American Institute for Security Research, Marina del Rey, California, pp. 5–9.

[9]For an expert critique of the GDR's economic performance under Mittag see the interview with Wilma and Rolf Merkel in *Die Zeit* (Hamburg), September 29, 1989.

during the 1970s the East German general standard of living equaled and then probably surpassed that of Czechoslovakia. This was largely due to a deliberate policy of "consumerism" initiated by Erich Honecker after he replaced Walter Ulbricht as leader of the Socialist Unity (communist) Party in 1971, Ulbricht having been removed because he opposed détente with the Federal Republic, the cornerstone of Brezhnev's new Westpolitik. Honecker's consumerism should partly be seen against the background of a general Brezhnev-inspired policy of increasing popular living standards throughout Eastern Europe as a response to the Prague Spring of 1968 and the workers' riots that toppled the Polish leader, Gomulka, in December 1970. But it also had a specific East German context. Honecker accepted Brezhnev's Westpolitik and the "normalization" of relations with the Federal Republic it entailed. But he immediately initiated a policy toward the FRG that became known as *Abgrenzung* (demarcation), designed to ensure that despite the new technical relations between the two Germanies, the GDR would more than ever go its own way, delineate its own socialist separateness, and have as little to do with West German capitalist contamination as possible. To strengthen whatever specifically East German socialist sentiment existed among the population (there was always precious little), and to further help ward off capitalist contamination from a prosperous Federal Republic, it was necessary to raise living standards.

The East German attempt to raise living standards and improve all-around economic performance was made unexpectedly difficult by the international economic crisis of the 1970s triggered by the two OPEC price explosions, in 1973 and 1979. This caused the Soviet Union to raise the price of its oil exported to the East European states. Its prices still remained well below the world price—at least until the 1980s, when international oil prices plummeted—but they still hit the East European economies very hard. The GDR, which got about 93 percent of its oil supply from the Soviet Union, was paying 25 dollars a barrel for Soviet oil at the beginning of the 1980s. Honecker complained in 1979 that the GDR was having to export three times more produce to pay the Soviet Union for a ton of its oil than it had before 1973.[10]

The most serious consequence of the crisis was the international hard currency debt the GDR began to accumulate. This debt, facilitated by the glut of petrodollars on the market, was caused partly by the need for protection against the rigors of the new international

---

[10]John M. Kramer, "Soviet-CEMA Energy Ties," *Problems of Communism*, July-August 1985.

economic climate and partly by the new overall East European policy of "import-led growth" that the states in the region, except Czechoslovakia, had embarked on with more enthusiasm than discretion. In 1971 the GDR's gross hard currency debt was $1.4 billion; in 1975 it was $5.9 billion; in 1981 it was $14.2 billion.[11]

In the early 1980s the difficulty of repayment was one of the GDR's most serious economic problems, and this caused it to lean more than ever on its West German "crutch." Honecker's *Abgrenzung* policy had never extended to refusing the West German financial payments and subsidies to the GDR, which related to a whole series of transactions between the two states but centered mainly on commercial relations and on the location of West Berlin in the heart of GDR territory. By the middle of the 1970s these payments were amounting to about 2.5 billion West German marks a year.[12] The East German government was able to manipulate the West German connection to advantage in its commercial relations. Exploiting the European Community provision giving it unhindered access to the West German market, the GDR conducted the bulk of its hard currency trade with the FRG. This trade was facilitated by special standing provisions, the so-called "Swing Credit" factor.[13] This longstanding West German crutch, sustained mainly by Bonn's determination—despite almost constant provocations over the years—to keep its hand out to the other part of the German nation, has sometimes been given the credit for the aspects of the East German economic "miracle" that were genuine. After the recent revelations about hitherto unsuspected weaknesses, it is beginning to be seen as the main buttress against a disaster that would otherwise have struck long before. However, its importance need not detract from the success, however temporary, of some of the GDR's own economic efforts.

Those efforts were seen at their best at the end of the 1970s and the early 1980s. The East European economies were seriously affected by the downturn of the world economy in the second half of the 1970s, the GDR's being no exception. Compared to the rest of Eastern Europe and the Soviet Union, its performance was still good, but in no single year could it meet its target for net material product. The Honecker

---

[11]*Neue Zürcher Zeitung* (Fernausgabe), March 27, 1985.

[12]Josef Joffe, "The View from Bonn: The Tacit Alliance," in Lincoln Gordon, *Eroding Empire: Western Relations with Eastern Europe*, the Brookings Institution, Washington, D.C., 1987, p. 157.

[13]Analysis of the Central Intelligence Agency, *East European Economies: Slow Growth in the 1980's*, Vol. 2: "Foreign Trade and International Finance, Selected Papers," submitted to the Joint Economic Committee, Congress of the United States, U.S. Government Printing Office, Washington, D.C., 1986.

leadership met this challenge with what, in East German terms, was a major economic reform, dubbed "the Economic Strategy for the Eighties." Essentially it was a major reorganization project with strong emphasis on economizing and rationalizing. Its principal organizational innovation was to attract world attention, and its early successes enabled the East German leadership to claim that it had reformed long before Gorbachev came on the scene. This innovation was the *Kombinaten*, some 130 large combines put together by grouping numbers of existing enterprises. Each *Kombinat* had between 20 and 40 factories and employed an average of 25,000 workers. Each had wide powers and responsibilities and incorporated research as well as spare-part manufacturers for the main product.[14] Many *Kombinaten* managers were competent, and many of their workers could still draw on the historic German reservoir of discipline and skill.[15]

The *Kombinaten*, the impact of the new economic strategy as a whole, the reorientation of Western trade even more toward the Federal Republic, the continuing West German crutch, plus the minor inundation of the GDR with West German marks as a result of increased travel between the two Germanies, all led to a better East German economic showing in the first half of the 1980s than many had expected. And, though the increase in living standards did not keep pace with the overall satisfactory economic performance (or the general smugness with which the GDR's leadership contemplated its own performance), it continued to compare well with the general East European level. Most significant was the East German performance compared to that of Poland and Hungary, the former having been through the upheaval of Solidarity and then martial law, the latter trying to reform its economy out of the morass into which it seemed to be irretrievably sinking. It was this mind-set of superiority based on performance and comparison that carried over into the Gorbachev era after 1985 and was to precipitate the undoing of communism in the GDR and ultimately the GDR itself.

THE LONG PASSIVITY

The 40-year history of Eastern Europe under communist rule was punctuated by upheavals caused by popular dissatisfaction. These began with the Berlin uprising in 1953, continued through the

---

[14]See Manfred Melzer and Arthur A. Stahnke, "The GDR Faces the Economic Dilemmas of the 1980's: Caught Between the Need for New Methods and Restricted Options," in *East European Economies: Slow Growth in the 1980's*, Vol. 3: "Country Studies on Eastern Europe and Yugoslavia," pp. 132–135 and p. 166.

[15]See "What It Takes to Be Boss," *The Economist*, February 22, 1985.

Hungarian Revolution and Polish October of 1956, the 1968 Prague Spring, the December 1970 riots in Poland, and Solidarity 1980–81, and came finally to the events of 1988–89 in Poland, Hungary, the GDR, Bulgaria, Czechoslovakia, and Romania that effectively brought about the end of communist rule. The East German population's contribution to this steady erosion and final collapse of communist rule occurred at the very beginning and the very end of the process—1953 and 1989. Why the long passivity in between? Several reasons present themselves, all of them interacting but some of obviously greater importance than others. Briefly, they were:

- The sobering memory of the 1953 riots.
- The resignation induced by the building of the Berlin Wall in 1961.
- The fact that the approximately 3 million East Germans who defected before the Wall was built were probably the people with the strongest oppositional spirit among the population.
- The presence in the GDR of 300,000 to 400,000 Soviet troops.
- The efficiency of the East German security apparatus (Staatssicherheitspolizei, or Stasis).
- The relative success of the regimes of first Walter Ulbricht and then Erich Honecker in neutralizing and even coopting crucial strata of society.
- The steady increases in the standard of living due to a combination of domestic policy and Soviet and (particularly) West German assistance.
- A conviction, once strong but steadily eroding, among considerable numbers of East Germans that whatever the faults and deficiencies of the GDR, the socialist bases on which it claimed to be built were superior to those of capitalist societies, most notably the Federal Republic.[16]

These were the factors that helped keep the East German population relatively quiet for so long. This quiescence simplified the task of the East German regime and emboldened Honecker to take risks in solidifying the GDR's future, risks that, though apparently successful in the short term, eventually helped bring on the final disaster.

The biggest early risk Honecker ran was the one from which his predecessor, Ulbricht, shrank: the normalization of relations between

---

[16]See Brown, *Eastern Europe and Communist Rule*, p. 234. See also David Childs, *The GDR: Moscow's German Ally*, George Allen and Unwin, London, 1983; and A. James McAdams, *East Germany and Détente: Building Authority After the Wall*, Cambridge University Press, Cambridge, 1988.

the two Germanies in the Basic Agreement (*Grundvertrag*) of December 1972. Honecker's own nervousness over the situation, shared to various degrees not only by the regime but also the total party membership of about 2 million, was evident in the strategy of *Abgrenzung* or demarcation. But the risk appeared to have paid off: The GDR was recognized almost immediately by well over 100 states around the world; it entered the United Nations simultaneously with the Federal Republic; and it was soon being counted—it was certainly counting itself—among the 10 most economically developed countries in the world. All this without the societal instability caused by the opening to the West that Ulbricht had dreaded and Honecker sought to head off through *Abgrenzung*. Again, the East German population was not totally passive, but it was never so unruly as to warrant the *Abgrenzung* measures themselves or some of the more hysterically brutal actions of the police authorities, either at the border with West Germany or in parts of the GDR itself.

Indeed, as it seemed that international détente was not working to the GDR's detriment but to its advantage, the regime tended to become more confident and relaxed. But it never lost its basic nervousness. In fact, Honecker's 18-year rule in the GDR can only be understood in terms of the interaction between boldness and nervousness, between the gambler and the neurotic. An almost staggering nonchalance about the dangers of West German television's saturation coverage of East German territory existed alongside a palpable insecurity about the possible consequences of the Helsinki Final Act of the CSCE process in 1975, an insecurity that recalled the overreaction of *Abgrenzung* just a few years earlier.

But into the second half of the 1970s it appeared that the confident tendency was prevailing. Helsinki certainly left its marks on the GDR and its international reputation. It moved many in the East German cultural milieu to be more active and demanding, which in turn provoked both severity and pettiness from the regime. Several of East Germany's best writers, for example, found their way, with various degrees of unwillingness, into the Federal Republic.[17] But Helsinki's bark, at least in the short term, seemed worse than its bite, and after a while it seemed no more dangerous than the *Grundvertrag* had been. Honecker could breathe more freely and concentrate more intensely on what had always been the main problem of any East German leadership: acquiring legitimacy.

---

[17]Brown, *Eastern Europe and Communist Rule*, p. 255.

THE STRUGGLE FOR LEGITIMACY

The initial hope of the founders of the GDR, not to mention their Soviet protectors, had been that ideology alone would provide the state's main legitimizing factor—the ideal of, and the quest for, the first German socialist state. Walter Ulbricht, though in other respects a pragmatic politician, seems always to have retained this ideal; and despite all the rebuffs of subsequent experience, many older East German communists, schooled in the earlier struggles for communism and against Nazism, held on to their belief that there need be no contradiction between legitimacy and socialism itself. Ideology certainly met a slower death in the GDR than in any other East European country.

But Honecker, more down-to-earth and aware of the realities around him, saw that ideology alone was clearly not enough. He was aware of what Stalin had known all along, what Yugoslavia in 1948 had reinforced, and what the satellites realized after Stalin's death: that communism becomes national communism, that it must at least pretend to a national coloration if it is to survive. Khrushchev had soon realized this and had promoted "home" communists in Eastern Europe to replace "Muscovites" in the leadership. But this was Honecker's dilemma: to promote nationalism in a state that was unique in its lack of any national foundation. As the Finnish diplomat, Max Jacobson, put it:

> The GDR is fundamentally different from all other Warsaw Pact members. It is not a nation, but a state built on an ideological concept. Poland will remain Poland, and Hungary will always be Hungary, whatever their social system. But for East Germany, maintaining its socialist system is the reason for its existence.[18]

History has been full of nations seeking statehood, but the GDR was a state searching for nationhood, a state in which almost 400,000 foreign troops were stationed, troops whom most East Germans considered to be a foreign occupier.

Honecker was helped by a few factors in his quest for legitimacy. In German history there was a strong historical tradition of regionalism. There had developed, it is true, some sense of East German "distinctiveness" on which it was hoped a sense of (socialist) nationhood could be based. More recently there had been the extraordinary, though meticulously prepared, successes of the GDR's athletes. But all this fell far short of a sense of nationhood. Honecker, therefore, realizing that it was history that molded the consciousness of nations, decided to

---

[18]*International Herald Tribune*, December 13, 1988, quoted by Barbara Donovan in "East Germany in the Gorbachev Era," internal Radio Free Europe Research analysis.

summon the past to try to stabilize the present and secure the future. Beginning modestly in the 1970s and culminating in the first half of the 1980s, he began the famous historical rehabilitation campaign, searching into German history for figures, even parts of figures—carefully selected phases in their careers—designed to fit the mold of a progressive German nationalist outlook. Thus, notables who had previously been vilified as the epitome of reaction, like Frederick the Great, Bismarck, even Wagner (or parts of him) and several other cultural luminaries were all solemnly placed into this new GDR pantheon. The high point of this historical rehabilitation campaign was the commemoration of the 500th anniversary of Martin Luther's birth in 1983, a gala event lasting months.[19]

The vast majority of East Germans greeted these displays with a mixture of cynicism and bemusement. They were somewhat more impressed, though, by a more courageous display of GDR nationalism in the summer of 1984, a display all the more genuine because it was directed against the Soviet Union. It arose from Honecker's determination not to let the GDR's improving relations with the Federal Republic be disturbed by the East-West imbroglio over INF and the subsequent Soviet freeze on relations with Bonn at the end of 1983. The GDR, as well as Hungary and Romania (with even Bulgaria showing signs of self-will), refused the Soviet demand to return to the Cold War atmosphere. The dispute, which involved obvious polemics between East German and Soviet media, came into focus on the subject of a long-planned visit to the Federal Republic by Honecker, due to take place in September. Eventually, at Soviet insistence, Honecker dropped the visit, as everyone expected he would. His show of independence, however, was the real high point of the GDR's nationalism and seemed to have elicited considerable sympathy from many East Germans.[20] Much of the sympathy, though, was felt because the Federal Republic was involved. Honecker thus owed much of his brief period of popular respect to the other Germany. Indeed, the summer of 1984 in the end only illustrated all the more the GDR's ultimate dual dependence—on the Soviet Union, which eventually did prevent the Honecker visit to West Germany, and on the Federal Republic.

The GDR's dependence on the Soviet Union was implicit not only in its very existence, but in its multifaceted role as a prime Soviet

---

[19]See Ronald D. Asmus, "The GDR and Martin Luther," *Survey* (London), Vol. 28 (Summer 1984), and "The Portrait of Bismarck in the GDR," *Radio Free Europe Research*, RAD BR/130 (German Democratic Republic), July 24, 1984.

[20]The best analysis of this episode is by Ronald D. Asmus, "East Berlin and Moscow: The Documentation of a Dispute," *Radio Free Europe Research*, RAD BR/158 (East-West Relations), August 25, 1984.

satellite. In its relationship to the Federal Republic, not only did the GDR more and more become an economic satellite, as East German needs became greater and its failure to meet them more obvious, it also became a psychological satellite. Much of what the GDR did, said, even thought, was predicated on its need to feel superior to or separate from the Federal Republic, to anticipate, preempt, equal, better, improve on, or denigrate what its western neighbor was doing. It was not so much a policy as a psychosis, of "me-too-ism," *moi aussi*, anything you can do we can do better (or, at least, we can do too). It was one of the ironies of the European postwar arrangement—and eventually its basic weakness—that the linchpin of its stability, the GDR, should be penetrated and dominated by the Soviet Union and West Germany, one the leader of the Warsaw Pact and the other the most powerful continental member of NATO, the two adversarial alliances that have maintained that stability, while that linchpin's existence also kept the postwar arrangement from becoming a settlement.

A PENETRATED SOCIETY

The GDR, in fact, furnishes a unique example of a penetrated society.[21] At first the penetration came largely from the Soviet side. It was comprehensive, but it had remarkably little effect on the essence of society. East Germany became much less russified than West Germany became americanized.[22] But the penetration from the West German side began in earnest only after the *Grundvertrag* of 1972, i.e., after the onset of détente. At first, as already mentioned, the dangers from the West, though recognized by the GDR leadership, seemed manageable—less than had been feared, certainly less than the advantages that seemed to be accruing. Eventually, of course, this turned out to be the fatal miscalculation. Western penetration helped bring about the final destruction—and sooner than anyone had anticipated. The three main instruments of West German penetration after the onset of détente were the West German mark, West German travelers, and West German television.[23]

The West German mark quickly became the currency that mattered in the GDR, and the regime made no bones about wanting to get its hands on as many of them as possible. It was impossible to tell how many deutsche marks there were in the GDR at any particular time—they were usually converted into goods and services very quickly or

[21]McAdams, *East Germany and Détente*, p. 119.

[22]On this point see Timothy Garton Ash, "Which Way Will Germany Go?" *New York Review of Books*, January 31, 1985. See also Ferdinand Hurni, "Deutscher als die Bundesrepublik?" *Neue Zürcher Zeitung* (Fernausgabe), July 27, 1987.

[23]Brown, *Eastern Europe and Communist Rule*, pp. 252–254.

simply hoarded—but they became an essential mechanism for large areas of social and economic life. But against their short-term convenience they had a gravely deleterious impact. They undermined the regime's legitimacy further by debilitating what must be one of the pillars of any state's credibility: its own coinage. The deutsche mark's popularity naturally debased the already shaky ostmark. But it also undermined social trust and cohesion. Those with access to deutsche marks, fairly or unfairly—often from relatives in the Federal Republic—could not only bribe their way to good service but also had access to the special shops, with good-quality Western merchandise, set up by the regime to soak up Western currency. Many of their countrymen, however, automatically became second-class citizens if they could not get deutsche marks. This led not only to outbursts of individual and sectional anger—workers, for example, demanding part of their wages in deutsche marks—but also to a deeper frustration just waiting for the opportunity to be unleashed.

West German visitors to the GDR had become a flood by the end of the 1970s. In 1979 alone, they numbered over eight million, bringing both their money and the West German way of life. On balance, these visitors did help subvert Honecker's ongoing attempts at legitimation. But some of them were far from being the best advertisement for the Western way of life. There were numerous complaints about their arrogance, ostentation, and insensitivity. Many did, in fact, tend to make East Germans feel a race apart, even becoming Honecker's unwitting agents in his legitimation drive.

Much more effective in the subversion of the GDR was the growing traffic the other way—the number of East Germans visiting the West. For many years, as a general rule, only East German pensioners were allowed to travel to West Germany; they would be no loss if they did not return, and the GDR would even gain somewhat financially. But the Helsinki agreements demanded more liberalization in this regard from everybody. The pressure for westward emigration increased sharply, and the regime had to respond. In 1984 emigration touched about 40,000, but the applications grew. Between 1 and 1.5 million were believed to have applied for emigration by 1989, and in that year some 200,000 were expected to leave legally. Beginning in 1986, however, restrictions on ordinary travel to the Federal Republic began to be relaxed noticeably. In that year 587,000 East Germans, many of them below retirement age, traveled to West Germany. In 1987 it was estimated that over a million below retirement age were allowed out. These concessions were seen at the time as not just a basic change of official policy but a sign of the regime's increasing self-confidence, which was obviously boosted by the remarkably low number of travelers who failed to return: 0.025 percent in 1987. The liberalized travel policy also appeared to be paying off in a (temporary) reduction in the number of applications for permanent emigration. In the first quarter of 1987 it was down almost two-thirds from the same quarter of the previous year.[24]

Liberalized travel, therefore, seemed to be a Honecker gamble that was paying off. But again, despite the immediate benefits, in the longer term it proved to be another gigantic miscalculation. It propped up a fatal self-confidence, a false sense of security that led to a distorted view of reality. This illusion that they could be sure of their population was a big factor in the East German leaders' refusal to follow Gorbachev's lead in reform. And it was that refusal that led to the final popular repudiation of the German Democratic Republic. Honecker and company might have taken note of the rising numbers of emigration applications after the brief downturn in 1987. They were a reliable barometer they chose to ignore.

The most intriguing form of penetration into the GDR was by means of West German television. All the communist states of Eastern Europe, including the Soviet Union, had been bombarded with Western radio programs for many years, and Austrian television could also be picked up by residents of adjacent parts of both Hungary and Czechoslovakia. But the East German situation was unique. From the beginning of the 1970s, 80 percent of the East German population could pick up West German television, 100 percent before the 1980s were out. Practically the whole of the East German population, therefore, could clamber into the Federal Republic through their television screens every night, stay there for a few hours if they wanted, and then clamber back.

In his previous incarnation as SED youth leader, Erich Honecker used to mobilize large numbers of East German young people in raids designed precisely to thwart the growing number of watchers of "subversive" television. Once in full power, though, he gave up that costly, practically impossible, struggle. Sociological and psychological evidence was apparently adduced to suggest that watching West German television might actually sublimate popular dissatisfaction and diminish yearnings for reunification. Certainly the seamier sides of capitalism that West German television showed in abundance would, it was hoped, make the East German citizenry thankful for its socialist law and order. Finally, any massive attempt to block off West German television, whether over the airwaves or in the homes of millions of

---

[24]Barbara Donovan, "Inter-German Relations: Political and Cultural Aspects," *Radio Free Europe Research*, RAD BR/75 (East-West Relations), May 8, 1987.

East Germans, would have involved the kind of humiliating loss of international and domestic prestige the Honecker regime simply could not afford to incur. On the other hand, allowing West German television to come in unimpeded and then actually facilitating its extension would suggest, it was hoped, an enviable sang-froid, a cool indifference to the kind of propaganda the other Germany could throw at the GDR.

It was another of Honecker's gambles, a big one, and a far cry from the *Abgrenzung* mentality of the early 1970s. And, for a time, it worked—at least in the sense that it seemed to do no harm. There was little serious political dissension that could safely be attributed to the seductions of West German television. The difficulties resulting from the Helsinki (CSCE) agreements of 1975 could hardly be blamed on West German "propaganda." (In any case, the East German official press was forced, under the terms of the agreements, to print the results of Helsinki in full.) The considerable increase in crime and lowering standards of social behavior in the GDR could, with some justice, be blamed on contacts with the capitalist West, and the authorities spared no effort to do so. But this was only grist to their propaganda mill—further proof of just how lucky the citizens of the GDR were.

The lack of obvious harm in the short run (or of evidence thereof) simply gave the regime one more chance to indulge in ruinous complacency. Constant exposure to the West German political, popular, and consumer culture undoubtedly did have an insidious effect on East German life, an effect unmeasurable but probably substantial, countering the communist ideology and undermining the regime's legitimacy. No one could predict when and how its effects would be felt. But few outside the East German leadership doubted they eventually would.

THE EVANGELICAL CHURCH: THE ALTERNATIVE AUTHORITY

The various forms of West German penetration, however undermining over time, were in themselves too diffuse to make a concentrated impact. What was needed was a domestic institution to channel and focus discontent, originating, festering, and growing inside the GDR itself. The institution that took on this role, very unwillingly at first, was the Evangelical (Lutheran) Church. It never aspired to a political role, and for many years it had a difficult job maintaining its religious role among a population that, although nominally Protestant, contained ever fewer practicing Christians. But in a state that aspired to totalitarianism, the church was steadily pushed into the position of being an alternative point of loyalty for the community as a whole, especially for the growing number of young East Germans ready to take a stand on important public issues. As a French commentator observed:

> These Germans have found their area of freedom in the Protestant churches. The comparison with Poland is tempting, but quite misleading. The Polish church was a refuge for the Poles' faith and a bastion of the resistance to communist ideology. The Protestant churches in the GDR have rediscovered their Reformation calling. They have taught the East Germans, by no means all of whom have a religious faith, to assert their individual freedom and their free judgment in the face of the state; they have given them the courage not to be afraid of either the authorities or their prohibitions.[25]

The Evangelical Church grew in strength by taking firm stands on issues of political and social significance. It strongly opposed the increasing militarization of East German life and pressed for arms reductions, nuclear disarmament, and the right of conscientious objection and alternative service. It also became a focal point for pressure on environmental issues, as the ecological health of the GDR worsened and the regime showed itself ideologically unable or unwilling to face up to it. And these were just two of a whole series of issues in which the Protestant churches became involved.[26] Already by the 1980s, the church had moved from the margin of East German society to the center. It never directly challenged the regime. In fact, it was continually offering its cooperation. Sometimes it seemed rather pliable, and often some of its leaders and local clergy were too ready to please the authorities. Honecker, as his confidence grew during the 1970s, was ready for his own kind of cooperation with the church, thinking that it could be useful to him as a safety valve. But the church steadily generated a spontaneity fatal to the totalitarian concepts on which the GDR was built. The final clash came after 1985 in the response to Gorbachev. While the regime resisted the new Soviet leader, the church welcomed him. In doing so it inevitably moved into the opposition, along with the rapidly growing number of East Germans who were demanding change. In November 1987 the increasingly nervous Honecker leadership raided an East Berlin church that was housing an

---

[25]Daniel Vernet, *Le Monde*, November 11, 1989.

[26]Brown, *Eastern Europe and Communist Rule*, pp. 255–258. See also Vladimir Tismaneanu, "Nascent Civil Society in the German Democratic Republic," *Problems of Communism*, Vol. 38, March–June 1989.

unofficial environmental library. It was a declaration of open hostilities that had been coming for many years.[27]

FAILING THE FINAL TEST

The popular image of the GDR throughout most of its history was that of a pliant Soviet satellite. But, like all of Moscow's East European allies, it was not without leverage in intrabloc relations, leverage stemming from both its strengths and its vulnerabilities.

Since its foundation the GDR has been involved in three major disputes with the Soviet Union. The first involved Ulbricht's objections to the role envisaged for the GDR in Brezhnev's Westpolitik at the turn of the 1970s. Ulbricht, who had irritated the Soviet leadership on several counts before this, was forced out of office as a result. The second dispute was the "summer of 1984" episode. After a well-publicized squabble, the Soviet leadership under Chernenko, such as it was, insisted that Honecker at least postpone his visit to the Federal Republic, and Honecker complied. Had he not, it is doubtful that the then Soviet leadership could have forced Honecker out, as Brezhnev had forced Ulbricht out. But Honecker chose not to make it an issue of survival. He may simply have considered it little more than a diplomatic defeat. And, over the longer run, he probably expected— correctly as it turned out—that détente between Bonn and Moscow would return.[28] (He made a state visit to West Germany in September 1987.)

These two disputes clearly centered on what the East German leadership believed to be the national interests of the GDR. So, in its own way, did the third, involving the rejection of *perestroika* that ended in October and November 1989 with the downfall of Honecker and the collapse of the communist system in the GDR. This was not a dispute like the other two, however, because the Soviet Union refused to be drawn directly into it. Obviously there were pressures of various kinds from Moscow designed to steer the GDR toward its own version of *perestroika*, but there appears to have been little or none of the direct intervention so obvious in 1971 and 1984. The pressure that did build up and prove directly decisive was popular, domestic pressure, generated not so much by Gorbachev as by Honecker's own obstinacy.

---

[27]See Donovan, "East Germany in the Gorbachev Era."

[28]Some observers saw the whole episode as a victory for Honecker. See A. James McAdams, "The New Logic in Soviet-GDR Relations," *Problems of Communism*, Vol. 37, September–October 1988.

Yet Honecker and the rest of the leadership were again acting in the GDR's national interests as they saw them.[29] For the GDR to move toward marketization and democratization would mean losing its raison d'être. Its very survival as a socialist state would also be threatened if Poland reformed to the point of shedding its own socialist system. This was truer now than it had been in 1981, when East Berlin got so disturbed about Solidarity. The matter was indeed of vital concern to the GDR, but the concern of the leadership was in no way shared by the majority of the East German people. Whatever they may have thought about the existence of the GDR and its social system—and some were not initially averse to either—they were not willing to be left out of the growing surge toward reform because of what their leaders told them its consequences would be. For them, better no GDR at all than the GDR of "real existing socialism." Finally and comprehensively, the first German socialist state had failed its legitimacy test.

THE LAST PHASE

Like the Czechoslovak and Bulgarian leaderships, as well as the Romanian, the East German leadership probably hoped initially that Gorbachev would be removed from power or at least would himself slow the impetus for reform in the Soviet Union. If this were to happen, then, despite Gorbachev's claims that *perestroika* was not necessarily for export, there would inevitably be a corresponding slowdown in Eastern Europe, too. But this was not happening. On the contrary, the political upheavals continued in Poland, Hungary, and the Soviet Union itself. The East German attitude, therefore, soon hardened into a clear anti-Gorbachev position. In April 1988 the SED leadership obviously took sides against Gorbachev in the Nina Andreeva affair, which was at the time the clearest dispute so far in the Soviet leadership. *Neues Deutschland* was the only East European party daily to reprint Andreeva's attack on Gorbachev and her defense of "Bolshevik principles."[30] It did eventually publish *Pravda*'s counterblast to Andreeva's attack, but only along with an article pointing to Gorbachev's alleged similarities with the Prague Spring "revisionists."[31]

---

[29]From what was subsequently revealed about the venality and self-serving characteristics of at least part of the SED leadership, it can be assumed they were also acting very much in their own interests. But the two are seldom easy to separate, particularly by the actors involved.

[30]*Neues Deutschland*, April 2, 1988.

[31]See Donovan, "East Germany in the Gorbachev Era."

By the end of 1989 the East German leaders were openly critical of the course of developments in the Soviet Union and Eastern Europe. In December, Honecker referred to the Soviet reforms as a "march into anarchy," and the prolific Otto Reinhold was lashing out in print at reformers in general and Hungarian reformers in particular.[32] East German spokesmen increasingly used what they obviously considered their most effective weapon against reform: comparisons between the perilous state of the Soviet, Polish, and Hungarian economies and the alleged stability of their own. Unemployment, inflation, crumbling social services, and creeping anarchy were held up to be the only tangible results reform could show.

But the more their official spokesmen railed, the less the East German population was convinced. Western visitors to the GDR during this period (end of 1988 and early 1989) were reporting a growing restlessness, even militancy, among many East Germans. The population was now convinced that the reform in Eastern Europe was taking root and that Gorbachev represented something genuinely new. This gave them the spirit to question, to demand, even to resist the actions of a leadership that no longer looked as impregnable as it had just a few months ago. Regime and population were already on a collision course.

One of the striking and ironic aspects of the SED's nervousness and isolation was its reintroduction in this phase of the old policy (or psychosis) of *Abgrenzung*. But this time the portcullis was lowered to keep out baleful influences not from the Federal Republic, but from the Soviet Union. It was from this direction that the more immediately dangerous contamination was now deemed to be coming.[33] The GDR's first attempt to insulate itself from the new threat had come in the fall of 1988 with its almost hysterical rejection of the Soviet anti-Stalin film, *Repentance*, made by the Georgian director Tengiz Abuladze and eventually shown in the Soviet Union through the good offices of Abuladze's compatriot, Eduard Shevardnadze. Its showing had been forbidden in the GDR, but it was carried on West German television. Enough East Germans obviously saw and were impressed by it for the SED leaders to lash out fiercely at what must have seemed to some of them a clear case of Soviet–West German ideological collusion. Critical reappraisals of communist history, it was argued, could be misused by "anticommunist forces" both at home and abroad; Abuladze's film, made by the Soviets, delivered by the West Germans, put into "the enemies' hands new material for demagogic tricks."[34]

---

[32]*Neues Deutschland*, December 2 and 3–4, 1988.

[33]See Donovan, "East Germany in the Gorbachev Era."

[34]*Junge Welt*, October 29, 1988.

The Abuladze film episode led to a continuing dispute between East German and Soviet ideologues and historians on the critical reassessment of history that was going on in the Soviet Union. But this was noticed by a relative few. What brought the SED-Soviet dispute to the forefront of national and even world attention was the announcement in November 1988 that the Soviet monthly press digest *Sputnik* had been effectively banned in the GDR, apparently for carrying "distorted" versions of history. What particularly angered the regime was *Sputnik*'s publication of articles discrediting German communists of past eras and containing interpretations that "violated" the constitution of the GDR. This may have been the nub of the whole issue, showing again the acute sensitivity of the East German leaders on the legitimacy question. Flaws in German communist history could not be admitted, particularly when suggested in the new spirit of spontaneity that was sweeping parts of the communist world.[35]

This, then, was the new *Abgrenzung*, reflecting the new realities of Soviet–East German relations and the quickening erosion of alliance unity. But the East German regime did not settle for total isolation. It rather tried to form a latter-day "little entente," this time comprising the GDR, Czechoslovakia, and Romania, like-minded states in their aversion to the reformist spirit. Especially strong efforts were made to strengthen links with neighboring Czechoslovakia. These were, after all, the two frontline states in Europe, the first line of defense against the capitalist West. The Czechoslovaks were apparently not nearly as keen as the East Germans on this kind of unity, preferring to keep their options more open. Still, both leaderships realized that if one of them began to give way to the reform surge, the other could not hold out for long. In the end, the event they both feared the most actually happened. But the first to buckle was not the Czechoslovak but the East German leadership, whose breathtaking collapse in October 1989 was followed within days by a similar collapse of the communist system in Czechoslovakia in November.

The GDR's most bizarre marriage of convenience, however, was with Romania, regarded since the middle of the 1980s (even more than Albania) as Europe's pariah state. In a perverse sense, the two states were simply continuing their alliance of the summer of 1984. Again, perceived national interest, with the Soviet Union as the adversary, was the nexus. But by now the context had changed completely. What had gained respect in 1984 aroused only disdain four years later. Honecker did himself no good, least of all among the East German population, by linking himself with Ceausescu. Now he seemed prompted by nothing but dogma and insecurity. *Neues Deutschland* even went so far as to praise

---

[35]*Neues Deutschland*, November 24 and 25, 1988.

Ceausescu's much-abhorred *systematization* program for transforming the Romanian countryside.[36]

What was unnerving Honecker, though, was not the mounting international opprobrium but the growing restiveness within the GDR. The party rank and file was asking more questions than it used to, and many were obviously not happy with the answers they got. The *agit-prop* apparatus had its hands full coping with this situation. The banning of *Sputnik* caused special perplexity and indignation; hundreds of local party organizations lodged official protests. A prominent East German writer (also a party member) told a West German magazine that the "unrest in the party" showed that "communists were becoming more mature." He continued:

> People are becoming more aware of what they actually are; of what role they should be playing in a socialist state. [They are aware] that they are not here to follow orders and to stand around with their hands in their pockets; but that they are free people and that important goals cannot be reached without broad discussion or without taking the risk of making mistakes.[37]

What statements like this also reflected was a growing mood of rebellion among some party intellectuals—not just writers and other creative artists, but social scientists and economists. The first example of a well-established member of the ruling elite breaking ranks and giving full support to *perestroika* was supplied by Markus Wolf, the GDR's longstanding "chief spy" who for many years had been considered second in the security apparatus behind the veteran minister for state security, Erich Mielke. In his autobiographical novel, *The Troika*, published in 1989 in both East and West Germany, Wolf enthusiastically backed both *perestroika* and *glasnost*. He was one of many East German communists trained in Moscow with a real loyalty to the Soviet Union and what it happened to be doing at any particular time. Many of these must have been puzzled by Honecker's line. After the fall of Honecker and the collapse of the system, an old "Muscovite" veteran explained what went wrong by saying that the SED did not do what the Soviet Union was doing.[38]

---

[36]*Neues Deutschland*, February 11–12, 1989.

[37]Stephan Hermlin, *Der Spiegel*, February 6, 1989, quoted by Donovan, "East Germany in the Gorbachev Era."

[38]This was Wolfgang Herger, elected Politburo member and Central Committee secretary after the fall of Honecker. The reason for the collapse, according to Herger, was that the SED leadership forgot one of its old, cherished slogans: "To learn from the Soviet Union is to learn how to win." Timothy Garton Ash: "The German Revolution," *The New York Review of Books*, December 21, 1989.

Wolf was the only top political establishment figure to speak up like this. No Politburo members, for example, were suspected of fully sharing his views. Günter Schabowski, however, the party leader in East Berlin, seemed inclined toward reform and played a leading role in the ousting of Honecker. The "white hope" in the top party ranks, however, had for a long time been Hans Modrow, SED first secretary in Dresden, who had been kept out of the Politburo because of his less than conformist views and had also become the target of considerable vindictiveness on the part of the Honecker coterie.[39]

It was symptomatic of the sclerosis of the SED leadership that its immediate uncertainty was not so much over Honecker's policies as over the question of his successor. In the summer of 1989, Honecker's robust health at last showed signs of failing. In July he was hospitalized and rumored to be dying of cancer. The succession question, therefore, became urgent. Schabowski was being mentioned, but so was the long-time "crown prince," Egon Krenz. It was, in fact, Krenz who would take over from Honecker and try to salvage something from the collapse. Krenz, age 49, had not only followed in Honecker's career footsteps—first as communist youth organization chief, then Central Committee secretary for security—but was an uncompromising supporter and articulate proponent of the hard line. The most recent example of this was his endorsement of the Chinese regime's bloody repressions in Tiananmen Square. Among many East Germans he was disliked even more than Honecker.

In view of the massive popular demonstrations in October 1989 protesting and then rejecting communist rule in the GDR, it seems extraordinary that only a few weeks before there had been little hint of such massive repudiation. From the beginning of the 1980s there had been a marked rise in open dissatisfaction over economic conditions, especially consumer goods shortages, rising prices, and the housing shortage. And the public was increasingly irritated when the regime belabored the point that things were still better in East Germany than in the rest of the Soviet bloc. Their yardstick was not Poland or Hungary but West Germany, which all of them knew through television and many were getting to know at first hand through the regime's more liberal travel policy.

The growing dissatisfaction over economic conditions was also one reflection of the rising expectations many East German citizens had been entertaining for several years. Objectively, conditions in the GDR had been improving, and not just economically. Despite all the irritations, politically, as well as in the sphere of human rights and personal

---

[39]A very good, brief portrait of Modrow was published in the *Süddeutsche Zeitung* (Munich), November 9, 1989.

freedoms, life had been getting easier. As mentioned earlier, this was due
to the increasing confidence of the Honecker regime from about 1978 on,
and to the regime's need to live up to (or at least appear to be doing so) the
prescriptions of Helsinki. Living up to Helsinki became the passport to
greater international respectability, something for which Honecker personally seemed to have developed a distinct craving.

Expectations thus had already been growing when Gorbachev came on
the scene. His appearance gave them a powerful boost, and for the
Honecker regime this was a most alarming development. Without Gorbachev and against a background of relative international calm,
Honecker would probably have continued his policy of gradual relaxation.
But now the Gorbachev phenomenon was not simply threatening the pace
of this relaxation; it was threatening to turn it in a wrong direction, sub-
verting the system and the principle of rule on which the GDR was based.
This mounting conflict, the "antagonistic contradiction" of which Gorbachev was unquestionably the catalyst, was what led so quickly to the
downfall of the system. Honecker had raised expectations; Gorbachev
hijacked them. Now they menaced Honecker, and the only recourse he
knew was suppression. This explained the new *Abgrenzung* against
Soviet "subversion." More seriously, it explained the punitive actions
already mentioned against the Evangelical Church, the increased nervousness and erratic behavior of the police, the regime's inconsistency. In
short, the SED was losing control, and the people knew it. They became
bolder, more critical, less resigned to accepting a situation dictated solely
by their ruling oligarchy. The GDR was slipping into a prerevolutionary
situation.

The event that set the erosion on an accelerating, irreversible slide was
the local elections on May 7, 1989. The official results—the usual massive victory for the SED—were achieved only by the most fraudulent
manipulation. Everybody knew there had been a considerable anti-SED
vote that the official results did not show; also, the regime's falsification
campaign had been unusually blatant. Its director was Egon Krenz.

Important though that episode was in arousing and concentrating
popular indignation, the regime was still strong enough to have survived
it through suppression. But then came the mass defections to the Federal
Republic through Hungary in the late summer, followed by more through
Czechoslovakia. The defections through Hungary were a fatal blow to the
Honecker regime—both the defections themselves and the action of the
Hungarian government in permitting them, with the acquiescence of
Moscow. Honecker could hardly have expected much from Gorbachev,
but he might have hoped the Soviet leader would forbid an action that so
clearly repudiated him and his leadership. He was now too weak and
unnerved to withstand any more.

The beginning of the end came with the mass demonstrations in Leipzig in October, which then spread to larger and smaller towns throughout the country. These had nothing to do with emigration or defections. They were conducted by East Germans intending to stay but demanding far-reaching changes that clearly meant a repudiation of the communist system. At the "40 years" celebrations in early October commemorating the founding of the GDR, there were the usual self-congratulations from the regime speakers, including Honecker himself, back on view after his severe illness. The principal guest, Gorbachev, was noncommittal on the crisis in public, but in private he is believed to have urged concessions, ruling out any interference from the Soviet troops stationed in the GDR. The celebrations only spurred the public anger that hastened the end.

There was still the possibility of a Tiananmen Square–style "solution," and Honecker and others appear to have considered it. This was apparently when Egon Krenz finally realized that the GDR's turning point in history had arrived. On October 9 in Leipzig he is reported to have been finally persuaded by local dignitaries to prevent the use of armed force against demonstrators, thereby avoiding a bloodbath.[40]

He succeeded Honecker very soon afterward and set about trying to shed the ballast of 40 years of communist rule in the GDR. In doing so he made the historic concession of November 9, 1989, the opening of the frontiers. The turning point in East German history had now become the turning point in European history. For Krenz, shedding the ballast, with the huge concessions that involved, was the necessary prelude to salvaging what could be saved. He set about his job with extraordinary energy and apparent self-confidence, seeking continually to stay ahead of the situation, meeting change by provoking more change. But his situation recalled the jibe made much earlier in Hungary about the Hungarian communist party behaving, in its policy of concessions, like the man being chased by a wolf and shedding his clothes to stay ahead.[41] More than any Hungarian, Krenz was very much in that situation—running faster, shedding more. And the wolf soon got him. On December 3, 1989, Krenz was unseated when the whole SED Politburo and Central Committee resigned. He had failed in his efforts to keep up with events and save the GDR. December 3 shattered all illusions about the GDR's having any future. The East Germans, it was now read, would not be satisfied with reform. They wanted reunification.

---

[40]Subsequent SED publicity made Krenz the main hero of this incident. It appears, however, that he was persuaded to intervene by a group of citizens of which Kurt Masur, director of the Leipzig Gewandhaus Orchestra, was the most prominent and active member. See *Frankfurter Allgemeine Zeitung*, November 21, 1989; also Timothy Garton Ash, "The German Revolution."

[41]See Sec. II.

IV. CZECHOSLOVAKIA

THE OBSTACLES TO REFORM

In January 1983 Antonin Dolejsi, by no means one of the less intelligent of Czechoslovak conservatives, wrote an article in the party monthly *Nova Mysl* entitled "The Revolutionary Epoch Can Last Centuries." The key to the article was in his flat statement that "the present and the future already belong to communism."[1] It was an orthodox, thoroughly "dogmatic" article, strongly against private farming, small-scale industry, whether private or public, and any concession to the growing East European fad for small privatization in any field. The communist party was the exclusive leader of society and must constantly be on its guard against infiltrations and subversion. The Soviet experience was of paramount importance, as was the concept of the dictatorship of the proletariat, "whose fundamental features have a general international validity." Dolejsi acknowledged the current difficulties that the movement and his own country were passing through, and the opportunities all this was giving to the "counterrevolutionaries." But socialism would survive this challenge, because socialism was right, and it would all work out in the end.

Dolejsi's article was intended as a counterblast to the doubts about the future that the deteriorating economic situation in Czechoslovakia was raising and to the calls for reform, usually along Hungarian lines, that were timidly being raised. Premier Lubomir Strougal, for example, was speaking about socialist entrepreneurship, and Jaromir Sedlak, a senior member of his staff, was writing the following:

> No really fundamental turning point in the economy can be reached in Czechoslovakia unless qualitative transformations are brought about in the overall social climate, at all levels and in all social groups. . . . The social climate that prevails at the moment is characterized by increased feelings of hopelessness. Many people are losing hope in the future.[2]

The conservative constituency represented by Dolejsi was strong in 1983. It had considerably weakened toward the end of 1989, but it was still a political force to be reckoned with. In this respect, there was a strong similarity between Czechoslovakia and the GDR, at least until the Honecker regime's dramatic collapse in October 1989. Dolejsi and

---

[1]*Nova Mysl*, No. 1, 1983.
[2]*Hospodarske Noviny*, No. 47, November 26, 1982.

his counterparts in East Berlin spoke for a strong left-socialist and communist political tradition. The East German tradition is often cited, but the Czechoslovak (here, "Czech" is more correct) is often ignored amid the acclamation of the democratic character of the interwar republic.

The point was that the large communist movement, breaking off from the former socialist mainstream after the establishment of the Comintern, prospered in the democratic tolerance of the first Czechoslovak republic. Even during the 1920s, when it obediently followed the Comintern's line against the newly founded Czechoslovak republic as an instrument of Western imperialism, the communist party of Czechoslovakia got solid electoral backing.[3] After the popular disillusionment with the West resulting from the Munich Agreement of 1938, and then bolstered by the Soviet victories in World War II, the communists' fortunes rose further; by 1946 they were clearly the strongest political party in the Czech Lands (though not nearly so strong in Slovakia). In the Czech Lands immediately after World War II, the leftist trend politically and the pan-slavic trend culturally were both very strong. The democratic, pro-Western trends, once personified and led so ably by Masaryk, were on the defensive, poorly led and disorganized. The liberal-democratic structure, reinstated in 1945, fell easy victim to the brilliantly led communist coup in February 1948.

The subsequent record of communist Czechoslovakia was a failure by any yardstick, and the communist and pan-slavic tradition was shattered. But in the 1980s, as represented by people like Dolejsi, it still had its hard core of adherents, whose defense of it seemed only to get more shrill as its credibility got weaker. This hard core now existed only in Czechoslovakia, the GDR, and probably in Bulgaria—the three East European countries that had a communist tradition. In Poland and Romania there had indeed been communists, but no communist tradition. In Hungary there had been a communist republic after World War I, but that was the beginning and the end of the tradition.

In Czechoslovakia since 1968 this hard core was supported by a large careerist bureaucracy put in place by the "normalization" process instituted after the Prague Spring. It amounted to a new governing class bent on preserving the status quo, less for ideological reasons than for holding on to power, place, and privilege. And to preserve the status quo the Czechoslovak leaders were not averse to reforms that at any other time—at least before the late 1980s—might have seemed

---

[3]H. Gordon Skilling, "Czechoslovakia Between East and West," in William E. Griffith (ed.), *Central and Eastern Europe: The Opening Curtain*, Westview Press, Boulder, Colorado, 1989, p. 243.

considerable, even extensive. But reform now had come to mean *systemic* reform, and in those terms what the Czechoslovak leaders would countenance was marginal, even irrelevant. In any case, the essential precondition of systemic reform in Czechoslovakia was the repudiation not only of the crackdown of August 1968 and the subsequent normalization, but also of those who had ruled for the last 20 years. For Czechoslovakia's governing class, therefore, the question was one of survival. Undoubtedly their counterparts in the rest of Eastern Europe were facing the same question. But nowhere else was the matter quite as poignant or momentous.

It was these mixed but converging motives that made Czechoslovakia's leaders so resistant to change. This resistance would not have been so effective for so long had there been persistent, concerted pressure from below. There certainly was some pressure from below, beginning in the late 1970s and mounting during the 1980s. But this pressure, involving intellectuals, large numbers of young people, and increasingly confident religious believers, lacked any component of working class support. The same, of course, had been true for Hungary. But in Hungary there was an effective combination of regime reformers and opposition intellectuals, and this brought the country toward parliamentary democracy and the constitutional state without strong worker support. In Czechoslovakia the workers had always been a stronger political force than in Hungary, and their attitude toward reform would be more important.

In this respect the developments in Hungary were reminiscent of the Prague Spring. In 1968 in Czechoslovakia it had been the party reformers and the opposition intellectuals who transformed the political scene while the workers remained unconvinced in the wings. For a long time in Czechoslovakia, there was no indication of worker alienation from the system sufficient to tip the scales away from the ruling leadership. What this signified in historical terms was continuing proletarian acceptance—as distinct from support—of the communist regime. Throughout its more than 40-year history, the Czechoslovak communist regime made a point of appeasing the working class, especially in the heavy industrial sectors. And in the last 20 years at least, this was one of the main reasons for the decline of the economy. Nevertheless, workers were not impressed by the economic performance of Eastern Europe's two reform pioneers, Hungary and Poland—a performance that only served to fortify traditional Czech smugness about the backwardness of their neighbors.

At the end of 1989, therefore, Czechoslovakia seemed some way from the classic prerevolutionary situation. To be sure, those who espoused reform were growing in numbers and were losing their previous fears and inhibitions. They were also affected by the spirit of reform that was sweeping parts of Eastern Europe as well as the Soviet Union. They were to be decisively affected by the remarkable upheavals in the GDR in October–November 1989. But their best hope of support in the shorter run lay not with the workers but in increasing numbers of defections to their cause from the ranks of the ruling elite. Because of 1968 and after, the ruling elite seemed to be locked into the conservatism of self-preservation. Still, after the East German debacle, the numbers of those ready to make the leap grew dramatically. And once they did, others would follow. Then, when self-preservation began to look like self-destruction, the trickle would become a flow, and then a flood.

MOVEMENT WITHOUT PURPOSE

For many years there were serious obstacles to systemic reform in Czechoslovakia. But the lack of systemic reform did not mean total immobility. During the 1980s, especially since the emergence of Gorbachev as a radical reformer, there was in fact considerable movement. Some of it was the result of economic necessity, some of popular pressure; it made Czechoslovakia a different place than it was at the beginning of the 1980s. The parameters became wider than they were, though they were still set well short of any systemic reform. The regime was in a difficult position. It realized it must go on widening the parameters for change, but knew they could not be so wide as to threaten the system they were designed to protect.

During the first half of the 1980s the leadership's favorite expression with regard to the economy was *intensification*, which essentially meant trying to squeeze more performance out of the existing system. This focus was not only because the Czechoslovak economy urgently needed intensification, but also because some political leaders (although very few real economists) believed that it could be done without basic reform. Intensification had been discussed ever since the middle 1960s in Czechoslovakia and had been very much on the minds of the Prague Spring reformers. They, however, knew that real intensification meant real reform. But after the August 1968 invasion, even the word "reform" disappeared from all but the most specialized journals in Czechoslovakia as the trauma of the Prague Spring had a local and immediate relevance.

Both the economists and the more perceptive political leaders, like premier Lubomir Strougal, realized how self-defeating it was for the economy to keep prolonging its extensive phase. Modernization had been slow and patchy. The manufacturing base was too broad, producing too many items. The employment rate was very high—many women were in the work force—but there was still a labor shortage. Absenteeism and loafing on the job were standard operational procedure. After all, "in an economy short on labor, laxity at work is a kind of fringe benefit the management is forced to concede."[4] Extensive economic development also led to priority being given to primary industry (e.g., mining, forestry) at the expense of more sophisticated forms of manufacturing. There was a huge waste of energy as well as manpower.

In retrospect, in view of all the blunders and procrastination, what was perhaps the most remarkable feature of the Czechoslovak economy was its capacity for survival, its ability to stumble along without the comprehensive breakdown so many predicted. (This ability, of course, long played into the hands of political conservatives.) It was this resilience that enabled Husak to achieve one of the essentials of his normalization policy: the promotion of the standard of living through "consumerism." Between 1971 and 1975, although real wages only rose by about 5 percent, personal consumption in Czechoslovakia rose by 27 percent. In 1971 one in 17 people had an automobile; in 1975 one in ten; in 1979 one in eight.[5] Figures like these do much to explain why the Husak strategy of normalization worked for as long as it did—and without the massive Western credits to which all the other East European countries resorted.[6]

By the middle of the 1970s the outlook was much less promising. The OPEC price explosion early in the decade and the Soviet response in sharply raising oil prices for Eastern Europe, then the second OPEC price explosion at the end of the decade, brought on a crisis in which Czechoslovakia and the GDR, as the region's two most industrialized countries, tended to suffer the most. By 1980 Czechoslovakia was paying nearly five times as much for a ton of Soviet oil as it had in 1971—and was importing about twice as much. Nor did the situation improve. In 1980 Czechoslovakia's Soviet oil bill was 8,600 million crowns (fifteen crowns to the dollar at the official rate of exchange). In 1986 it was 23,500 million crowns.[7]

[4]Vlad Sobell, "The Running Battle with Labor Discipline," *Radio Free Europe Research*, Czechoslovak SR/8, Item 3, May 13, 1985.

[5]Vladimir V. Kusin: "Husak's Czechoslovakia and Economic Stagnation," *Problems of Communism*, May–June 1982. See also the same author's *From Dubcek to Charter 77*, St. Martin's Press, New York, 1978.

[6]In 1988 the Czechoslovak net debt was estimated at $4.2 billion, the lowest in Eastern Europe except for Romania. The Czechoslovak per capita debt was $270, the Polish $900, the Hungarian $1470. *Liberation* (Paris), September 19, 1989.

[7]*Statisticke Prehledy* (Prague), No. 5, May 1987, pp. 143, 151.

This was a crippling disability that helped produce, and partly coincided with, the economic depression many had predicted. Economic output fell in 1981 and 1982. It all recalled the beginning of the 1960s, when difficult economic conditions had helped set off the chain of events leading to the Prague Spring. Indeed, in some key respects it was worse now than it was then. At the beginning of the 1960s both industry and important elements of the infrastructure were 20 years younger, and the price of Soviet raw materials was cheap and expected to stay cheap. The deterioration since then, in infrastructure and in external and internal economic conditions, had been both cumulative and accelerative. But the biggest single problem was domestic: the huge numbers of unfinished investment projects. At the end of 1981, about 30,000 industrial building sites stood unfinished—tied-up capital representing just over 20 percent of all capital funds in the Czechoslovak economy for that year.[8]

It was an alarming state of affairs, emboldening an increasing number of economists to claim that basic reform could no longer be delayed. Even the regime leadership was prompted to act, but its action was very disappointing, even to relative conservatives. It was the so-called "Set of Measures," which, though allowing for some degree of decisionmaking decentralization in both industry and agriculture, merely recalled the remedial steps taken 23 years before in 1958, actions that even then had been considered inadequate to the need.[9]

But some regime leaders and apologists were to claim that the "Set of Measures" was by no means the only part of their early 1980s strategy. It was in this context that "intensification" came into its own. An economic official defended the allegedly "do-nothing" policy of those years as follows:

> If the word stagnation is to be used, then it must be said that we gave preference to stagnation over growth, or to be more precise, to internal and external balance over excessive growth.[10]

Hungary, said the same official, echoing a widespread Czechoslovak opinion, "was not for us."[11] The decision to stagnate, or to let stagnation take its course, should really be seen as a decision to intensify.

Leaving aside the complacency of remarks like these, it remains a moot question just how much control the regime had over the course of economic development in the first half of the 1980s. The poor

---

[8]Brown, *Eastern Europe and Communist Rule*, pp. 302–303.

[9]Kusin, "Husak's Czechoslovakia and Economic Stagnation."

[10]Vaclav Vertelar, quoted by William Echikson and Elisabeth Pond, "Experiments in Eastern Europe," *Christian Science Monitor*, January 8, 1986.

[11]Ibid.

performance of the economy during that period was due more to the accumulation of past mistakes than to any deliberately planned reorientation. All the same, some of the desired effects of intensification did become apparent by mid-decade. The cutbacks made earlier in the imports of energy and raw materials (some of them made necessary by the 10 percent cut in Soviet oil exports), the reduction of investments and of the already small imports of Western technology—all these undoubtedly contributed to the very slow rate of growth. When the economy began to pick up again, from 1983 to 1985, it showed signs of intensive growth, i.e., growth sustained by the mobilization of reserves and the better processing of available inputs.

The year 1985 was considered crucial in the whole intensification process. Domestic net material output was scheduled to grow faster than the volume of output, i.e., value added was more important than growth in quantitative terms. Increases in national income were to be achieved mainly through increased productivity and continuing reductions in the use of energy. More automation, electronic innovations, and whatever modern technology was available were to be introduced into the economy as quickly as possible.

Whatever the motives or the exaggerated claims made for it, "intensification" did have some effect. But it only scratched the surface of Czechoslovakia's economic problems and made the debate about further reform all the more acute and urgent. Broadly speaking, by the economic crossroads of 1985 there were three options: basic reform, the "halfway-house" approach, and doing nothing. Although there was much militant conservatism, and probably even more inertia, favoring the do-nothing option, the serious, practical debate tended to center on the first two. Thus began the third important debate on the economic structure since the invasion of Czechoslovakia in 1968. The first had been at the beginning of the 1970s and had resulted in a complete victory for the reactionaries and the return to the command structure. It was this structure, with a few subsequent modifications, that the do-nothing school was defending. The second debate had been in the early 1980s and had brought forth the "Set of Measures." Now, as the Czechoslovak economy deteriorated and reform was gathering pace in the Soviet Union and parts of Eastern Europe, the advocates of basic reform were more numerous, more courageous, and with a palpably stronger case than ever. What they appeared to have in mind were some of the proposals being implemented in Hungary and those contained in the Polish Reformed Economic System (RES) prepared during the Solidarity period and then shelved after martial law. (Compared with the Hungarian, Polish, and even Soviet reforms of the late 1980s, such proposals barely qualify, of course, as basic or systemic reform, being much closer to the "halfway-house" variety.)

The principal political champion of this first option was Premier Strougal, although, typically, he never specifically committed himself.[12] The boldest reform champion in the governmental ranks, however, was Leopold Ler, the finance minister. Ler had been closely associated with the 1981 "Set of Measures" but had since realized their inadequacy and apparently wanted to go much further. He was forced to retire in October 1985, not for political reasons but for genuine reasons of health. Lower down the hierarchy was a whole bevy of professional economists who became more audacious as the decade wore on and the economy wore out. The best known of them was probably Valtr Komarek, of the Institute for Economic Forecasting in Prague. Komarek had almost certainly been an advocate of basic reform long before he considered the political climate ripe enough to declare himself one.[13]

The pressure for at least some basic reform was obviously strong enough in 1985 for communist party leader Husak to step in with one of his ex cathedra pronouncements. It showed both his awareness of the political implications involved and the continuing impact of the trauma of the Prague Spring.

> We will not take the road of any of the market-oriented concepts that would weaken [the system of] socialist collective property and the party's leading role in the economy. We have had bad experience of that kind of thing.[14]

Husak in 1985 was not nearly as powerful as he had been even five years earlier, but he certainly had strong enough apparatchik backing when he disparaged anything that smacked of the Prague Spring. In such remarks Husak was not, however, ruling out reform. He was simply warning any actual or potential "wild men" not to go too far. In practical terms he was conniving at the "halfway-house" option. In typical fashion, he was not saying what should be done, but what should not.

A Yugoslav journalist, Lazar Martinovic, summed up the situation well, revealing also a keen insight into Prague's political mores. The problem, he said, in an article entitled "Subtle Indications of Change," was how to introduce a certain amount of decentralization "without basically disturbing central planning as the key regulator of the

---

[12]For a brief biographical sketch of Strougal, see Brown, *Eastern Europe and Communist Rule*, pp. 483–484.

[13]For a review of Komarek's earlier articles, see Vlad Sobell "Fundamental Change in the Economic Mechanism Advocated," *Radio Free Europe Research*, Czechoslovak SR/10, Item 6, June 27, 1985.

[14]*Rude Pravo* (Prague), June 19, 1985.

country's economic life." However, "even the most responsible personalities do not have a clear-cut idea of what should be done." The notion of "market socialism" was being generally criticized, continued Martinovic, but "such criticism is generally accepted more as a theoretical point of departure than a categorical negative precept for practical economic policy." Martinovic added that when the economic journal *Hospodarske Noviny* was recommending neither "exaggerated centralization" nor "absolute decentralization," this was a reliable indication that some changes were being prepared. The sense of expectancy had aroused considerable public interest in the subject, according to Martinovic: "This is why the public has recently been agitated by such a development and everybody wants to speak his mind."[15]

What had happened over the previous two years was that the official mood of opposition to basic reform had changed to one of ambivalence, even resignation. And with the change of mood, many Czechoslovaks engaged in the economic process began evading or ignoring the official restrictions. Again, Martinovic captures perfectly the Czech way of doing things:

> You can see in Czechoslovak towns stalls from which the owners of gardens sell their fruit and vegetables. Gradually, private services are also being allowed, especially for people working after normal hours in the socialist sector of the economy. True, there is not much talk about the full-fledged revival of the private sector, but there are signs that this will be done gradually and cautiously.[16]

Subsequently, in 1986 minor reforms were introduced in agriculture, as a result of which only the procurement of grain and of slaughter animals was left obligatory. At the same time there was a general reduction in state subsidies for agriculture. To show how necessary such a reduction was, milk prices provide a good example. In 1985 one liter of milk on some farms cost six crowns to produce, but it was sold at a retail price of between 1.90 and 3 crowns. The idea behind the new reforms was that some of the money saved by the reduction in subsidies should be used to increase procurement prices for high-quality products.

There had also been some movement in trade policy toward the West. By the middle of 1986 eight joint ventures were being conducted with Western partners, and the permitted foreign share of the equity had been raised from 40 percent to 49 percent. (Again, to keep such progress in perspective, it might be mentioned that in a matter of two years the Hungarian government was permitting 100 percent foreign

---

[15]*Borba* (Belgrade), November 23–24, 1985.

[16]Ibid.

ownership of equity.) By 1988 joint *production* ventures with Western companies now numbered 100. Such ventures had the advantage of giving the Czechoslovak companies involved access to Western technology without their having to pay for it. Not surprisingly, the Federal Republic of Germany was the biggest Western operator in this field, participating in 46 percent of Czechoslovakia's Western joint production ventures.[17]

As the 17th Czechoslovak party congress in March 1986 approached, there was an air of expectancy about economic reform. Some expected far-reaching reforms to be announced at the congress, others warned of the enormous dislocation such reform would entail. In late 1985 *Nova Mysl*, the party's main theoretical monthly, wrote that "the reconstruction of the economic mechanism represents a task comparable in its complexity with the reconstruction of the economy in the period of industrialization and the collectivization of agriculture."[18] Many were prepared to settle for intensification and give it a chance to work. For them, basic reform was a risky leap in the dark.

THE GORBACHEV FACTOR

The sides being taken in the economic debate generally reflected the main political alignments in public life, in which the Gorbachev factor was now beginning to play an important and unsettling role. Gorbachev had been elected Soviet party leader in March 1985 and quickly became a disturbing element for the long-established Czechoslovak leaders. Although he did not emerge as a radical systemic reformer until about two years later, right from the beginning he stood for change and modernization and was considered to have little sympathy or patience with several of the East European leaderships, of which the Czechoslovak was unquestionably one.

For many Czechoslovaks the question of reform—economic reform in the first instance—became closely linked with the question of how to respond to Gorbachev. Responding to Gorbachev would break up the established pattern of Czechoslovak politics, sharpen existing divisions, and let some much-needed fresh air into the stifling atmosphere. But it would be wrong to conclude that Gorbachev began the reform process in Czechoslovakia. What he did was to give a political edge to the economic process already underway. He dramatized it and gave it a

---

[17]See Economic Commission for Europe, "East-West Joint Ventures," United Nations (New York), 1988. See also Leslie Colitt, "West Woos Orders from Prague," *Financial Times*, September 17, 1985.

[18]*Nova Mysl*, No. 11, 1985, pp. 85–94.

note of urgency, also raising the question of how long one or more of the current Czechoslovak leaders would survive politically.

Not unexpectedly, the Czechoslovak leaders divided on Gorbachev the way they had over economic reform. Strougal and his followers lower down the ladder (he was virtually isolated in the Politburo itself) saw Gorbachev as both an ally and an opportunity. At the other end of the ruling spectrum, Vasil Bilak, with several supporters in the highest leadership, instinctively rejected Gorbachev's *perestroika*; Bilak himself at first sounded almost East German in his tone of rejection.[19] In between there was a group of several senior leaders who, whatever they may have thought initially about the necessity for change, had now come to regard it as unavoidable. For them the question now was what kind of change and how much. At the center of this group was Husak, standing before yet another new phase in his variegated and turbulent career.

At the 17th party congress in March 1986, Strougal's speech reflected the differences inside the leadership over reform. He complained that the question of "perfecting the economic mechanism" had been on the agenda for the last five years, i.e., since the introduction of the "Set of Measures," but that precious little had been done about it. "Intensification" had not been carried far enough, nor had the federal agencies of government "seen to the necessary systemic requisites." Czechoslovakia and its economy were not keeping up with the needs of the time.[20]

Although, characteristically, the 17th congress reelected the same old leadership virtually intact, the divisions between the supporters of reform and those expressing various degrees of "moderation" and caution were evident throughout. (The degree of *moderation* expressed was a generally accurate measure of the *opposition* the speaker felt toward reform.) Husak, steadily becoming persuaded of reform's inevitability, argued that the country "must not be afraid of reforms."[21] He was voicing the conclusion of the reluctant majority that there was little point in resisting the irresistible. Even Bilak concurred with this, while in his resourceful and tactically astute way he began a delaying action, partly to dilute as much as possible whatever reforms might be enacted and partly hoping that Gorbachev, *perestroika*, and *glasnost* would turn out to be yet another nightmare aberration—like the Prague Spring.

---

[19]Brown, *Eastern Europe and Communist Rule*, p. 305.

[20]*Rude Pravo*, March 26, 1986.

[21]*Rude Pravo*, March 25, 1986.

Actually, Bilak (and the many like him) was not averse to even a considerable degree of "socialist" economic reform, one that preserved the command structure and safeguarded the leading role of the party. Nor did he believe that a socialist state should resort to "administrative measures" unless absolutely necessary. Despite his severity toward the enemies of socialism he did not advocate anything like a return to the terror of the 1950s. He was fond of describing himself as a "man of January," i.e., he had heartily welcomed the downfall at the beginning of 1968 of Antonin Novotny, the veteran communist leader (against whom he carried a strong personal animus), and had favored federal status for Slovakia. But he had been adamantly opposed to the way the Czechoslovak reform developed into the Prague Spring.

Bilak and most of his supporters drew a sharp line at *political* reform. This, they considered, could lead to the weakening of party rule that they associated with the Prague Spring. It would also begin the undermining of the whole post-1968 normalization regime. It was on this score that they abhorred the very notion of *glasnost*. Just as *glasnost* in the Soviet Union had unavoidably led to yet another inquest on the Stalinist period, in Czechoslovakia it would lead to a reexamination of 1968, the invasion, and after. In their vehement opposition to this, the Bilak conservatives were joined by the moderates around Husak as well as many, if not most, of the supporters of economic reform itself. It was this factor that kept Strougal, for example, from emerging as a full-fledged reformer. The refusal to repudiate the past remained the nexus in Czechoslovak public life, binding together all but a few of the ruling elite. As the 1980s progressed, more and more members of that elite broke away from the nexus and embraced broad reform. Their numbers would multiply, but toward the end of 1989 it still seemed as though it would be some time before they would become a determining factor on the political scene.

In the course of their delaying action Bilak and his followers also resorted to another stratagem, one that involved a seeming reversal of a deeply held principle affecting the Soviet connection. During the Brezhnev era no one had outdone them in holding up the Soviet Union as the universal paragon and model. This, of course, had been a Czechoslovak communist tradition since Gottwald, carried on by Novotny and by the post-1968 Husak. Bilak, personally, had elevated it to a canon of "normalized" behavior. Now, however, to the derision of many of his opponents, he became an ardent upholder of the principle of "own roads to socialism." While ostensibly (if only occasionally) praising Gorbachev, and even *perestroika* in its Soviet setting, he became almost "Romanian" in his insistence on national solutions. What was good for the Soviet Union was no longer automatically good for Czechoslovakia. Bilak actually went further than this. The Czechoslovak experience, he argued, might even be useful for the Soviet Union. Having gone through 1968, the Czechoslovak comrades might act as a moderating influence on the "impulses" of their Soviet colleagues, as well as on any others who might be similarly tempted.[22]

The disturbing impact of Gorbachev reached a peak in Czechoslovak politics during the first half of 1987. In January of that year, at a CPSU Central Committee plenum, Gorbachev made the first of the great speeches that stamped him as a radical systemic reformer. It was also announced that the following April he would make a state visit to Czechoslovakia. To prepare for his arrival, Soviet Foreign Minister Eduard Shevardnadze and Politburo member Lev Zaikov paid separate visits to Prague amid great speculation about how far the Czechoslovak leadership would follow Gorbachev's lead. The Soviets, for their part, were anxious for their East European allies to follow their reform lead but were also at pains to stress both state and party independence within the alliance. Valentin Falin, for example, the deputy head of the Soviet Central Committee's International Department, told the West German daily *Die Welt* that they were not "writing prescriptions." "Our friends will decide themselves," he continued, "what they consider appropriate. I am sure that whatever happens in Czechoslovakia will not happen in a Soviet way."[23]

But no matter how different the approach was in Prague from that in Moscow, the Czechoslovak leadership was anxious to see the forthcoming visit of Gorbachev go off without serious signs of division between the two countries. Moreover, whatever the Czechoslovak leaders, collectively or severally, may have thought about the new Soviet leader and his policies, they had to take into account the increasingly important factor of public opinion—and this was solidly behind Gorbachev. There was some popular skepticism about the Soviet leader, it was true. However impressive his reform credentials might be in Moscow, many Czechoslovaks would judge him mainly in reference to the Prague Spring. Indeed, the Prague Spring and the Soviet-led invasion cast its shadow over the entire visit, much as the Czechoslovak leaders tried to behave as if neither had ever happened. But overall, the public's view of Gorbachev was one of positive curiosity, and this was enough to make its leaders nervous.

---

[22]Bilak comprehensively responded to *perestroika* in an article in the party daily *Rude Pravo* on February 20, 1987, an article immediately carried by the East German party daily, *Neues Deutschland*. It was also significant that Ivan Hlivka, a well-known hard-line official at the International Department of the Central Committee, wrote an article in *Rude Pravo* on February 28, 1987, on the "new thinking" in the international communist movement without mentioning Gorbachev by name and referring only vaguely to Soviet international policies.

[23]*Die Welt* (Hamburg), February 10, 1987.

They showed their nervousness, as they usually did on occasions of tension, by both concession and repression. At the beginning of 1987 a long-term economic reform program was announced amid considerable publicity. Its main aspects will be discussed later, but it is worth noting here that its character and timing were at least partly designed to appease any impatience in Moscow. On the eve of Gorbachev's visit, Husak, at a Central Committee plenum in March, almost sounded like a genuine reformer—at least more like Strougal than ever before. He referred not only to economic reform but also, however vaguely, to some aspects of political reform. For example, he promised that the possibility of conducting party elections by secret ballot was being examined. Finally, in an obvious reference to reform in the Soviet Union, he said the Czechoslovak regime was "studying the experience of the fraternal countries" and "looking for optimal forms suitable to our condition."[24]

In the same month that such promises were being made at the Central Committee plenum, the trial of the leaders of the Jazz Section of the Czechoslovak Union of Musicians took place. The regime had always regarded the activities of this Jazz Section as a political provocation. Years of persecution had culminated in the arrest of its leading officials in September 1986. Their being brought to trial so soon before Gorbachev's visit was obviously not coincidental. The aim was intimidation, particularly of the more active young people. The two main defendants, the president and secretary of the Section, were sentenced to 16 and 10 months respectively.[25]

Actually, the period just before Gorbachev's arrival was in some ways more exciting than the visit itself. The public rumors and the signs of official nervousness themselves demonstrated the Soviet leader's impact. Both the hopes and the fears surrounding the visit turned out to be exaggerated. Despite the fears of many officials, high and low, Gorbachev did not try to enforce a reformist policy or a top-level purge. On the other hand, the "wishful-thinking" rumors that he would meet Alexander Dubcek, rehabilitate the Prague Spring, and condemn the Soviet-led invasion turned out to be totally groundless. (The three-day delay in his arrival, purportedly due to influenza, only served to stoke the wildest conflicting rumors.)

Compared to these vivid expectations, the visit itself could not avoid being an anticlimax. Neither the best hopes nor the worst fears were fulfilled. Gorbachev's clearest reference to the Prague Spring certainly disappointed many:

---

[24]See *Radio Free Europe Research*, Czechoslovak SR/4, Item 1, "Husak Reluctantly Reaffirms the New Course," April 6, 1987.

[25]See *Radio Free Europe Research*, Czechoslovak SR/4, Item 5, "The Trial of the Jazz Section Ends," April 6, 1987.

It did not grow out of nothing. Problems had been allowed to pile up in society. Some people declared that the working class was a conservative force. See what kind of revolutionaries and zealots of renewal surfaced at that time! According to them the revolutionary force included artists and journalists, while the communist party was a party of the working class, and useless. They also made all manner of other claims such as that the economy had to be returned to private hands.[26]

It seemed to most observers at the time that with this remark, Gorbachev was clearly, even if not directly, rejecting the Prague Spring. At no time during his visit, however, did he endorse the Soviet-led invasion of August 1968. But neither did he reject the Brezhnev Doctrine. In brief, on all the painful issues, Gorbachev was deliberately ambivalent. The regime must have been relieved. It could not have expected more. The public, on the other hand, had hoped for more.

On the more immediate issue of following his own example of reform, Gorbachev was also equivocal:

One can say that the most reliable yardstick by which to measure the seriousness of a ruling communist party today is its attitude not only to its own experience but also to the experience of its friends. As regards the value of this experience, we consider that the following is the only criterion: social practice and the results of socio-economic development, the strengthening of socialism in practice.[27]

That was the kind of formulation even a Bilak could live with. There was no pressure here, at least in public, for the regime to change its basic course—perhaps just to accelerate it somewhat. And this is what it could say it was already doing with its major economic reform program.

That program, "The Concretization of the Principles of the Restructuring of the Economic Mechanism of the CSSR" ("Principles of Reconstruction"), had been announced in January 1987.[28] But the program as a whole was only due to begin with the start of the next five-year plan (1991–95). Before this, however, some important preparatory experiments were to be carried out. Among them were decentralization as applied in selected enterprises; a reform of wholesale prices, to be prepared by January 1989; and more flexible forms of "socialist enterprise" involving the greater use of indirect indicators, exchange rates, etc.

---

[26]The entire Gorbachev visit to Czechoslovakia is covered in the complete issue of *Radio Free Europe Research*, Czechoslovak SR/5, Items 1 through 9, May 4, 1987.

[27]Ibid.

[28]The entire program was published in a supplement of the economic journal, *Hospodarske Noviny*, No. 13, March 27, 1987.

In the context of "normalized" Czechoslovakia since 1968, the "Principles of Reconstruction" did represent a real step forward. A significant shift was envisaged toward enterprise autonomy, away from the central and intermediate agencies. The central agencies were to concentrate on strategic planning and would henceforward issue guidelines rather than directions. There was an element, of course, of déjà vu about much of what was planned. It looked less like systemic reform and more like the old practice of tacking bits of capitalism onto what was still basically socialism. Looked at from the perspective of 1989, with Hungary, Poland, and even the Soviet Union in mind, the "Principles of Reconstruction" looked very tame indeed. But for the Czechoslovak regime, which had virtually avoided reform since normalization, it was a real effort to address both the domestic needs and the perceived new requirements of Soviet-Czechoslovak relations.

The growing number of basic reformers in Czechoslovakia, along with the opposition, continued to criticize the new plans as inadequate. Strougal himself was constantly assailing the "excessive caution" of the regime. But Gorbachev seemed satisfied with the Czechoslovak situation. In an interview in May 1987, shortly after his visit, he told an Italian correspondent:

> The evaluation of the events of 1968 is primarily up to the Czechoslovak comrades themselves. The leadership of the CPCS, headed by Comrade Husak, has accomplished a great deal since then. Czechoslovakia has made remarkable progress in many fields and I witnessed this personally in my recent visit there.[29]

The Czechoslovak regime's attempts at *economic* reform were, indeed, often underestimated, not only inside the country but by many Western observers. But the few who watched Czechoslovakia closely, especially those aware of the formidable obstacles to change, were not unimpressed. A Radio Free Europe analyst, for example, wrote in June 1987 that "contrary to many Western reports, the Czechoslovak 'normalization' regime's adaptation to the new reformist line has been one of the swiftest."[30]

In retrospect, the Gorbachev visit in April 1987 was a watershed not only in the reform process but also in relations with Moscow. And it led to quite the opposite results from those generally expected. Rather than further stimulating reform along lines conforming to the Soviet pattern and binding the Czechoslovak policy closer to Moscow's, it resulted in a slackening of urgency for reform and less Soviet direction rather than more.

[29]*L'Unita* (Rome), May 20, 1987.

[30]Vlad Sobell, "'Restructuring' versus 'Normalization': A Transient Accommodation," *Radio Free Europe Research*, Czechoslovak SR/7, Item 1, June 12, 1987.

Actually, the Husak regime had begun to benefit from what turned out to be one of the great paradoxes of Gorbachev's rule. The period of greatest Soviet danger to Eastern Europe's aging, Brezhnevite leadership, including Czechoslovakia's, was the first phase of Gorbachev's rule—between March 1985 and early 1987. During those months there are grounds for believing that he intended to "shake up" the Eastern European leaderships and have appointed new, younger leaders in his own image, which was then one of a reorganizer and modernizer, not a systemic reformer. But when Gorbachev turned in early 1987 to systemic reform at home, he did not insist that Eastern Europe follow suit. On the contrary, the East European leaderships were now left very much to themselves. They could take systemic reform, partial reform, or no reform. Nothing was mandatory. As for leadership changes, if they occurred they would be the result of local, not Soviet, initiative. This remained true even in the fall of 1989, when both Honecker and the veteran Bulgarian leader, Todor Zhivkov, fell from power. What pushed them was not so much Moscow but the actual or potential groundswell for change in their own countries. This Soviet laissez faire certainly meant relief for the Czechoslovak leaders, most of whom had become very nervous. The country was now left with a freedom in its relations with Moscow that no leadership in the entire history of communist Czechoslovakia had ever enjoyed.

As to how it was to use its unexpected liberty, it took a typically equivocal stance: it neither embraced radical reform, like Poland and Hungary, nor rejected virtually any reform, like Romania and the GDR. It stuck with its comprehensive, but far from radical, economic reform and avoided political reform. Husak, for one, seemed content with the results of Gorbachev's visit. There would be change, but it would be defined, and timed, in Prague and not Moscow. "Everywhere," he said in August 1987, "an effort is being made to change deep-rooted notions and habits. Each socialist country is proceeding in this effort in accordance with its own conditions, needs, and experiences."[31]

No one seemed more satisfied with the significance of the Gorbachev visit than Bilak and the conservatives. In an article demonstratively entitled "For Our Common European Home," he strongly supported Gorbachev, making an almost fervent plea for the "new thinking," being careful at the same time to extol the right of every country to proceed according to its own conditions.[32] Actually, Gorbachev's new views on the East European relationship vindicated Bilak's line on

[31]Radio Prague, July 28, 1987.
[32]*Rude Pravo*, August 13, 1987.

independence, which he had been espousing ever since Gorbachev became Soviet leader. His conversion to "own roads to socialism" had been very timely.

THE CHANGE AT THE TOP

It is this new situation that must be taken into account when trying to explain Husak's stepping down from the party leadership in December 1987, only eight months after Gorbachev's visit. Many observers assumed, almost automatically, that the Soviet leader was behind the change. Although one may assume that Gorbachev was consulted, the evidence that exists—direct and circumstantial—points to the change being initiated domestically, in fact largely by Husak himself.

There were important differences between Husak's resignation and Janos Kadar's in Hungary the following May. The situation in the two countries was obviously quite different. Hungary was heading toward comprehensive and groundbreaking reform, and Kadar was standing in its way. His political demise, though the result of a carefully laid plan, took place openly, and much to his surprise, at a Central Committee plenum. Husak was certainly not standing in the way of any groundbreaking reform in Czechoslovakia, and his departure was less "democratically" arrived at than Kadar's. It was, in fact, first hinted at by the classic Kremlin game of "nonappearance." Husak's failure to appear on the reviewing rostrum in Red Square in Moscow at the October Revolution celebrations in November 1987 prompted the expectation of his departure.

However different the two resignations were, they had the basic similarity of being initiated and engineered domestically and not in the Kremlin. Still, neither leader could have been a favorite of Gorbachev. For his part, Husak stood for reaction or, at best, foot-dragging change, which in the Czechoslovak context was a particular embarrassment for the Soviet leader. For the many in both Eastern Europe and the West who were skeptical of the seriousness and depth of Gorbachev's reform intentions, the Prague Spring, the August 1968 invasion, and the Brezhnev Doctrine together formed a crucial test of his real intentions. Yet, as was seen most poignantly during his May 1987 visit to Czechoslovakia, Gorbachev could not vindicate the one and condemn the other two without repudiating the whole normalization process as well as the Czechoslovak leadership that had implemented it. This he did not want to do because he was not ready, and because the resulting instability would almost certainly not be confined to Czechoslovakia alone. It was a problem to be avoided, therefore, rather than confronted.

Better for Gorbachev, then, if Husak and Kadar melted away as a result of essentially domestic processes, with the advanced age and failing health of both men given as an important factor. His approval for their removals was presumably still needed, and in Kadar's case there were clear signs of the withdrawal of favor from a man who for 32 years had become accustomed to enjoying Soviet favor. In Husak's case, it had to be remembered that his resignation did not mean his complete withdrawal from Czechoslovak politics. He remained president of the Czechoslovak republic and a member of the party presidium (Politburo). Two years later many observers were commenting on the considerable role he still played. Strong rumors earlier in 1989 that he would retire completely for health reasons were premature.[33]

One look at Husak's successor should have been enough to dispel any notion that it was Gorbachev who masterminded the change. Milos Jakes, aged 64 on his accession, was of the postwar communist generation and had had a conventional career in the Czechoslovak provincial party apparatus. Under Novotny he first served as head of the Czechoslovak Komsomol, then was deputy chairman of the governmental body responsible for the local economy, and from 1966 to 1968 was deputy minister of the interior. (There were persistent rumors about his longstanding links with the KGB.) He supported the Soviet-led invasion of August 1968, and his ascent to the heights began soon afterward. As head of the party control commission he led the witch hunt that resulted in the expulsion of about 450,000 party members between 1969 and 1971. Jakes was particularly zealous in rooting out from their jobs actual or suspected reformers. He joined the presidium as a candidate member in 1977, moving to full membership in 1981.

During the 1980s several Prague "insiders" were reporting that Jakes had become a supporter of economic reform and was gathering around him a group of experts with a view to its implementation when the political moment was right. But very little survived of these expectations. Jakes's past stamped him as an uninspired reactionary without any of Husak's political ability and stature. Had Gorbachev been set on actively interfering in Czechoslovak leadership politics to promote reform and national reconciliation, the result of his exertion would not

---

[33]The fact that these rumors were reported by the well-informed West German correspondent, Michael Frank, suggests there was probably something behind them: "Ablösung von Präsident Husak steht bevor," *Süddeutsche Zeitung*, March 20, 1989.

have been Milos Jakes. And in the event, Jakes himself proved anxious to dispel any notions about any late conversion to reform.[34]

In the case of a change in the party leadership, some Czechoslovaks had been hoping that Strougal would move over from the premiership and then begin to lead a significant reform movement. Speculation on this point increased when Strougal visited Moscow and conferred with Gorbachev shortly before Husak's resignation was announced. Even after Jakes's appointment, Strougal continued in a buoyant mood and was more in the public view than he had been for several months. On the eve of Chancellor Helmut Kohl's visit to Prague in January 1988 he gave an exuberant interview to a West German newspaper, urging better relations between East and West and making frank disclosures about differences over reform within the normalization regime, projecting himself throughout as the champion of progress.[35]

This may have been his undoing. He seemed to have thoroughly alarmed most of those with vested interests in the status quo, who now gathered round Jakes and proceeded to isolate Strougal. In the late spring there were even rumors about his forthcoming purge, coinciding with an obvious downplaying of the theme of reform in the media and in the statements by regime leaders. The expectation of at least some in the Prague leadership was that Gorbachev's days might be numbered; hence reform might be shelved. There was nothing like the reform publicity that had existed, say, between the 17th party congress in March 1986 and the visit of Gorbachev in April 1987. This shift in the official climate for reform proved detrimental and, in a short time, fatal to Strougal's position and political career.

THE PRESSURE FROM SOCIETY

As these changes were taking place at the ruling elite level and between Prague and Moscow, an important new element had begun to emerge in Czechoslovak politics: the societal factor and the force of public opinion. For many it had taken a depressingly long time coming. As Gordon Skilling has written:

> For some years after the [1968] occupation, a profound malaise gripped the entire country, and the great majority of people relapsed into what the internationally famous playwright and dissident Vaclav Havel called a state of anomie. Disillusioned by the experience of

---

[34]See Richard Davy, "Czechoslovakia Under Jakes," *The World Today* (London), April 1988.

[35]*Frankfurter Rundschau*, January 22 and 26, 1988. The interview was reported in *Rude Pravo* on January 22, 1988, but with all obviously controversial parts excluded.

1968 and by earlier disasters such as Munich and the Prague coup, most Czechs saw no prospect for early change and were not ready to risk their own futures through any kind of opposition or open criticism.[36]

In this context, a distinction must be made between the mood in the Czech Lands and that in Slovakia. For most Slovaks, however much may have been lost in the 1968 invasion, something very important did survive: federal status for Slovakia. This meant the fulfillment of at least part of their national aspirations. It was this, not democracy, that had given the Prague Spring its true meaning in Slovakia. Moreover, it followed that since the reforms of 1968 had been largely of Czech provenance, the subsequent repression would fall mainly in the Czech Lands. In fact, normalization in Slovakia was relatively light. Only against the Catholic Church, with its traditionally strong support in Slovakia, its intimate connection with Slovak nationalism, and historical associations with "clerical-fascism," was normalization applied severely. Many Slovaks suffered for their faith. But on the whole most Slovaks suffered less than did many Czechs, and Slovak home rule was not unwelcome in Slovakia, even for many of its uncompromisingly anticommunist citizens. And many Slovaks, however much they may have hated Gustav Husak, did not mind him "lording" it over the Czechs in Prague. Generally, the Slovaks played a relatively small part in the political and cultural currents of opposition in Czechoslovak society in the 1980s. In the growing religious opposition, however, they had an important role that steadily grew.

Husak's normalization succeeded rapidly in Czechoslovak society. A simple comparison between Czechoslovakia in the 1970s and the failure of Jaruzelski in Poland in the 1980s illustrates how successful Husak was. Building on the Czech national mood of despondency, he applied his own combination of compulsion and incentive. Vladimir Kusin has seen this combination as consisting of the "three Cs"—coercion, circuses, and consumerism. The coercion, in which Milos Jakes played a notable part, has already been mentioned. Kusin describes circuses as "the toleration of a widened range of individual entertainment [that] formed another factor in the depolitization scheme." It consisted of "mild" pop (not jazz, which came to be considered political), Western television features, movies, soap opera sagas, and organized sport. Consumerism meant a considerable rise in the standard of living, backed by the availability of not only cheap foodstuffs but also consumer durables such as automobiles, washing machines, television sets,

---

[36]In Griffith (ed.), *Central and Eastern Europe: The Opening Curtain*, p. 252.

and the like.[37] For many Czechs it meant most importantly a small country cottage, a place for weekend escape.

The first serious sign of restlessness came in January 1977 with the publication of Charter 77, the famous declaration calling for greater freedoms in the spirit of Czechoslovak democracy and signed by nearly 250 men and women of almost all political persuasions. Vaclav Havel was the most prominent of the signers, but they included many of the most notable supporters of the Prague Spring (all but two or three were Czechs). Closely connected with Charter 77, but institutionally separate, was VONS (the Committee for the Defense of the Unjustly Persecuted), founded in 1978. VONS issued regular communiqués on cases of persecution of all kinds, and it was not surprising that it was the object, even more than Charter 77, of relentless police curiosity.[38]

Charter 77 and VONS, although they spoke for society as a whole, were elitist in composition and were regarded as such by the population. It was religion—Catholicism—that inspired the first mass movement of opposition. This began with the election in 1978 of Pope John Paul II, the Slavic Pope, which inspired and emboldened many Slovak Catholics. It also stiffened the attitudes of many Catholics, especially younger ones, in the Czech Lands, where Catholicism had rarely been deeply felt and had often been regarded as an antinational creed. The aging Cardinal Frantisek Tomasek, Archbishop of Prague, always considered a passive, even compliant figure, now became a stout defender of the church's interests.

The most massive demonstration of religious feeling—antiregime by implication—came in 1985 with the 1100th anniversary of the death of St. Methodius, the apostle of the Slavs. In what some observers considered to be a turning point in state-society relations, over 150,000 Czechs and Slovaks gathered to mark this event at the burial place of St. Methodius in Velehrad in Moravia.[39] This commemoration created a movement in religious-inspired civic activity that gathered pace. In December 1987, for example, a 31-point petition was presented to the regime authorities by Cardinal Tomasek, demanding the rectification of injustices and the independence of the church from the state. Similar demonstrations of religious strength and determination continued throughout 1988 and 1989. They not only served to strengthen the resolve of society as a whole in all parts of Czechoslovakia, they helped

---

[37]Kusin, "Husak's Czechoslovakia and Economic Stagnation."

[38]The discussion of Charter 77, VONS, and other opposition groups in Czechoslovakia is based on H. Gordon Skilling, "Independent Currents in Czechoslovakia," *Problems of Communism*, January–February 1985.

[39]See the analyses under the general title, "Saints Cyril and Methodius" in *Radio Free Europe Research*, Czechoslovak SR/7, April 19, 1985.

press the regime into making specific concessions. As a result of an agreement in July 1989 between the Czechoslovak state and the Vatican, three of the country's 10 vacant bishoprics (out of 13 total) were filled after years of waiting and pointless negotiations. The regime, of course, was under various pressures to soften its image, internationally and internally, but it would not have done this without popular pressure.

In the second half of the 1980s, the number of independent dissident groups multiplied, particularly in the Czech Lands—social, cultural, religious, and covertly and overtly political. The political groups covered almost every persuasion, from social democratic to nineteenth-century bourgeois-liberal capitalist. They all had one common denominator: a demand for self-expression, reflecting the acute dissatisfaction with the stagnation of normalization. Charter 77 remained the best known and most prestigious of them all, both at home and abroad. Some of its most prominent members had gone, or had been forced, into exile and had continued their activity from the West. Many of the Charter's situation papers on crucial contemporary topics also found their way to the West, and their contents were broadcast back into Czechoslovakia by Western radio stations.

But Charter 77 was now only one group of many, and in terms of popularity it was beginning to pay the penalty of simply having been the first. It was the younger Czechs who now dominated dissent; although they paid tribute to Charter 77, some tended to regard it as too elitist, not radical enough, too careful in its methods, and somewhat passé. Many considered it too much associated with the past, the Prague Spring, and reform socialism. The conviction had rapidly gained ground that socialism in Hungary, Poland, even the Soviet Union (not to mention Czechoslovakia) was beyond both reform and repair.

The growing militancy among many of these young Czechs and Slovaks was indeed a product of the domestic situation and the ferment among Czechoslovakia's neighbors. It is illustrative of the evolving mood to compare Czechoslovak reactions to the changing fortunes of Solidarity in Poland. The birth of Solidarity in 1980 was greeted in Czechoslovakia with skepticism, and its demise in December 1981 with unmistakable *Schadenfreude*. This strongly reflected the continuing post-1968 mood of self-centered dejection. Seven years later the response to Solidarity's revival and then victory was quite different. Here was something to be admired and, before long, emulated.

Once again, however, it was Gorbachev who did the most to dispel the cloud hanging over Czechoslovak society. In the first place, the very emergence of a reformist Soviet leader weakened the Prague regime. The bedrock of the normalization regime in Czechoslovakia, its raison d'être almost, had been the continuance of an orthodox—better still, reactionary—regime in Moscow. This had now not just been swept away but was being almost totally repudiated by its successors. Though not as dramatic as Khrushchev's attack on Stalin, the shift was even more basic.

The Czechoslovak population was not slow in grasping the discomfiture of its regime. Nor did it fail to see the significance of the leadership's resulting decline in confidence. And, as the regime's response to growing societal militancy became less resolute and more erratic, so the awareness of its weakness spread. People, especially the young, were just not intimidated any more.

Allowing for variations in national temperament, the Czech and Slovak response to Gorbachev was not dissimilar to that of the Poles and the Hungarians. There was some astonishment that the Soviet system could throw up such a leader, and no time was lost comparing him with their own leaders. Many placed in him early, unrealistic hopes for quick, sweeping changes, these being a measure of their own frustration. Disappointment on this account led some to become disillusioned and to relapse into the previous certainty that nothing good could come out of the system. The normalization regime, however weakened, was still strong enough to do nothing. On his visit to Czechoslovakia in April 1987, Gorbachev had seemed to equivocate on issues like political freedom and national independence. But whatever the disappointments, for most Czechoslovaks Gorbachev still personified the acceptable, and the not-unattainable, alternative. With the 1989 collapse of the GDR's Honecker regime, which had seemed so invulnerable, the alternative began to look not just attainable, but immediately so.

All through 1989, as further cracks appeared in the regime's determination, so the streams of popular discontent poured into them; as the regime became less confident, so many sections of society became bolder. However repressively it might have wanted to respond, the regime was inhibited by the various agreements on human rights it had been obliged to sign as part of the CSCE process and by the increasing international attention Czechoslovakia was receiving from Western journalists and through interviews given by Havel and others.

Nothing attracted more international publicity than the return to public activity of Alexander Dubcek, the Czechoslovak party leader during the Prague Spring. Dubcek had lived in obscurity in Slovakia for nearly 20 years, and—another reflection of the collapse of popular morale after 1968—had enjoyed no great respect for the role he had played during that time. Nothing better reflected the recovery of morale, then, than his return to public favor. Young demonstrators in

Prague and elsewhere now habitually invoked his name along with that of Másaryk. In January 1988—another sign of the times—the regime did not choose to stop him from giving an interview to the Italian communist party daily *L'Unita*, in which he drew a parallel between *perestroika* and the Prague Spring, spoke enthusiastically about the new Soviet leader, and criticized the Czechoslovak regime for paying lip service to reform but then doing nothing about it.[40] Subsequently, Dubcek was almost lionized by both the Western press and reformers in Hungary and Poland. A frank, extended interview he gave in spring 1989 to the official Hungarian radio in April made the Czechoslovak authorities wonder what the world was coming to, and it elicited a hefty protest from the Prague Foreign Ministry.[41]

Nothing illustrates the interaction between increasing societal militancy and growing regime nervousness better than the "Just a Few Sentences" episode in July 1989.[42] "Just a Few Sentences" was the (very Czech) name given to a petition demanding democratic reforms and the opening of a dialogue between the authorities and the population. The appeal had more than 1800 signatures when it was released to the press at the end of June, and during July the number rose to over 10,000. Not only the petition itself, but also its timing and the publicity it received were embarrassing to the Prague regime. The Western press had by now been primed to look for newsworthy material from Czechoslovakia—after a lapse of some 20 years—and gave the event considerable coverage.

Czechoslovakia had also now become the object of much attention from the democratic movements in Poland and Hungary. Over several years a network of consultation and mutual support had operated among Polish, Hungarian, and Czechoslovak dissidents. Clandestine meetings had occasionally been held, usually in border areas of the countries concerned. As the political situation eased greatly in Poland and Hungary, and somewhat in Czechoslovakia, the cooperation became more open and widespread. The authorities in Poland and Hungary had long since become inured to such activity, but the Czechoslovak regime still regarded it as outrageous and seditious. Much as it might rail, however, it was becoming increasingly powerless to stop it.

The most galling incident of all occurred in July 1989, when an unofficially invited Solidarity delegation, including Jacek Kuron (soon to become minister of labor in the new Solidarity government), Adam

---

[40]*L'Unita*, January 10, 1988.

[41]See *Radio Free Europe Research*, Czechoslovak SR/10, Item 3, "Dubcek's Interview in Hungary," May 5, 1989.

[42]See *Radio Free Europe Research*, Czechoslovak SR/16, Item 4, "Support for Petition for Democratization Grows Despite Fierce Official Attacks," August 12, 1989.

Michnik, and Zbigniew Bujak, the former Warsaw underground leader, came to Czechoslovakia to visit Havel, Dubcek, and others. (That they were able to enter Czechoslovakia was itself one of the clearest indications of change.) Inevitably, the public statements issued at the end of the conversations between the Poles and their hosts were deemed imprudent and inflammatory by the Czechoslovak authorities. Nor were their feelings softened by remarks made by Bujak on his return to Poland. Helping to put Czechoslovakia onto the reform road was, according to Bujak, crucial for reformers in neighboring countries. Without genuine *perestroika* in Prague, change in the rest of Eastern Europe would be crippled. He suggested that reform-minded parliamentarians in Poland, Hungary, and the Soviet Union might issue a formal condemnation of the 1968 invasion, and this might force those responsible for the stagnation in Czechoslovakia to begin stirring themselves or to move on.[43]

The Czechoslovak media instantly inveighed against this Solidarity "invasion," the party daily *Rude Pravo* repeating the kinds of charges Prague and East Berlin had always leveled against recent developments in Poland: The Solidarity delegation and its hosts in Prague and Bratislava were trying to force "Polish" reform onto Czechoslovakia and to create "economic anarchy" with the aim of destroying socialism. It was premature for Solidarity members to give advice to Czechoslovakia, for they themselves "had not yet achieved anything positive." Nobody needed lessons from "the Michniks, the Bujaks, and others." *Rude Pravo* continued: "The majority of Czechoslovak population does not pine for the kind of disorders which Solidarity has caused in Poland, does not yearn for economic chaos, empty stores, and inflation."[44]

In the meantime, the authorities stepped up their campaign against "Just a Few Sentences." A criminal investigation was begun to undermine its originators, with the warning that, when caught, those responsible would be charged with sedition and severely punished. "Countercampaigns" were organized, complete with "voluntarily" signed petitions denouncing "Just a Few Sentences," a few of whose signatories were pressured into withdrawing their names. The determined activity all tended to belie the nonchalance with which the regime tried to pass off the incident to the outside world. Jakes, for example, in an interview with a Spanish newspaper, dismissed "Just a Few Sentences" as being supported by "barely a couple of thousand people."[45]

---

[43]*Gazeta Wyborcza* (Warsaw), July 25, 1989.

[44]*Rude Pravo*, July 27, 1989.

[45]*Radio Free Europe Research*, Czechoslovak SR/15, Item 6, "Petition Calling for Democratization Angers the Regime," July 14, 1989.

The 21st anniversary of the Soviet-led invasion turned out to be a still bigger international embarrassment for the regime. It saw the biggest street turbulence in Prague since the previous January, when thousands of young Czechs had taken to the streets on successive nights and many of them had been brutally beaten by the police. In August, similar demonstrations attracted an estimated 3000 to 5000 people—big turnouts for a Czechoslovak demonstration. Police brutality and, in some cases, clear lack of discipline brought the authorities much unwanted international publicity. Even more embarrassing was the presence of several young Hungarians, all connected with democratic movements back in Budapest, in the thick of the melee. A minor diplomatic incident between two fraternal allies was touched off when two of the Hungarians were arrested, tried, convicted, sentenced, and then expelled, with indignation in Budapest rising with each stage of their highly publicized ordeal.[46]

Incidents like this—and they were increasing in frequency—invariably involved the Prague authorities in a no-win situation. The more they railed, the sillier they looked. The Czechoslovak regime was not losing its capacity to suppress. It could still quell disorder when it wanted to. But it was losing something more important: its credibility and right to be taken seriously. The international situation by itself was ensuring that the days of normalization were numbered. The regime, by its behavior, was actually hastening the end.

However, having given all due stress to the stirrings of Czechoslovak society and to the deepening and broadening of the opposition to the regime, the fact remained that toward the end of 1989 only a relatively small number of citizens were fiercely committed to change. The number was small in terms of the Czechoslovak population as a whole, and very small compared to those who had initiated reform in either Poland or Hungary. On October 28, 1989, in a demonstration in Prague marking the 71st anniversary of the founding of the first Czechoslovak republic, 10,000 people turned out. It was the biggest demonstration since 1948, but it was puny in comparison to the hundreds of thousands of East Germans on the streets at the same time. It was after the fall of Honecker that many Czechoslovaks must have become convinced that their hour would strike soon. In the event, it struck sooner than they could have expected.

But to repeat, large sections of Czechoslovak society, most heavy industrial workers, and most farmers were still some way from feeling the kind of pinch that would elicit a mass, angry response. Many felt

---

[46]*Radio Free Europe Research*, Czechoslovak SR/18, Item 6, "Thousands Demonstrate in Prague," August 24, 1989.

little in common and less sympathy with demonstrating students, and few Czech workers have ever felt strongly enough about religion to go to the barricades for it. Still, the regime could no longer afford to be complacent about the mood in the factories and the countryside. The workers, for example, did not have to be provoked into active opposition, and still less into the kind of worker-intellectual alliance that developed in Poland, for them to become a danger. All they needed to do was to become indifferent to the point of feeling they no longer had any stake in the status quo. All the farmers had to do was to feel it was no longer worth their while to sell as much to the state procurement agencies, and advantageous to sell more on the free market instead.

If, or when, the workers and farmers reached this stage of indifference, they would at once become the ally or at least the silent partner of the forces bent on change. The regime, in the meantime, would have lost its biggest and most protective cushion. And, despite the sophisticated and honest opinion polls it was now using to gauge public opinion, it was simply not sure how far the workers, especially, really were from this curious stage of menacing indifference. The uncertainty was another important cause of its growing nervousness. After the collapse of the Honecker regime, the nervousness inevitably grew.

STIRRINGS AMONG THE RULING ELITE

The growing restlessness among various sections of the population had two contrasting effects on the ruling elite. A small group under premier Strougal considered it more necessary than ever to catch the rising tide and press for more economic, political, and rhetorical changes. However, the much stronger group of conservatives led by Jakes, alarmed at the effects elsewhere in the Eastern Bloc of the interaction of discontent and reform, seemed resolved more firmly than ever to resist the tide. For these conservatives the issue, more clearly than ever, was not one of policy but of survival.[47]

In this predicament they drew what comfort they could from the continued support—or passivity—of most of Czechoslovakia's workers and farmers, and from the one remaining stronghold of orthodoxy in East-Central Europe, the German Democratic Republic. As long as the East German leaders stood firm in their rejection of *perestroika* and *glasnost* and kept a secure grip on their own society, the Czechoslovak

---

[47]See *Radio Free Europe Research*, Czechoslovak SR/19, Item 1, "Fojtik Defines CPCS Stand on Reform," September 20, 1989. See also Viktor Meier, "Der Prager 'Betonbunker' zunehmend unsicherer," *Frankfurter Allgemeine Zeitung*, August 24, 1989.

leaders had at least some strong support. And up to the fall of 1989, the GDR appeared to be precisely the bastion it had always been. Indeed, it seemed to many that after the avalanches in Poland and Hungary, Gorbachev was more than happy for the conservative stability in the GDR and Czechoslovakia to continue. These "islands of Brezhnevism," as Zdenek Mlynar has aptly described them,[48] had their uses. They provided a breathing space—at least as long as they lasted.

The fall of 1988 saw the most serious power struggle in the Czechoslovak leadership in 20 years, since the clean-out of Dubcek and the Prague Spring reforms in the second half of 1968 and the first half of 1969.[49] The struggle actually began in the spring of 1988 at the 9th Czechoslovak party Central Committee plenum. Rumors circulating for several weeks before had suggested that Husak might retire from active politics, leaving both the Czechoslovak state presidency and the party presidium. It was also expected that Bilak would retire, ostensibly on grounds of age—he was over 70. If anything, the rumors pointed to a reformers' advantage.

The reality, however, was different. Husak stayed, presumably because he was the only Czechoslovak politician (except perhaps Strougal) with any real international standing, and his departure at this time of uncertainty could have sparked precisely the kind of instability that nobody wanted, in Prague or, probably, in Moscow. But Bilak also stayed. In fact, the only notable casualty was Karel Kapek, presidium member and for many years head of the Prague party committee, the most powerful machine in the country. One longstanding hard-liner, Jan Fojtik, a Central Committee secretary, was actually promoted from candidate to full presidium member. It subsequently turned out, however, that this was in preparation for when Bilak did retire. Fojtik took his place as the regime's top ideological official.

The April plenum was indecisive, and it was followed by more signs of struggle and uncertainty. Moreover, the Czechoslovak struggle was bound to be influenced in some degree by the continuing leadership uncertainty of the Soviet Union, where Gorbachev and the conservatives were engaged in another trial of strength, the end of which would be signaled by another round of personnel changes. Those changes came at a Soviet Central Committee plenum early in October 1988 and resulted in a further strengthening of Gorbachev's personal position. The changes also meant the departure or weakening of some Soviet leaders who, personally, politically, or institutionally, had had a

---

[48]Interview with Radio Free Europe, Munich, September 1, 1988.

[49]The following discussion of the changes, their background, and their implications is based mainly on *Radio Free Europe Research*, Czechoslovak SR/16, Items 1 through 6, October 14, 1988, which is entirely devoted to the changes.

considerable bearing on the Czechoslovak scene. Gromyko, for example, was relieved of the presidency, which was to be assumed by Gorbachev himself. Ligachev, on whom most of the Prague leaders had pinned their hopes, lost his ideology portfolio and went to take charge of agriculture, an evident demotion. Also transferred was Chebrikov, head of the KGB, an institution with which several of the top Czechoslovak leaders (including Jakes) were reputed to have had intimate associations.

If the Soviet changes were anything to go by, it looked as if a reformist victory would be on its way in Czechoslovakia. But quite the contrary occurred. Gorbachev's writ did not extend to Prague, or he made no effort to extend it there in this particular case. The Czechoslovak reformers were hoping that, affected by the Soviet example, enough conservatives would switch or weaken to enable them to win a victory or, more realistically, to make inroads into the conservative majority. This did not happen. The Jakes leadership refused to be impressed, and it got enough support to not only hold its own but inflict a decisive defeat on the reformers.

The principal victim was Strougal, who was forced out of the premiership he had held for 18 years. He also left the Czechoslovak party presidium. Strougal had never been a "liberal," not even in the sense that some of Janos Kadar's followers had been, or even Kadar himself. But in the context of Czechoslovak leadership politics during normalization, at least since the beginning of the 1980s, he had been pragmatic—and that had meant progressive. Whether this was out of conviction or opportunism is difficult to say. Probably, as in most cases, it was a combination of both. From reliable, unofficial reports it would seem that his opponents had been trying for about a year to have him dismissed. If this was true, he was probably helped by two things: the fact that reform had now become a crucial issue, one of survival for the conservatives, and Gorbachev's protection, or inferred protection. Strougal's demise, therefore, came when the question of reform—to proceed or not to proceed—could be postponed no longer and, even more important, when the question of Gorbachev's protection ceased to be as important as was once thought.

The question of Soviet protection, involving as it did the whole matter of Soviet influence, had for 40 years been paramount in Soviet–East European relations and in the domestic affairs of every East European country. Now, however—and this was a momentous change—it was of less importance as a result of Gorbachev's conscious decision, from about the beginning of 1987, to leave the East Europeans pretty much on their own in domestic affairs and in their relations with the West. In Strougal's case, the Kremlin's new laissez faire, combined with the urgency of the reform and the conservative determination (and freedom), led to his isolation and defeat. In getting rid of him the conservatives may have been defying the Kremlin's wishes, but they could hardly be defying its orders if such things did not exist.

Though Strougal was the principal victim, he was not the only one. Peter Colotka, Slovak prime minister and Czechoslovak party presidium member, also lost his positions. Colotka had originally supported the Prague Spring and was considered lucky to survive the purges of 1968–69. In Slovakia during normalization he had helped conduct the relatively mild regime there. Probably the most telling and symptomatic removal was that in November of Miroslav Valek, the Slovak minister of culture. A cultivated man and a gifted poet, he had been a tolerant minister and was known to favor more openness in cultural affairs. In November 1988, soon after the falls of Strougal and his own immediate protector Colotka, he publicly called for "guarantees" with any restructuring that might take place, and demanded a "thorough analysis" of normalization and an examination of why Charter 77 and other dissident manifestations had been considered necessary.[50] Just a few days after these remarks an official announcement said that Valek, "a poet, had asked to be replaced so as to be able to spend more time on his literary activities."[51]

All in all, the changes during this short period involved several dozen officials, and not all the "victims" were reformers. To give an impression (which deceived no one) of evenhandedness, a handful of conservatives left office, too. Bilak went at last, but Fojtik, his successor, was a more consequential dogmatist than he was. Bohuslav Chnoupek, another Slovak, foreign minister during most of the normalization period, also retired.

One of the most significant *changes* (not losses) of position involved another veteran Slovak, Josef Lenart, first party secretary of the Slovak party since the early 1970s. Lenart, always a Czechoslovak party presidium member, was now brought back to Prague as a Central Committee secretary, a position he had occupied for several years during the 1960s. He was persistently being mentioned as successor to Husak when the latter eventually retired. Apart from experience, of which he had plenty, and a certain disarming geniality, Lenart's chief qualification for the post of president was his being a Slovak. The Czechoslovak party leader, Jakes, was Czech, as was Ladislav Adamec, Strougal's successor as prime minister. To maintain national symmetry, at least at the top level, the next president should be a Slovak. Just below this

---

[50]Reuter (from Prague), December 16, 1988.
[51]Radio Prague, December 19, 1988.

apex, however, there was less pretense now to symmetry than ever since the days of Novotny, who had made no secret of his contempt for Slovak aspirations. Czechs overwhelmingly outnumbered Slovaks in the top party and governmental positions. This was causing unease among many Slovaks, some anticommunists among them. Unpopular as a Husak might have been, as long as a man of his stature continued in the presidency there was some reassurance in Slovakia. But when he departed—and this could not be far off—the question of Slovak representation in the federal framework might become an awkward one. Lenart could satisfy nobody on this score.

In assessing the fall 1988 personnel changes and their potential significance, it should be stressed that although they did represent a striking victory for conservatism in the context of the time, they did not signify immobility on every front. The Jakes leadership made it clear that the political status quo must now be accompanied by greater movement and vigor in pursuing economic reform. The leadership almost seemed to be saying that the political status quo was *contingent* on economic reform. Change in one sphere preserved immutability in the other.

Strougal's successor as Czechoslovak prime minister, Adamec, was a good representative of the economic/technocratic elite that developed under "modernization." Formerly prime minister of the Czech Lands of the Czechoslovak Federation, he had spent most of his career in economic management and administration. His dedication to comprehensive economic reform was sincere; he had certainly had occasion to see the need for it. But with regard to political reform, though by no means a conservative like Jakes or Fojtik, he did not seem convinced of its value or its necessity as an accompaniment to economic reform. He was an able, circumspect, Czech senior official, but hardly the type to break the conventional mold of normalization politics.[52]

In economic reform there were grounds for believing that Adamec would have preferred to be bolder, but unlike Strougal he was not ready to fight his colleagues on the issue. He complained about "obsolete and bloated" smokestack industries, Czechoslovakia's lack of competitiveness on world markets, and the huge government subsidies on foodstuffs and public services. He insisted that the Czechoslovak economy should be opened up (within limits) to the West and that most industries should be drastically "restructured," a term he used often. He also indicated that restructuring could mean relocation for many workers, and was fairly open in his warnings that the "easy

---

[52]The best discussion of the political "block" on systematic economic reform in Czechoslovakia is by Francoise Lazsare, "Tchecoslovaquie la peur du choix," *Le Monde* (Paris), August 15, 1989.

times" were over. But his bolder warnings were usually hedged with cautionary provisions designed to convey reassurance rather than realism. He stressed, for example, that administrative means would always be available to monitor market forces and that every worker would ultimately be taken care of.[53] This prudence could, of course, be defended as not only morally estimable but also politically necessary, considering the sentiments of his colleagues. But it signaled to everybody that in the last analysis, the regime would flinch from unpopular measures.

Moreover, on one basic issue that came to be seen as the divider between dogmatism and pragmatism—private property—the leadership continued on the course of 1988. Poland, Hungary, and Yugoslavia substantially eased restrictions on the number of employees in the privately owned sectors of the economy. In Poland and Hungary the number was raised to 500. By contrast, according to reliable private reports from Prague, a proposal supported by many economists calling for the Czechoslovak ceiling to be raised to 200 was rejected at the Central Committee level as being "inconsistent with socialism." Similar efforts to increase the amount of privately owned land in agriculture also foundered.

Small wonder, then, that many Czechoslovak economists became discouraged. Adamec's ideas of radical reform seemed to them nothing more than radical reorganizations, containing much common sense but nothing like the necessary depth and boldness. "The blueprint of the report represents only a very small, just a half step," one of them complained.[54] Many Czechoslovak economists during 1989 also joined the dissidents in favoring extensive political reforms.

The "Principles of Reconstruction," the basic program for economic reform, originally approved (as mentioned earlier) in 1987, were originally to begin operation in 1991, the first year of the next planning cycle, but that was subsequently brought forward to 1990. In preparation for this, all enterprises were supposed to go over to "self-financing" (*khoszrachet*) on July 1, 1989, but there were many complaints that this was being done only halfheartedly. One of the problems was that many of Czechoslovakia's most famous companies, like Skoda in Pilsen and Tatra in Koprovnice, had been insolvent for many years.[55] In this case, self-financing would have meant instant closure as well as social problems of a nature and complexity that—all questions of ideology aside—the regime was not prepared to face.

---

[53]See, for example, his speech on "Miners' Day" in Prague, September 2, 1989; reported in *Rude Pravo*, September 4, 1989.

[54]Reuter (from Prague), July 6, 1989, quoting Vladimir Dlouhy, deputy director of the Institute for Economic Forecasting.

[55]Reuter (from Prague), August 30, 1989.

Even more inhibiting was the reality of political influence. The large enterprises had powerful political backers, locally and in Prague and Bratislava, in the party and government bureaucracy. The backers would not see their political constituencies dissolve and would fight tooth and nail for sufficient subsidies. Thus the question of reform became neither an economic nor an ideological question, but one of bureaucratic politics and established procedures. One critic put it succinctly: "Unless you solve the problem of political unwillingness to close down bankrupt firms, unless we really see it, and the population has the expectation that it will happen, I won't believe in the reform."[56]

Change was indeed a matter of political will, a will that, even among most of the regime reformers, was not there. Neither, at the end of 1989, was it there among considerable sections of the working population. But change came nonetheless. The economic situation, like the one in the GDR, was universally expected to worsen. It could not keep workers safe in their illusions for long. Societal dissatisfaction was increasing, as were its manifestations. Junior and middle-level regime officials were speaking up. Some of the satellite political parties, taking their cue from Poland, were no longer as submissive as they had been. Above all, the Czechs as a nation were beginning to take heart. And the pride was returning. The example of Havel and others was taking hold.

The collapse of the East German regime in October 1989 was decisive. It produced a revolutionary mood among the Czechoslovak people and broke the confidence of their regime. Demonstrations began, not only in Prague but in other Czechoslovak cities, including—significantly—Bratislava, the capital of Slovakia. At first the demonstrations seemed small, even tiny, compared with the massive demonstrations going on at the same time in the GDR. But the numbers grew. Havel and others formed the "Civic Forum," a move designed to direct and coordinate the growing popular surge. Severe police brutality on the night of November 17 against a large number of demonstrators in Prague angered the whole country and gave the necessary element of passion to popular feelings.

The real turning point came with the great success of the two-hour general strike called by the Civic Forum for November 27. The massive worker response removed the last plank from under the sinking regime, whose leaders may have been consoling themselves that however great the disaffection among the youth and the intellectuals, the

---

[56]Vladimir Dlouhy, deputy director of the Institute for Economic Forecasting, Reuter (from Prague), July 6, 1989.

mass of the workers remained, if not loyal, then at least passive. The worker response to the strike thoroughly disabused the regime of this notion. The two main, often opposing, trends in Czechoslovak politics—the intellectual "liberal" and the worker "socialist"—had joined in their disgust with the regime that had ruled for 20 years. And, just as important, the demonstrations in Slovakia showed that the Czechs and Slovaks, the two nations of Czechoslovakia, had also joined in opposition. How long these unities would last was something for the future. The important thing for now was that they had produced the collapse of the communist system in Czechoslovakia.

V. SOVIET ECONOMIC POLICIES TOWARD EASTERN EUROPE

As the Soviet structure of power crumbles in Eastern Europe, the Soviet Union and its partners in the Council for Mutual Economic Assistance (CMEA) are trying to create a new set of rules under which to conduct their economic relations. On January 9–10, 1990, one of the most important meetings in the history of the CMEA, the primary institution for the implementation of Soviet economic policy toward Eastern Europe, was held in Sofia, Bulgaria. The Session, a meeting of the prime ministers of the member countries, is the highest policymaking body of the CMEA. The Session finally held in 1990 had been postponed repeatedly since the last meeting in Prague on July 5–7, 1988. It culminated the series of policy disputes and rethinking that occupied East European and Soviet officials for much of 1989. It also displayed the mark of the revolutions of that year on economic policy in the CMEA.

The 1990 Session was important because it formally recognized the failure of the old institutions and mechanisms of the CMEA and declared new ones necessary. It also aired the divergent views of the CMEA members on the future shape of the organization and the mechanisms for intra-CMEA trade. It placed most members on record as advocating the replacement of the current mechanisms with markets in which goods would be traded for convertible currencies and priced at world market prices.

This section traces the outlines of the emerging economic relations between the democratizing countries of Eastern Europe and the Soviet Union. It begins by analyzing the evolution in Soviet economic policy that led to these changes. It then describes the recent proposed changes in the CMEA, concluding with an assessment of the likely success of those proposals.

SOVIET POLICIES BEFORE 1980

The Stalinist Period

After World War II, Soviet economic policy initially focused on extracting resources from Eastern Europe. German-owned property in all countries (even property the Germans had themselves expropriated) was seized. Reparations were demanded of Hungary, Romania and, of course, Germany, where whole factories were disassembled and transported to the Soviet Union. Subsequently, joint stock companies owned by the Soviets and the indigenous government were set up in Hungary and Romania, in which the Soviet contribution usually consisted of expropriated German capital. The Soviet Union benefited from the repatriation of profits from these companies. The Soviet Union also set advantageous prices on some important commodities traded with the East Europeans. For example, it paid far below market prices for Polish coal for several years. Khrushchev eventually partially compensated the Poles by forgiving some substantial Polish debts incurred during this period.

The Thaw

After the crises of 1956, Soviet policies changed. The Hungarian Revolution and the Polish crisis drove home to the Soviets that continued economic exploitation of Eastern Europe, despite the short-term benefits, could be very costly in the long run if Soviet forces were to be repeatedly drawn in to quell local conflicts. Consequently, the Soviets began to emphasize mutually beneficial economic relations. In 1957 at the 9th Session of the CMEA, a price reform was introduced that was designed to make economic relations more equitable. In the new system, foreign trade prices were set for the entire five-year plan period on the basis of the average of world market prices during the previous five-year plan period. The CMEA, moribund since its founding in 1949, was also given some bureaucratic life.

In the early 1960s, Soviet policy focused on increasing economic integration in the CMEA. Khrushchev sought to pursue this goal through joint planning, and he had visions of setting up a super Gosplan for the entire region. He lobbied for trade on the basis of factor endowments: the less developed countries such as Romania and Bulgaria were to specialize in the production of raw materials and agricultural products; the more developed countries such as Czechoslovakia and the GDR were to specialize in the production of manufactures. Due in large part to the open intransigence of the Romanians and the quiet opposition of other East European countries, the project died.

The Comprehensive Program

In the 1970s, Soviet economic policy goals for the region were embodied in the "Comprehensive Program for the Further Deepening and Improvement of Socialist Economic Integration of the CMEA

Member Countries" (henceforth the Comprehensive Program), approved by the 25th Session of the CMEA on July 27, 1971. Those goals were

- To promote the further deepening and perfection of cooperation and development of socialist economic integration.
- To promote the systematic development of the national economies.
- To promote the acceleration of economic and technological progress.
- To increase the level of industrialization of the countries with a less developed industry and the gradual drawing together and equalization of the level of economic development.
- To promote the uninterrupted growth of the productivity of labor.[1]

The Soviet Union faced a number of obstacles in the effective pursuit of these goals, the most important of which was the near absence of decentralized forces pushing for integration. In contrast to Western nations, CMEA countries have not benefited from the spur to integration provided by wholesalers and retailers searching for low-cost sources of supply and producers looking for profitable markets. Annual trade plans limit exports and imports, and the negotiated price system deprives producers and consumers of any signals to tell them who the most efficient supplier is and where the greatest demand lies. Thus the Soviet Union has increasingly turned to the CMEA to provide the institutional framework to pursue the goals of the Comprehensive Program.

The CMEA facilitates the use of the Soviet Union's considerable economic clout. Despite the ostensibly multilateral nature of the institution, economic relations are generally bilateral. Trade is conducted with transferable rubles, a nonconvertible currency. Consequently, trade surpluses with one country cannot be used to offset deficits with another. Prices are set through bargaining between the foreign trade ministries, not by markets. Because the Soviet Union is the most important trading partner for each of the CMEA countries, the yearly bilateral trade negotiations with the Soviet Union to determine prices and quantities are, naturally, critical for each country.

The Soviet Union, through the CMEA, employs a battery of policy instruments to achieve its economic goals. The most important of them are discussed briefly below.

---

[1]These goals were extracted from *Osnovnye dokumenty Soveta Ekonomicheskoy Vzaimopomoshchi*, Moscow, Vol. 1, 1981, p. 10.

Trade Protocols. Currently, most trade is conducted through annual bilateral trade protocols. These are hammered together in the fall of the preceding year (e.g., during fall 1989 for 1990). The protocols specify quantities and prices of major trade items and set quotas by value for other items. Quantities and prices are determined through bilateral bargaining between the ministries of foreign trade.

At the beginning of each five-year planning period (the current plan runs from 1986–90), the Soviet Union and Eastern Europe draw up bilateral five-year trade protocols as well. These agreements define the terms under which trade is to be conducted over the five-year plan. They set down the quantities and pricing formulas for the entire period for some of the most important commodities, such as oil or iron ore. Countries also agree on overall trade volumes and trade-related projects to be embarked on during the course of the next five years. Annual trade plans are supposed to be drawn up within the framework of these treaties.

Plan Coordination. In 1971 the Committee for Cooperation in Planning, one of three Council Committees, was created. It has attempted to coordinate plans among the member countries but does not have the authority to function as a supranational planning authority.[2] Most real coordination takes place in high-level meetings between heads of planning commissions and other government and party leaders, which are held when five-year plans are being drawn up. However, actual investment and trade decisions are made in the planning authorities and ministries of the participating governments. These production and investment plans form the basis for the negotiation of the five-year trade agreements.

Specialization Agreements. Specialization agreements are treaties signed between two or more countries within CMEA, under which one (or more) of the participating countries agrees to specialize in manufacturing a specified product to satisfy not only its own needs, but also those of the other participants. The nonspecializing countries agree to either limit or eliminate production of the product to be imported from the specializing country. Specialization agreements are designed to exploit economies of scale and accelerate technological advances by concentrating production and research and development efforts.

Cooperation Agreements. Specialization agreements are closely related to another policy instrument called cooperation agreements, which involve two enterprises from different countries in the production of a single commodity. One enterprise usually supplies the other

---

[2]J. M. van Brabant, *Socialist Economic Integration: Aspects of Contemporary Economic Problems in Eastern Europe*, Cambridge University Press, London, 1980, pp. 187–189.

with components. Cooperation agreements may involve joint development work, sharing designs, sales networks, parts supply, joint operation of service networks, etc. They are usually signed by the heads of branch ministries or associations.

Specialization and cooperation agreements differ in that cooperation stresses direct relations between producers, whereas specialization does not. Nonetheless, the two types of agreement are frequently intertwined. Exports of products under specialization agreements are frequently balanced against imports under a cooperation agreement. For example, Hungary exports its Ikarus bus to the Soviet Union under a specialization agreement, but the Soviets supply the front axles for these buses through a cooperation agreement.

Long-Term Joint Investment Projects. These projects became popular in the 1970s and are the most spectacular instrument for Soviet–East European economic integration. They are designed to assure long-term supplies of important industrial materials. Major projects include the Ust-Iluminsk cellulose mill, the Friendship oil pipeline, the Orenburg gas pipeline, and the ore enrichment plant at the Kursk magnetic anomaly, all located in the Soviet Union. In these projects the East European countries agreed to supply investment goods (actual physical capital) and in some cases hard currency in exchange for a share of the project's output at negotiated prices for a specified number of years. They have been partially financed through the International Investment Bank (IIB) of CMEA. A project itself belongs to the country in which it is located, i.e., generally the Soviet Union.

Target Programs. Target programs are an invention of the late 1970s. These programs identify priority industrial sectors or groups of products and provide a framework for joint development and trade within these sectors. At the time of their origin, five programs were set up: fuels, agricultural and food products, raw materials, machine tools, and consumer durables. Joint investment projects and specialization agreements were often devised for the purpose of fulfilling the goals of these programs.

What were the results of the Comprehensive Program? Despite or perhaps because of the plethora of policy instruments, the CMEA failed to produce the large economic benefits that have been ascribed to its West European counterpart, the European Community. Specialization and cooperation agreements failed to increase integration substantially.[3] Gosplan remained the primary determinant of specialization

---

[3]Keith Crane and Deborah Skoller, *Specialization Agreements in the Council for Mutual Economic Assistance*, The RAND Corporation, R-3518, February 1988.

and cooperation. It focused on filling gaps while ignoring costs, and it took a technological as opposed to an economic approach. Very often the Soviets imported components even though domestic substitutes were cheaper. The East European countries have complained bitterly over the cost of large investments in the Soviet Union. Plan targets have been missed, new capacities were outmoded when completed, and the gap between the technologies in the CMEA and those in the West yawned wider and wider. By the end of the 1970s, the Comprehensive Program had borne little fruit.

More galling for the Soviets was the increasing opportunity cost of trading with the East Europeans. After the OPEC oil price rises of the early 1970s, the Soviets delayed raising the price of their oil exports to Eastern Europe until 1975. In that year they unilaterally increased oil prices, breaking the terms of the 1971–75 trade accords. However, to cushion the shock of adjustment for Eastern Europe, they introduced a new pricing formula for the 1976–80 five-year plan. Instead of fixing prices for the entire five-year planning period, new prices were calculated each year based on the average of the preceeding five years. As oil prices spurted upwards again in the late 1970s, the disparity between prices in CMEA trade and those on the world market grew. The Soviets had to ship much larger amounts of energy to Eastern Europe than to Western Europe for the same amount of machinery and consumer goods imports. Furthermore, the East European products were of much lower quality. These beneficial terms of trade constituted an implicit subsidy to Eastern Europe that, by various estimates, totalled billions of dollars by the early 1980s (see Table 1). As the Soviet Union's domestic economic problems worsened, Soviet policymakers were unwilling to maintain this state of affairs.

SOVIET POLICY IN THE 1980s

The Soviets Take a Harder Line

By the early 1980s the Soviet willingness to bear large opportunity costs in its economic relations with Eastern Europe had worn thin. The Soviet Union first cut deliveries of crude oil to Czechoslovakia, the GDR, Hungary, and Poland between 1981 and 1983. In 1984 the heads of the various communist parties in Eastern Europe met for a special CMEA summit designed to forge a new approach to economic relations. The communiqué of the summit, "Statement on the Main Directions of Further Developing and Deepening the Economic, Scientific and Technical Cooperation of the CMEA Member-Countries" listed several new

Table 1

ESTIMATES OF IMPLICIT SOVIET TRADE
SUBSIDIES TO EASTERN EUROPE
(Millions of current transferable rubles)

Year	M-V[a]	Dietz[b]
1973	1019	251
1974	5163	2704
1975	5065	2007
1976	5906	2287
1977	6150	1731
1978	5851	889
1979	9037	NA
1980	14987	NA
1981	15552	NA
1982	13107	NA
1983	10165	NA
1984	10700	NA

[a]Michael Marrese and Jan Vanous (M-V);
figures for 1973–78 from *Soviet Subsidization of
Trade with Eastern Europe*, Institute of International Studies, University of California,
Berkeley, 1983; figures for 1979–84 from
"Soviet Trade Relations with Eastern Europe,
1970–1984," mimeo, 1985.

[b]Raimund Dietz, *Advantages/Disadvantages
in USSR Trade with Eastern Europe—The
Aspect of Prices*, The Vienna Institute of Comparative Economic Studies, Paper 97, August
1984.

NA-Not available.

goals for the CMEA. Of particular interest are those contained in the
following paragraphs:

> In order to create economic conditions ensuring the carrying out and
> continuation of deliveries from the Soviet Union of a number of
> types of raw materials and energy sources to satisfy import require-
> ments in amounts determined on the basis of coordination of plans
> and long-term accords, the interested CMEA member-countries,
> within the framework of agreed-upon economic policy, will gradually
> and consistently develop their structure of production and exports
> and carry out the necessary measures to this end in the field of capi-
> tal investments, reconstruction and rationalization in their industries,
> with the aim of supplying the Soviet Union with products that it
> needs—in particular, foodstuffs, manufactured consumer goods, some
> types of building materials, and machinery and equipment that is of
> high quality and meets world technical standards.

Mutually acceptable decisions on these questions will be worked out with consideration for the objective economic conditions of the USSR and the other CMEA member countries, as well as for the structure of these countries' production and mutual trade turnover.

This statement and the rest of the final communiqué implicitly contains the following Soviet policy goals:

- A reduction in East European trade deficits.[4]
- Continued improvement in Soviet terms of trade, especially through deliveries of better quality goods for Soviet exports of raw materials.
- Increased East European participation in the development of Soviet natural resources.[5]
- Restructuring the East European economies so that they are better attuned to Soviet needs.

The Soviets also put the East Europeans on notice that future supplies of raw materials and energy would depend on Soviet domestic demand and the availability of supplies. In addition, the Soviets continued to see economic relations with Eastern Europe as a means of lessening economic dependence on the West. Despite opposition from some East European states, most notably Hungary, the 1984 summit pushed for a fifth goal:

- Consolidate the socialist states' economic independence from the West.[6]

Reasons for the Change

The Soviets' new emphasis on their own economic needs within the CMEA was due in great part to the economic slowdown of the late Brezhnev years. Increases in capital and labor inputs, the primary sources of growth in the Soviet economy over the past several years, were declining. More worrisome was the decline in factor productivity,

---

[4]The document contains the passage "Planning and foreign-trade agencies . . . should coordinate . . . measures to increase mutual deliveries of goods, the main proportions and structures of reciprocal trade turnover," which we interpret as calling for balanced trade.

[5]The statement goes on to say "They [the member countries] will carry out appropriate measures, including the participation of interested countries in capital investments and in providing exporter countries with other economic incentives on a bilateral or multilateral basis by the interested countries." Policy goal three seems implicit in this passage.

[6]"Statement on the Main Directions of Further Developing and Deepening the Economic, Scientific and Technical Cooperation of the CMEA Member-Countries," final communiqué of the 1984 CMEA summit.

which has been traced in part to transportation bottlenecks, especially problems with the railroads, the accelerated depletion of natural resources coupled with rapidly increasing costs of developing new deposits, and the concomitant shortages of raw materials.

Changes in trade and credit policies toward Eastern Europe were seen as mitigating these problems. Reductions in energy and raw materials deliveries, if coupled with unchanged deliveries to the West, would ease pressures on supplies in the Soviet Union and diminish demand for investment in the development of new deposits. Improvements in imported machinery from the bloc, which accounts for a considerable share of Soviet machinery investment, could help reverse the decline in factor productivity.

A second factor was the lack of effectiveness of past Soviet policies. Eastern Europe was always a flawed asset. Trade credits and favorable terms of trade had been rewarded with civil strife in Poland, greater foreign policy independence in Hungary and the GDR, and continued Romanian unwillingness to conform to the Soviet foreign policy line. Economic growth in the region had been slow, Poland had to reschedule its debts with the Soviet Union as well as with the West, and the quality and technological levels of East European manufactured exports lagged those of many Third World countries. Soviet policymakers rightly wondered what benefits past economic assistance had brought.

New Policies

Soviet concerns over the losses in Eastern Europe led to the creation of new policies on two fronts. The first was a concerted effort to close trade deficits with the East European countries and reduce outstanding credits. In bilateral trade protocols, especially those in the 1986–90 five-year plan period, targets were set for the East Europeans to close their trade deficits and pay their debts to the Soviet Union. In addition, the Soviet Union attempted to "harden" the terms of trade. Soviet factories and wholesalers were encouraged to return faulty goods to the East Europeans, and foreign trade officials were told to stop purchasing obsolescent products. The policy was given some teeth by the new domestic policy of *gospriemka*, which focused on improving the quality of Soviet goods by penalizing manufacturers of defective products.

The second front was the "Comprehensive Program for the Scientific and Technological Progress of the CMEA, Member Countries through the Year 2000." This program, which to some degree superseded the 1971 Comprehensive Program, was signed at the 41st

Extraordinary Session of the CMEA, held in Bucharest in December 1985. The program specified intensification and cooperation in research in computerization, automation, nuclear power, biotechnology, and the development and use of new materials and their associated technologies. In contrast to past attempts at cooperation in research, the program focused on the development and introduction of new technologies into the production process, as opposed to pure research. It emphasized direct ties between research institutes and enterprises both within and across countries.[7]

The primary policy instruments in the program were called "long-term agreements on science and technology," designed to provide a framework for joint research and, more importantly, development. They appear to define priority tasks and outline a division of labor. Under these umbrella agreements, member countries enter into projects that stipulate the roles of the participating research institutes, the scientific exchanges, and how the proceeds from inventions are to be divided among the participating countries. Theoretically, this policy would gear East European research and development toward the needs of Soviet industry, provide Soviet control over much of East European research and development, and lead to standardization in the CMEA, currently a major problem because of the proliferation of standards. It would also work toward improving the quality of East European exports.

Another change in Soviet policy was introduced in the decree embodying the Soviet foreign trade reform issued on August 19, 1986. Besides creating the State Commission on Foreign Economic Relations (GKES), the decree made it possible for Soviet enterprises to set up joint ventures with enterprises in other countries, socialist and capitalist alike. This new policy exemplified the new emphasis on "direct links" that has been so prevalent in the Soviet literature. Aside from creating the possibility for joint ventures, the reform signalled a Soviet willingness to decentralize economic decisionmaking and make greater use of markets. Reportedly, the governments of the CMEA countries were worried about the decree. If Soviet enterprises were to be given more freedom, they might purchase Western-made goods rather than traditional imports from their CMEA partners. The commercial attachés reportedly flocked to CMEA headquarters to complain about the new law. However, most of the governments understood that something had to be done.

---

[7]Steven W. Popper, *Eastern Europe as a Source of High Technology Inputs for the Soviet Union*, The RAND Corporation, R-3902-USDP, forthcoming.

The 43rd Session of the CMEA was held in Moscow on October 13–14, 1987. This Session resulted in a reform of the CMEA bureaucracy. The number of standing commissions was reduced from 23 to 15. One-third of the CMEA staff was to be laid off; at this writing, however, no confirmation has been received that this decision was carried out. The following Session, held in Prague in July 1988, was more important. At this meeting all the CMEA member countries, except Romania, signed an agreement to work toward a socialist market.[8] The attempt to insert content into this commitment generated the policy debates of 1989 and contributed to the 1990 decision to drastically reform the CMEA.

Results

The policy changes of the 1980s had some tangible effects, but in general they have been judged a failure. The Soviet Union has been able to rechannel oil production by reducing the volume of oil exports to Eastern Europe. The East Europeans have been pressured to export higher-quality goods. The implicit trade subsidies to Eastern Europe have dramatically declined, primarily because of the fall in the world market price of oil.[9] Soviet trade surpluses with Eastern Europe turned into deficits, and some countries paid off their ruble debts (see Table 2). In fact, Czechoslovakia has become a net creditor to the Soviet Union.

Despite these improvements, the Soviets did not attain their policy goals. They continue to pay substantially more in terms of oil and natural gas for East European exports of machinery than they would from the West. The East Europeans have not agreed to participate in any new, large Soviet investment projects. Science and technology agreements as a means for integration have been judged a failure.

Joint ventures between the Soviet Union and Eastern Europe have also functioned poorly. As of 1988, 67 joint ventures had been set up with East European countries out of a total of 418 joint ventures concluded by the Soviets with other countries (since risen to 600). These joint ventures are very modest. Soviet enterprises have had more interest in cooperative ventures with Western companies, because those companies are easier to work with, there is no ministry on the other side governing relations, and they have technologies unavailable in Eastern Europe. Intra-CMEA joint ventures also suffer because of

---

[8]"Towards an East European Common Market?" Centrally Planned Economies Service, WEFA Group, January 1989.

[9]Because intra-CMEA trade is still priced using a five-year moving average, prices of oil have declined less rapidly than world market prices, thereby improving Soviet terms of trade.

Table 2

SOVIET TRADE BALANCES WITH EASTERN EUROPE
(Millions of rubles)

Year	Bulgaria	Czechoslovakia	GDR	Hungary	Poland	Romania
1970	−128.5	−27.8	181.2	36.7	80.0	−29.4
1971	−100.7	13.4	−11.6	101.0	64.9	−82.5
1972	−102.4	−118.5	−363.9	−74.5	−188.9	−112.1
1973	−93.2	−51.6	−252.5	−112.3	−110.3	−92.1
1974	52.9	−7.3	13.9	−13.3	92.8	−33.8
1975	128.4	127.8	337.2	41.7	41.1	−121.6
1976	87.9	97.7	438.6	181.0	265.2	−59.5
1977	164.1	243.5	594.9	156.0	323.8	−18.4
1978	147.0	−56.6	270.8	203.3	−150.4	2.4
1979	139.0	179.5	299.5	187.2	102.0	117.4
1980	221.3	112.2	546.8	403.9	809.7	131.1
1981	677.6	277.5	371.5	244.3	1710.5	146.9
1982	596.5	315.6	643.4	267.6	715.9	−254.4
1983	457.5	451.2	202.1	466.8	487.6	−16.2
1984	506.8	566.7	113.8	−239.1	763.6	48.7
1985	394.7	226.0	98.7	−143.0	991.7	−327.7
1986	561.0	390.6	756.1	−195.2	686.6	408.1
1987	−275.4	−130.7	542.7	−480.3	212.9	192.0
1988	−779.4	−432.7	168.8	−458.9	−811.3	−86.8

problems in resolving differences in pricing and enterprise control between the participating countries, repatriation of profits, and valuation of capital contributions. A few tripartite agreements between the Soviet Union, the West, and Eastern Europe are in the offing, however. Only time will tell how they fare.

More disappointing has been the stagnation and, in some cases, declines in Soviet–East European trade in the 1980s (see Table 3). Soviet exports to Eastern Europe by volume were only 7 percent higher in 1988 than in 1980. The value of Soviet exports and imports with the CMEA has fallen since 1986.

THE 1989 POLICY DEBATE

The failure of the Soviet Union to achieve the policy goals set forth at the 1984 and 1987 Sessions, along with ongoing problems of CMEA trade, led to an intensified policy debate in the second half of the

Table 3

SOVIET TRADE FLOWS WITH EASTERN EUROPE
(Millions of transferable rubles)

	Exports		Imports	
Year	Value	Volume %	Value	Volume %
1980	24339	100	21438	100
1981	28566	100	23619	102
1982	31150	96	27552	117
1983	34449	96	30812	123
1984	38167	100	34622	127
1985	40053	101	37639	135
1986	42157	106	40696	137
1987	40696	107	38856	139
1988	39049	107	39830	139

SOURCE: *Vneshnyaya Torgovlya*, various years.

1980s. In 1989 this debate charged to center stage, due in part to the political changes in Eastern Europe and in part to the problems posed by the Soviet economic decline. Below is an examination of the evolution of this debate in 1989, focusing on the Soviet, Polish, and Hungarian views. Because of the enormous and recent political changes in the other countries, their former policy positions have little relevance for the future of the CMEA and are therefore mentioned only very lightly. Because the political changes in Poland and Hungary occurred earlier, their views still have some relevance.[10]

Soviet Thoughts on New Economic Policies for Eastern Europe

CMEA Reform. By July 1989 a consensus had emerged in Moscow that CMEA reform was imperative. Although the CMEA Secretariat, as opposed to the member countries, was not seriously planning reforms, objective factors were pushing the institution toward them. Many Soviet economic policymakers believed that if structural reform were not forthcoming, the East Europeans would turn to cooperation with Western Europe or among themselves rather than with the Soviet Union. Past CMEA development policies had failed. Growth had

---

[10]Many of the perceptions presented here were garnered from interviews held in Moscow, Prague, Warsaw, and Budapest in the summer of 1989.

failed to accelerate in the countries that received preferential treatment and aid: for example, the investment and specialization agreements signed with Mongolia contributed little if anything to development. Soviet planners also believed a market-oriented CMEA was needed to stimulate the creation of an internal market in the Soviet Union itself.

Soviet economists took the European Community as one potential model. Under such a model, the Soviets and East Europeans would create a common market in which goods would be traded on the basis of competition and comparative advantage. There would be no barriers to trade. Joint ventures would be an important integrative mechanism. An institution analogous to the EC Commission, but operating on the principle of majority vote, would be created and endowed with supranational rights to coordinate trade policies. The organization would have political as well as economic components, with an institution akin to the European Parliament.

Other Soviet proposals were less ambitious. Some economists argued for the creation of free-trade zones, followed by the gradual development of a common market over 15 to 20 years.

Trade Flows and Pricing Systems. Despite the consensus among policymakers on the need for reform, no decision had been made concerning the new CMEA system in July 1989. Both the East Europeans and the Soviets were engaged in intensive bargaining over trade volumes and planning procedures for the 1991–95 five-year plan. Plans remained bilateral and would contain targets for commodity trade by volume. Some East European countries had already agreed with the Soviet Union to preserve some quotas until 1995 and contemplated a ten-year transition period that would contain both old and new elements. In the new system, clearing trade would account for about 40 to 50 percent of trade by 1995. Quotas would cover energy, industrial raw materials, some types of machinery, and goods falling under specialization agreements. Consumer goods and most machinery would be freely traded. Soviet policymakers thought most changes would be made bilaterally rather than in the CMEA as a whole.

The Soviets advocated using world market prices but did not believe they could be introduced overnight. They were considering using prices based on a two- to three-year moving average of world market prices, eventually moving to yearly averages or the actual price. If they were to have some success introducing markets, they believed they would also have to use tariffs.

Some changes in the trade payments system had already been introduced in 1989. Czechoslovakia, Poland, and Bulgaria had agreed to the use of domestic currencies for trade in some products. For example, if a Soviet enterprise exported to Poland it could receive payment in zlotys and use those zlotys to make purchases on the Polish market. The system did not work well. The Poles dropped transferable ruble retention quotas because enterprises had difficulty using the rubles to purchase goods on the Soviet market. They were forced to approach Gosplan and bargain for a quota to purchase a product. Soviet enterprises eagerly purchased goods from Czechoslovakia with koruna, but Czechoslovak enterprises, like their Polish counterparts, had difficulty in purchasing anything from the Soviets.

A major problem will be managing trade balances in the new system. Formerly, Gosplan, the Ministry of Finance, the Ministry of Foreign Trade, and the Central Bank controlled trade. Gosplan incorporated goods in the trade plan into the annual production and consumption plans. The Ministry of Foreign Trade signed the trade agreements and created balances of trade flows in physical units. It also factored in price changes. The Ministry of Finance then accepted the foreign trade plan and incorporated it into its own financial plans. Finally, the Ministry of Foreign Trade reached agreements with foreign partners on quotas and concluded protocols. In the new system, these ministries would no longer be able to use direct instruments to control trade, so balances could get out of control.

In the next five-year period the Soviets expect trade volumes to fall from 5 to 10 percent for each country, for an average of 7 percent. (Hungarian and Polish foreign trade policymakers believed the decline would be larger.) The Soviets expect to run trade deficits with all the East European countries and to eventually be a net debtor to each. These deficits would be generated primarily by the declines in prices for fuels and raw materials caused by the fall in the world market prices of these commodities in 1986–87. Oil exports are likely to fall because of overexploitation of the Tyumen fields, which will result in production shortfalls, which will lead to delivery cutbacks to Eastern Europe. The Soviets will also reduce imports from Eastern Europe of machinery (55 percent of total imports) because of the decline in Soviet investment. The Soviets are also likely to continue to impose tougher quality standards on Eastern Europe because of *gospriemka*. Enterprise managers already return poor-quality goods more frequently.

The Soviets understood that reform in the CMEA will most likely create severe adjustment problems for the East European countries. If Soviet enterprises are free to choose their own suppliers, they will probably stop buying many goods from Eastern Europe. An analogous development has already taken place domestically, among Soviet agricultural machinery producers. They faced a sharp decline in demand because their traditional customers, state and collective farms, have more freedom to make their own purchasing decisions and are more sensitive to costs. Despite enormous overcapacity in the industry, Soviet agricultural machinery equipment producers have raised prices. Not surprisingly, the farms no longer buy as much machinery. Soviet economists feared that the Bulgarian electronics industry may face the same fate, as Soviet enterprises become more quality-conscious and demand products that are competitive on the world market. Adjustment may also be difficult in shipbuilding in the GDR and Poland, bus manufacturing in Hungary, and the railway car industry in the GDR. Because of these problems of transition, the Soviets were seeking ways to spread the costs of reform. To minimize the disruption, they wanted to reduce central and guaranteed purchases and trade volumes slowly. Some argued for continued annual agreements to cushion adjustment.

Despite the potential problems, the Soviets reported that the Hungarians have asked to trade in dollars at world market prices. Hungary would have a trade deficit and could suffer terms-of-trade losses of $1.5 billion a year after such an agreement. Hungarians will have the advantage, however, of no longer coordinating plans in physical terms and will have no obligations within trade plans.

The Impact of the Soviet Foreign Trade Reform. Because trade mechanisms are so tightly linked to domestic economic mechanisms, and because the Soviet Union is the main trading partner of all the CMEA countries, Soviet economists argue that without a successful Soviet economic reform, CMEA reforms will fail. If, however, the Soviet Union changes, other countries will be forced to adjust. They do not believe that economic reforms have to be identical, but they expect economic liberalization in the Soviet Union to push Eastern Europe along similar paths. Soviet change will also force changes in economic organizations and trade patterns.

Despite their increased freedom, the role of enterprises in CMEA trade is still up in the air. In value terms, Gosplan was to fix 50 percent of the plan targets for trade; other targets would be set by the branch ministries. Branch ministries create an additional obstacle to liberalizing CMEA trade. They control the allocation of major commodities. If they face a target, they can give orders to enterprises to fulfill it, regardless of the enterprise manager's preferences.

The main mechanisms for managing trade remain the five-year and annual plan agreements. State orders for enterprises by the ministries and Planning Commission are still the primary means for filling export orders. Although state orders were down 30 percent in 1989, enterprises were still forced to supply other enterprises and fulfill trade agreements. Because of supply shortages in consumer goods, the State Committee for Material and Technical Supply (Gossnab) prohibited some exports.

Although the Soviets are shifting toward trade without quotas, Soviet enterprises are still not very interested in exporting. If they do export they receive part of the proceeds in transferable rubles, but they have found it difficult to purchase anything with these rubles; the other country was often not interested in selling.

The Polish View

Trade with the Soviet Union. In 1989, Polish exports to the Soviet Union grew faster than desired. Polish exporters found the Soviet market more profitable and easier to sell to than the West. Simultaneously, the Soviet Union fell behind in promised counter-deliveries. This created a fairly sizable problem for the Polish government. Although the Poles owe 6.5 billion rubles to the Soviet Union and other East European countries, the increased trade surplus with the Soviet Union resulted in Poland repaying its Soviet debt more quickly than need be. Poland would have preferred to repay the debt at a slower pace, especially as it faced severe internal economic problems and pressure from its Western creditors to service its dollar debts.

The Poles attempted to slow down ruble export growth by devaluing the zloty at a slower pace against the ruble than against the dollar. The government also denied some export permits. The Soviets, however, took a very hard line on trade, cutting their own exports by each ruble the Poles cut theirs. Perhaps with the coming devaluation of the ruble, the Soviets were afraid Polish debt would diminish in real terms and wanted to reduce their exposure as quickly as possible.

Polish trade policymakers were interested in making Poland a bridge between the European Community and the Soviet Union. Because Polish enterprises would accept both rubles and dollars, deals might be done in Poland that could not be done elsewhere. Polish policymakers also envisaged Poland as a middleman for trade with individual Soviet republics. If Poland could codify its access to the Soviet market and reach an agreement with the European Community, it would be able to assure overseas investors privileged access to the Soviet market.

In 1989 about one-third of total Polish trade was with the Soviet Union. Polish policymakers expected Soviet trade to fall by 20 percent in volume by 1995. The decline would occur partly in response to the fall in oil prices in 1986 and 1987, which is feeding into CMEA prices. It would also occur because of the lack of Soviet exports. The Soviets have nothing else they want to trade. The Soviets have already made small reductions in exports of cellulose and metals.

Because Poland exports some things to the Soviet Union that cannot be exported for dollars and cannot be used domestically, the Soviet market helps keep some factories open. However, this production is precisely what Poland should be eliminating.

Soviet demand has also changed. Demand for more modern machinery has increased while aggregate demand for machinery has fallen, although if Soviet enterprises could obtain the financing, in most cases they would continue to demand East European machinery. The structure of Polish exports to the Soviet Union continues to run 58 percent machinery, 20 percent consumer goods, and the rest other products.

There have been intense discussions on the pricing system. The Soviet Union and Poland would like to reduce the period over which prices are averaged to two to three years, although they are still discussing the use of five-year moving average prices. The Poles would like to increase that part of trade conducted in dollars. They have agreed in principle to liberalize trade in "B" goods, i.e., "soft" goods. This trade would be decided between enterprises, would be offered at contract prices, and would not be included in the annual trade protocol. The state would not have a role in this trade. Trade in "A" goods ("hard" goods) would be decided at the government level, but enterprises would decide whether or not to fulfill these contracts. In 1989, 80 percent of trade was not subsidized; in 1990, all remaining subsidies were to be eliminated. The exchange rate was to be set in negotiations (not through market forces).

Because subsidies have disappeared and prices are to be determined through contracts, trade will be healthier, but will decline. Some exporters will stop exporting because of the lack of profitability. The process of transition may be very difficult for two to three years. However, well-managed enterprises do not fear the new system; poorly functioning enterprises will have problems.

There will be increased problems with Soviet trade because there is little incentive for Soviet enterprises to export. However, those who wish to import will be forced to export. If enterprises become truly independent, enterprise managers will find goods they can profitably exchange for other items. In the new system, specialization agreements can be renewed. However, the enterprises themselves, not the state, will decide how to cooperate with those in other countries.

Border trade with the Soviet Union expanded dramatically in 1989 because of the relaxation of travel restrictions and the increased independence of enterprises.

The CMEA. The Polish government has been very dissatisfied with the CMEA because it is primarily a barter arrangement. At the 43rd and 44th CMEA Sessions it agreed to a number of changes: Plan coordination became a three-step procedure that takes place at the government, ministry, and enterprise levels. Enterprise-to-enterprise contacts have been liberalized. Enterprises now possess their own foreign trade funds and are free to make contracts. The Minister of Foreign Trade is to concentrate on facilitating the fulfillment of the plans by acting as a go-between for the top and enterprise levels. Trade protocols will continue to be bilateral, although actual contracts lie in the hands of enterprises.

Polish policymakers hoped to take steps toward partially liberalizing trade. Poland has already begun to use convertible currencies more, but such trade still accounts for less than 10 percent of intra-CMEA trade. Clearing agreements, like those it has with Yugoslavia and China, have not been especially successful.

Poland and Hungary were to liberalize trade in 1990. "A" goods were to be traded through quotas. Everything else was to be traded at market prices to be freely determined by the enterprises involved. Trade was to be settled in zlotys or forints; the exchange rate would be determined by market forces. Because the zloty has become partially convertible, this arrangement would improve the convertibility of the forint, but it could also make managing Polish and Hungarian exchange rates more difficult. The Poles hoped to gradually introduce convertible currency trade in the CMEA as well.

Polish policymakers were supportive of CMEA reform but were unhappy with the CMEA at its lowest level. They perceived Soviet reform efforts as mistaken and too slow. They argued that the pace of reform in Poland and Hungary was qualitatively different from that in the Soviet Union and is perceived as such.

There was concern throughout the CMEA, including Poland, about the repercussions for the domestic economies when the Soviet Union stops subsidizing them. They were especially concerned about obtaining the financing needed for restructuring. A number of East Europeans want guaranteed raw materials and prefer the same system, although they are willing to take a lower level of profits. They see this as less disadvantageous than a rapid reduction in trade. The Polish official view is that the old instruments should be eliminated and replaced with market forces. The Soviets as well as other countries supported this position. The Poles had some concerns that the Soviets would be able to use their market power to take advantage of the East Europeans. They noted that if Poland does not provide world-market quality and quantities, the Soviets will trade with countries interested in preserving their CMEA connections.

Polish policymakers cautioned that even if the CMEA trades in dollars, the national currencies will not become immediately convertible. Moreover, direct links do not imply a market because many countries would preserve state orders, quotas, and export and import permits.

The Hungarian View

CMEA Policy. Many Hungarian economists and economic policymakers have long advocated radical changes in the CMEA. For
them, CMEA reform has taken on greater urgency because they believe
the Soviets are facing a period of deep economic decline. Reform is
also necessary because Hungary needs to integrate CMEA trading
mechanisms with its domestic economic reform if the reform is to function.

Because the Soviet economy is collapsing, little credence should be
given to Soviet promises concerning trade for the next five years,
because the Soviet Union will be unable to fulfill these promises. In
1989 many Hungarian economists believed the Soviets had not yet
realized the extent of their future economic problems. They predicted
that Hungary would suffer major economic losses if it tied its economic
development to the Soviet Union. Thus, these economists argued
against Hungarian participation in the coordination of five-year plans.
Five-year plan coordination channels investment. By participating in
this process, the bulk of investment would be allocated for the production of products traded with a region that accounts for less than 40
percent of trade and facing a massive economic crisis. Such a policy
could have disastrous consequences for the Hungarian economy.

Another problem facing the Hungarians is that the system of
managing CMEA trade is totally inconsistent with the Hungarian
economic system. As Hungary continues to liberalize, divergences
between CMEA commitments and marketization will grow. Hungary
cannot afford this path any more. If Hungary is serious about using
markets, it has to cut its ties to the old CMEA institutions and its
dependency on the CMEA. It cannot continue with the current system
under the hope that Soviet economic reforms will eventually force a
change in the CMEA, especially since Soviet understanding of markets
and free trade is muddled. Therefore, Hungary has to trade at world
market prices in hard currency with its CMEA partners.

Trade with the Soviet Union. Four models were proposed for
trade with the Soviet Union:

- The current system
- Bilateral clearing in dollars using world market prices
- Bilateral clearing in rubles along the Finnish model
- Free trade in convertible currency

The official Hungarian position has been to ask for free trade in dollars, a position the Soviets had not yet accepted at the time this section
was written. The decision had been reached in late May 1989 after a great

deal of infighting. A draft program arguing for convertible currency trade had been sent to the state administration in early 1989; it had been emasculated by spring. The administration argued that trade with the Soviet Union was a highly stabilizing factor in the Hungarian economy. The reform committee resubmitted the proposal, and for the first time the government (Nyers, Pozsgay, Nemeth) voted down the administration's proposal and adopted the reform committee's.

The second possibility, trade in clearing dollars where only surpluses are covered in convertible currency, was deemed likely to lead to a return to barter. The third model, trade in clearing rubles or forints along the lines of the Finnish model, diminishes costs in convertible currencies but reintroduces the inefficiencies generated by quotas so prevalent in the current model. The fourth model was proffered by the Planning Office. They argued that half of trade should be conducted in the current manner and the other half freely traded. Hungarian economists were afraid that this system would quickly degenerate to the current system. They argued that the Planning Office has no sense of the opportunity costs of Soviet trade; it focuses on the short-term benefits.

Most Hungarian economists preferred free trade in convertible currency with the Soviet Union. First, this solution would lower debt/export ratios and ultimately would lead to more flexibility. Second, the Soviet Union is likely to be an excellent market, if trade is conducted in convertible currencies. Hungarian industries can offer goods that are superior to Soviet products but cheaper than Western substitutes. Ultimately, trading in convertible currencies will make it easier to increase convertible currency trade surpluses. This solution also makes Hungary more attractive for direct foreign investment. Hungarian enterprises can use their knowledge of the Soviet market to become an export platform to the Soviet Union for Western firms.

A major drawback of convertible currency trade is the losses that will be created by changes in terms of trade. Hungarian economists estimated the cost of a decline in net export receipts at $500 million to $1.5 billion. The Hungarians hope to persuade the Soviets to lend money to cover this deterioration in their balance of payments but are afraid the loans would be tied to trade flows—which could reinstitute barter via the back door. Alternatively, the Hungarians may ask for Western credits to cover the costs of transition.

Specialization agreements and long-term investments like the Yamburg pipeline would probably survive a move toward dollar trade. However, the Soviet-Hungarian aluminum agreement is likely to become unprofitable. The arrangement whereby Hungary exports Ikarus buses and the Soviets export Lada cars in return is likely to continue.

The Hungarian Planning Commission believed that ten to twelve companies would encounter serious difficulties. However, the general managers of Videoton, a large electronics firm highly dependent on the Soviet market, and of Ikarus, the bus manufacturer, argued that trade in convertible currency would be beneficial, not detrimental, to their businesses. The chief engineer at Danubius, a builder of cranes and small ships, argued that past agreements with the Soviet Union had been unprofitable. Danubius would have preferred not to sign a five-year trade agreement on ships in 1985. If it had not, the workforce would have shrunk from 12,000 to 6,000 employees, but the company would have become more profitable and efficient.

Economists feared that if Hungary does not push for all trade with the Soviet Union to be settled in convertible currencies, the Hungarian bureaucracy will foreclose options. It will rearrange priorities and return to old methods, and Hungary will lose this political and economic opportunity. Hungary has to increase its export capacity by 1991 because it faces a very heavy debt service burden. If it participates in joint planning from 1991–95, it will find that it has geared its priorities to the CMEA markets once again, and will not have the export potential it needs. At the same time, those capacities will not be used on the Soviet market because of the Soviet Union's inability to generate exports in return.

Czechoslovakia, the GDR, and Romania

In 1989 the leaderships of the GDR and Romania wanted to continue to use quotas, trade agreements, and five-year moving averages to set prices in CMEA trade. The Honecker government in particular wanted no changes in the CMEA. Direct connections between enterprises were to be conducted within the framework of the plan. Czechoslovakia, on the other hand, was ready to abandon its support for the old system and was willing to change.

THE 45TH SESSION OF THE CMEA

The debates on the future of the CMEA have been superseded by the revolutions of 1989. The old governments and policies have disappeared. These debates, however, formed the background for the 45th Session of the CMEA held in January in Sofia, Bulgaria. This Session laid the groundwork for a fundamental transformation of the Soviet Union's economic relations with Eastern Europe. The debates at the Session outlined the probable future course of Soviet–East European economic relations.

The Session communiqué called for fundamental changes in CMEA trade mechanisms, activities, and goals. It also called for the establishment of a special commission to discuss proposals for new methods of cooperation and to draft a new charter and other basic documents of the organization.[11] The report of the special commission is to be presented at the next Session, now scheduled for the fall of 1990 in Budapest.[12] All parties have agreed that the next meeting needs to be held shortly.

The Soviet Position

The major change at this Session was the new stance of the Soviet Union. Premier Ryzhkov stated that despite the past successes of the CMEA, the organization has to change. The directive system of economic management in the CMEA countries and the concomitant way of organizing trade through bilateral trade accords are outmoded and impose large costs on their practitioners. Therefore, intra-CMEA trade needs to be conducted using convertible currencies and markets.[13] An optimal solution would be to make the currencies of the CMEA countries convertible. However, this is likely to be a slow process, and each country will proceed at its own pace. Consequently, the members of the CMEA should trade in convertible currencies (such as the dollar or deutsche mark) at world market prices. In short, the final Soviet proposal was substantially more radical than the proposals discussed in Moscow in the summer of 1989. Ryzhkov acknowledged that the process of change will be more difficult for some countries than others. Therefore the process should be gradual, with a three-year transition period. He gave the example of Polish-Soviet trade, in which initially only 15 percent of total trade will be conducted in hard currencies, as one alternative path.[14]

The Group of Three

The Czechoslovak, Hungarian, and Polish prime ministers argued that trade should only be conducted through markets; bilateral trade protocols specifying trade volumes and prices should be a thing of the

---

[11]"CMEA Session Communiqué," TASS, January 10, 1990.

[12]Kyodo News Service, April 8, 1990, as translated in *FBIS-EEU-90-068*, April 9, 1990, p. 44.

[13]Text of the speech by N. I. Ryzhkov, chairman of the USSR Council of Ministers, entitled "CMEA: On the Verge of Great Changes," as translated in *FBIS-SOV-90-007*, p. 6.

[14]Ibid.

past. Trade should be conducted in hard currencies, and all trade decisions need to be made at the enterprise level. These countries had decided not to participate in plan coordination, but to rely on market-based cooperation among enterprises to harmonize economic policies. If the rest of the CMEA countries are unwilling to agree to these changes, Poland, Czechoslovakia and Hungary have stated that they will create a smaller, "experimental" group with those countries that are willing to do so. Trade would be conducted through markets established among themselves by 1991.[15]

Although the policymakers of these three countries are committed to marketization, all three premiers qualified their statements by noting that the transition to the new model will be a gradual one. Premier Miklos Nemeth of Hungary, the country that has gone the farthest to change its trade relations with the CMEA, said:

> Transition to the new model should be a gradual process, taking the different situations, levels of development and systems of economic management of the member states into account.[16]

Premier Marian Calfa of Czechoslovakia and prime minister Tadeusz Mazowiecki of Poland echoed Nemeth.

The Rest

Bulgarian policymakers were less radical than the "Group of Three." Andrei Lukanov of Bulgaria, the chairman of the CMEA Executive Committee, stated:

> We must leave countries free to use their own combination of a convertible currency and the transferable ruble and see from experience how that works. With regard to five-year plans, there is currently no question of eliminating them, but of making them the tools of economic regulation rather than directives.[17]

The Bulgarians appear to be pushing for a mixed system, trade through protocols, as well as markets and a mixed-price system, rather than complete liberalization.

---

[15]"Mazowiecki's Address to CMEA Session (Abridged)," *PAP*, Warsaw, January 9, 1990, as printed in *FBIS-EEU-90-007*, January 19, 1990, p. 6; "Calfa Speech," *CTK*, Prague, January 9, 1990, as printed in *FBIS-EEU-90-007*, January 19, 1990, p. 4; "Nemeth Speech," Budapest Domestic Service, January 9, 1990, as translated in *FBIS-EEU-90-007*, January 19, 1990, p. 3.

[16]Nemeth speech (cited in note above).

[17]*Liberation*, Paris, January 10, 1990, pp. 12–13, as translated in *FBIS-SOV-90-012*, January 18, 1990, p. 8.

The East German premier, Hans Modrow, argued for a transitional solution but noted that market relations will need to supersede the current arrangements. This policy has changed after the March elections. As of April 1990, the East Germans had not ruled out German participation in a revamped CMEA but noted that all CMEA regulations would have to be compatible with European Community directives. They reassured their East European trading partners that all contractual commitments would be upheld, but continued German membership in such an organization is highly dubious.[18]

At the time of the Session, Romania did not appear to have had time to create a new economic policy. The speech by Petre Roman, the new prime minister, was devoted to explaining the economic and political situation in Romania. He noted that Romania would stress the development of bilateral relations with member countries because these can be improved more rapidly and efficiently.[19] Roman also argued against changing the institutions of the CMEA, adhering to the traditional Romanian policy of supporting the institutions of central planning and also opposing changes in the CMEA that might impinge on Romania's freedom of action.

PROSPECTS

As with everything in Eastern Europe in 1989, CMEA policy changed dramatically. By the beginning of 1990, the hesitant, partial consensus for reform had become a clarion call for change. Given the speed of past events, what is this change likely to be?

First, there is a rapidly emerging consensus that CMEA members will have to trade at world market prices in convertible currencies, although the countries have differed on what is meant by such trade. The Soviets have advocated clearing accounts and a long transition period during which trade quotas are phased out. Initially, the Soviets argued for the maintenance of annual and five-year plans.[20] The Hungarians want free trade conducted in convertible currency. Until such time as their individual currencies become convertible, this means trade will be conducted in dollars, ECUs, or deutsche marks. In fact, the Hungarian government signed an agreement with the Soviet Union in March to trade only in convertible currency beginning in 1991.

---

[18]Norbert Schwaldt, "Plan Methods Are Put to Sleep," *Neue Zeit*, April 21, 1990, p. 3.

[19]*BTA*, Sofia, January 9, 1990, as translated in *FBIS-EEU-90-007*, January 19, 1990, p. 9.

[20]Marie-Laure Colson, "Interview with CMEA Executive Committee Chairman Andrey Lukanov," *Liberation*, January 10, 1990, pp. 12–13.

Ruble claims will be converted to dollars.[21] Poland is taking similar steps in this direction. Bulgaria has signed agreements to trade in convertible currency with Czechoslovakia and the Soviet Union but has stipulated a transition period during which plans and trade quotas would be utilized. Even Romania now supports market reform. By 1991 all CMEA trade will probably be conducted in convertible currencies, although some countries may still resort to clearing accounts.

Such a move is likely to be fairly costly for Eastern Europe because of the declines in exports and terms of trade losses caused by the shift to convertible currency trade. Because of Poland's, Hungary's and Bulgaria's precarious financial situations, Poland and Bulgaria have expressed a willingness for a slower transition to world market prices in trade with the Soviet Union, even though other statements argue for an immediate shift. Poland has especially opposed moves to convert its ruble debts into dollars. Hungary has sought financial assistance to cushion the shock. The Czechoslovak government has also argued for a transitional period. This period is unlikely to be long. The Soviet Union's financial problems are increasing, and it has much less reason to subsidize Eastern Europe as those countries move away from the Soviet sphere of influence; marketization of the East European economies will make it very difficult to sustain a mixed hard currency/transferable ruble trading regime.

The costs of transition may be large. Past estimates of the terms of trade benefits derived from trade with the Soviets have been on the order of billions of dollars (see Table 1). The Hungarians estimated their cost of moving to world market prices in convertible currencies with the Soviet Union at $500 million to $1,500 billion. This includes declines in exports as well as the terms-of-trade losses. This figure may be used to estimate the costs of transition for the region as a whole. Multiplying it by the ratio of the absolute value of the sum of each country's net trade in machinery and energy trade with the Soviet Union to this same sum for Hungarian-Soviet trade, one may derive estimates of potential trade losses (see Table 4). The costs are very large, on the order of 20 or more percent of current hard currency export earnings. Such an adjustment will impose a substituted additional burden on the East European countries just when they are moving to market systems.

However, many of these costs would be unavoidable under the old system as well. Soviet economic turmoil has already led to curbs on exports of energy and raw materials; East European manufacturers

---

[21]Budapest Domestic Service, April 10, 1990, as translated in *FBIS-EEU-90-070*, April 11, 1990, p. 36.

Table 4

POTENTIAL COSTS OF SWITCHING TO TRADE IN
CONVERTIBLE CURRENCIES
(Millions of dollars)

	Low Estimate	High Estimate	As a Percent of Machinery Exports[a]	
			Low	High
Hungary	500	1500	12.6	37.7
Bulgaria	659	1976	10.9	32.6
Czechoslovakia	912	2737	14.5	43.5
GDR	945	2834	13.0	39.1
Poland	654	1963	12.2	36.5
Romania	251	753	13.2	39.7
Total	3921	11763	12.7	38.1

[a]Converted at the official ruble/dollar rate of exchange.

have already felt the decline in Soviet demand. As of early 1990, all the East European countries were experiencing less-than-promised shipments of Soviet raw materials and energy. Many were responding with export embargos to curtail exploding ruble trade surpluses.

Poland, Czechoslovakia, and Hungary have held some talks on multilateral economic cooperation within the CMEA. At the Sofia Session they espoused their willingness to set up an "experimental" reform group that would move to trading through markets and with convertible currencies more rapidly than other countries that prefer a slower pace. These three countries do not want their reforms slowed by other, less reformist countries. Such a "group within the group" is likely to emerge, but it may be outside rather than inside the CMEA. Government officials from all three countries have made scathing comments about the organization. If the group of three remains inside, it, coupled with the Soviet Union, will dominate the CMEA of the future. The GDR was the only major economic power in the CMEA that appeared to favor the "go slow" approach. As the GDR disappears, so will its role in the CMEA. The other members, Bulgaria, Romania, Vietnam, Cuba, and Mongolia, will either attempt to emulate the reformist three or are too small economically to have an important influence on the organization.

What then of Soviet economic policy toward Eastern Europe? With the fading of Soviet dominance in Eastern Europe, the Soviets are likely to adopt an even more commercial and self-interested economic policy toward the region. They may seek to hold the CMEA together as a group that provides its members with preferred access to each other's exports. The new group may even attempt to facilitate improved economic relations. Whatever emerges, however, will be a ghost of its former self.

VI. CONCLUSION

The year 1989 saw the collapse of communist rule in Eastern Europe and, with it, of Soviet hegemony. The collapse was sudden, unexpected, and almost total. In some respects the sheer speed of events was almost as important as the events themselves, generating a momentum that, toward the end of 1989, made the so-called "domino effect" a historical reality. The collapse of the communist regimes in Eastern Europe was caused by six interrelating factors, summarized below.

1. The most obvious and all-encompassing factor was simply *40 years of failure*. It was a multifaceted failure in which the incompatibility between Soviet interests and East European national aspirations became increasingly evident. But this incompatibility might have receded, or become less corrosive, had the system been able to establish a rational and satisfactory economic basis, one that consistently ensured higher standards of living and met rising popular expectations. As it was, the system was shot through with economic failure, and this had become fatal as early as the second half of the 1970s. By then it was obvious that this was not just another periodic malaise but a terminal condition. During the 1980s, drastic remedial reforms might have given the patient an extra lease on life. Since such reforms did not come, the situation rapidly deteriorated beyond repair. And this time the Soviet Union, however ready in the past to prop up its faltering satellites, was unable or unwilling to help. It had its own terminal illness to contend with. By the end of the 1980s the great economic failure was pervasive. All the East European regimes, except the Romanian, had tried to shelter their people from the worst effects of their ineptitude. But now they had finally run out of time.

2. It was this failure that made the *illegitimacy* of communism inescapable. Basically, the communist regimes had been illegitimate from the start, but they had encountered only brief periods of active opposition. Most of the over 40 years of communist rule in Eastern Europe was characterized by popular passivity, or at least resignation. Even Nicolae Ceausescu, who qualifies (in the face of severe competition) as the worst East European ruler, had his moments of actual legitimacy. As the 1980s came to a close, however, the very notion of legitimacy in Eastern Europe was tragicomic. Economic failure was not, of course, the sole cause of the all-embracing illegitimacy. But it brought the others into focus, it was tangible, and it was primary. Above all, while

173

economic success might have dulled the edge of East European nationalism, economic failure sharpened it and gave it coherence.

3. The most significant effect of the economic failure was that it stimulated and consolidated *societal opposition* in most East European countries. It brought together, though in different degrees of unity and cooperation, intellectuals, many young people, and many workers, the combination needed to challenge communist rule effectively and consistently. Just as important, economic failure turned other sections of society away from their support of the regime. This support, however passive, self-interested, or reluctant, had sustained the regimes during previous crises.

4. It was hardly surprising, then, that the communist elite, challenged by its opponents and deserted by its supporters, intimidated too by the immensity of its own failure, began *to lose confidence in its ability to rule* and, more to the point, to *lose the willingness to use the means to maintain it.*

5. However inexorably the East Europeans states moved into the classic prerevolutionary situation, their progress was also helped by external factors. The *improvement in East-West relations*, begun in earnest in the late 1960s, gathering force in the 1970s, interrupted in the early 1980s and subsequently resurging, was an important factor. Détente did not strengthen communism in Eastern Europe, it softened it.

6. The Western impact was slight, however, compared with that of the other external factor, the Soviet Union. It was this that made the revolutions inevitable. The tinder was already there, but it needed *Gorbachev* to light it. Gorbachev's effect on Eastern Europe was at once galvanizing and demoralizing, depending on the perspective:

- It was galvanizing for certain elements in East European societies, especially the youth and the dissidents, and for reform groups within the regimes, where they existed. Where such reform groups were strong—as in Poland and Hungary—change occurred progressively and evenly. In countries where they did not exist, the changes were tumultuous.
- It was demoralizing for regime conservatives. A "liberal" in the Kremlin was a development few had anticipated. Even more demoralizing was their growing realization that come what may, however much the regime, even the system, was in danger of collapsing, there would be no Soviet intervention. No tanks would roll this time. The Brezhnev Doctrine was, indeed, dead.

It was the realization of this that caused the dominoes to begin to fall. Poland and Hungary went quietly in the second half of 1989, seeming almost to race with one another in pursuing the civil society. Then came the GDR and Czechoslovakia, within a few weeks of each other. When one went, the other could not survive. The next domino was Bulgaria, in early November. And then the bloody culmination: the Romanian uprising in December.

The East European response to Gorbachev, therefore, had been swift and unexpected—not least for Gorbachev himself. This last point should be stressed in view of the Soviet leadership's subsequent claims that it anticipated, almost predicted, the communist collapse in the region. Foreign Minister Shevardnadze, in particular, has heatedly rejected charges of failure and lack of foresight in Eastern Europe. In a CPSU Central Committee debate in February 1990, for example, he traced the failure of communism in Eastern Europe right back to its imposition in the late 1940s and early 1950s:

> It was back then, not in 1985, that the undermining of faith in socialism began as a result of oppression and violence. Today people are asking: Why did we not foresee the events in these countries?

> We did. And that was why, starting in 1985, we fundamentally restructured the nature of interstate ties with them, abandoned interference into their internal affairs, and stopped imposing our solutions. Yet, as our own experience attests to, it is easier to change policy than to change people. Many leaders in these countries were cut from the same cloth—and it is well known who cut and sewed that cloth. Some of them came to power with the help of former Soviet leaders but after 1985 they could not be removed from power by the current Soviet leadership as, I repeat, it had foresworn interference in the internal affairs of other countries.[1]

The clearest example of Soviet miscalculation was probably on the German question. "New thinking," notwithstanding, the Soviets always made it clear that reunification was not an option for them, at least not in the short run. Gorbachev always spoke of the two German states as the reality from which one had to proceed. This was to be the cornerstone of the common European house: two German rooms, though with greater flow and exchange between them.

The Soviets, therefore, saw no inconsistency in urging the continuing division of Germany. One of the more liberal of the "new thinkers" on foreign affairs, Vitalii Zhurkin, spelled this out in a passage worth quoting at length.

---

[1]*Pravda*, February 8, 1990.

We are talking about two separate divisions. One is Europe's division into two political, military and economic alliances. The other is Germany's division and the existence of two German states. It seems to me that this is not the same problem.

As far as Europe's division is concerned, the blueprint for a "common European home" clearly envisages its gradual attenuation. Of course this is a difficult process. However, if we achieve real disarmament, genuine understanding, and real progress in the area of human rights, it will be possible to attenuate the military nature of the alliance and to reduce them to political alliances. In the future they could even disappear.

The issue of Germany's division is another matter, however. I believe that Gorbachev has clearly explained the Soviet position on this. There is a political reality, namely the two Germanies—one in the East, the other in the West. There is a zone, rather an entity—called Berlin which is recognized by an international accord and bilateral treaties, including with the FRG. This reality exists and will continue to exist. However, relations between the two German states are developing and they could develop further within the context of a common European home. Thus, the asperity of the so-called "German Question" could be attenuated in the future. In any case, this is the position of the GDR, which is our ally and which we support 100 percent.[2]

Zhurkin was speaking over a year before the breaking of the Berlin Wall and the subsequent collapse of the communist regime. But even up to the end of 1989, after the actual collapse of communism in the GDR, there is enough evidence to suggest that the Soviet leaders were deluding themselves that East German socialism was still somehow reformable and that the division of Germany could be preserved.

East German socialism could not be preserved, nor could the GDR itself. Both had to be surrendered eventually, along with the rest of Eastern Europe. The emasculation of German power, represented by the division of Germany, and Soviet domination in Eastern Europe— the two great Soviet Russian gains after World War II—were lost.

Although Soviet hegemony is over, the Soviet–East European connection, or interaction, need not be. It is already drastically and dramatically reduced, but it is hard to imagine that the East European rejection of communism and Soviet hegemony (and its accompanying westward gravitation) also means anything like a reversion to the kind of mutual isolation that characterized Soviet–East European relations before World War II. This is what the Soviets might well be fearing: Eastern Europe's integration into the West without them, a common European home indeed, but one stopping at the Bug, beyond which

---

[2]Interview in *Corriere della Sera*, October 31, 1988.

Russia would be on its own, fighting nationalist fires within the Soviet Union itself, partly stoked by the East European example.

Barring a comprehensive domestic collapse making external preoccupations almost irrelevant, such a nightmare is not likely to materialize. Future Soviet relations with its former East European allies are likely to pass through a difficult and perhaps drawn-out process of extrication into longer-term bilateral relationships based on mutual advantage. First, the multilateral relationship expressed in CMEA and the Warsaw Treaty Organization is already being totally revised. Both organizations in their present form are being scrapped. The Warsaw Pact will probably not survive; it may eventually be formally dissolved or just lapse into desuetude. The aim of most of the East European states is neutrality, to escape the responsibilities, the burdens, the very essence of the commitment to the Soviet alliance. CMEA, too, cannot survive as such. But the Soviet–East European economic relationships, in modified form, will almost certainly remain practical, even essential, for all concerned, especially the East Europeans. Economics will be the bedrock of the Soviet Union's future East European connection— but on a bilateral, not a multilateral, basis.

But economic relations have always had political implications; there is no reason to believe that whatever emerges from the present Soviet crisis—a stable Soviet Union, Soviet-Russia, or just plain Russia—will not wield some political influence, at least in parts of the region it once dominated. Nor need this influence spring solely from an economic basis. The new European order dominated by a reunited Germany, however strong the international framework and its stability-promoting mechanisms might be, will generate enough uncertainty and apprehensiveness to necessitate the continuance, even the revival, of traditional nation-state relationships. The European international environment will be such as to ensure a role for Russian activity and influence. The new role, though, will be based more on diplomacy than domination.